The Beginning Was the End

SERIES ON OHIO HISTORY AND CULTURE

Series on Ohio History and Culture
Kevin Kern, Editor

Steve Love, *The Indomitable Don Plusquellic: How a Controversial Mayor Quarterbacked Akron's Comeback*
Robert J. Roman, *Ohio State Football: The Forgotten Dawn*
Timothy H. H. Thoresen, *River, Reaper, Rail: Agriculture and Identity in Ohio's Mad River Valley, 1795–1885*
Mark Auburn, *In the President's Home: Memories of the Akron Auburns*
Brian G. Redmond, Bret J. Ruby, and Jarrod Burks, eds., *Encountering Hopewell in the Twenty-first Century, Ohio and Beyond. Volume 1: Monuments and Ceremony*
Brian G. Redmond, Bret J. Ruby, and Jarrod Burks, eds., *Encountering Hopewell in the Twenty-first Century, Ohio and Beyond. Volume 2: Settlements, Foodways, and Interaction*
Jen Hirt, *Hear Me Ohio*
S. Victor Fleischer, *The Goodyear Tire & Rubber Company: A Photographic History, 1898–1951*
Ray Greene, *Coach of a Different Color: One Man's Story of Breaking Barriers in Football*
John Tully, *Labor in Akron, 1825–1945*
Deb Van Tassel Warner and Stuart Warner, eds., *Akron's Daily Miracle: Reporting the News in the Rubber City*
Mary O'Connor, *Free Rose Light*
Joyce Dyer, *Pursuing John Brown: On the Trail of a Radical Abolitionist*
Walter K. Delbridge and Kate Tucker, editor, *Comeback Evolution: Selected Works of Walter K. Delbridge*
Gary S. Williams, *"No Man Knows This Country Better": The Frontier Life of John Gibson*
Jeffrey A. John, *Progressives and Prison Labor: Rebuilding Ohio's National Road During World War I*
John W. Kropf, *Color Capital of the World: Growing Up with the Legacy of a Crayon Company*
Steve McClain, *The Music of My Life: Finding My Way After My Mother's MS Diagnosis*
Jade Dellinger and David Giffels, *The Beginning Was the End: Devo in Ohio*

Titles published since 2016.
For a complete listing of titles published in the series,
    go to www.uakron.edu/uapress.

The Beginning Was the End

Devo in Ohio

Jade Dellinger
and David Giffels

The University of Akron Press
Akron, Ohio

All new material copyright © 2023 by the University of Akron Press
All rights reserved • First Edition 2023 • Manufactured in the United States of America.
All inquiries and permission requests should be addressed to the Publisher,
The University of Akron Press, Akron, Ohio 44325-1703.

ISBN: 978-1-62922-251-6 (paper)
ISBN: 978-1-62922-252-3 (ePDF)
ISBN: 978-1-62922-253-0 (ePub)

A catalog record for this title is available from the Library of Congress.

∞ The paper used in this publication meets the minimum requirements of ANSI/NISO z39.48–1992 (Permanence of Paper).

Cover photos: Courtesy of Bobbie Watson Whitaker. Cover design by Amy Freels, with Rhye Pirie.

The Beginning Was the End was designed and typeset in Minion with Cooper Hewitt display type by Amy Freels and printed on sixty-pound white and bound by Bookmasters of Ashland, Ohio.

Produced in conjunction with the University of Akron Affordable Learning Initiative. More information is available at www.uakron.edu/affordablelearning/

Authors' note: This text is heavily abridged and somewhat revised from our 2003 book *Are We Not Men? We Are Devo!*, which is now out of print. This edition contains numerous photographs and other images that did not appear in the previous book.

What we call the beginning is often the end
And to make an end is to make a beginning.
—T. S. Eliot, *Four Quartets*

No one can come onto my island without a mask.
—Eric Mottram, "Left for California: The Slow
   Awakening"

DEVO at a bus shelter in downtown Akron. *Courtesy of Bobbie Watson Whitaker*

Introduction

With Devo, everything is a question. Here's one:

Could this band have come from anywhere else except Ohio?

It seems impossible. While the group was rhapsodically embraced by the New York hipster elite upon their 1977 arrival at Max's Kansas City (introduced onstage by David Bowie as "the band of the future"), there's no way they ever could have gestated anonymously in the East Village for nearly a decade prior as they did in the hinterlands of Northeast Ohio. If the members had encountered one another in, say, Boise, what would have substituted for that which founding member Gerald V. "Jerry" Casale called the "art-directed backdrop" of Ohio's leaden, German Expressionist, industrial landscape?

Where else but Akron, a center of synthetic research, could they have found a janitorial supply house with an abundance of yellow DuPont Tyvek polyolefin jumpsuits? Did other schools besides St. Patrick's Elementary in Kent have ziggurat-shaped Art Deco light fixtures—inspiration for the red energy domes? How would Devo's twisted humor and penchant for media manipulation have galvanized without Ghoulardi, the schlocky Cleveland late-night B-movie host who primordially influenced a generation of musicians and artists? And is there any conceivable parallel for the triggering

1

impact of the May 4, 1970, student massacre on the Kent State campus, which Casale would describe as "the most Devo Day in my life?"

Time and place. Those are the foundations of Devo. Random chance brought together the talented, ambitious personalities that would mesh into one of the most advanced and misunderstood entities in pop music history. Certainly one can imagine an alternate universe in which Mark Mothersbaugh meets Jerry Casale, each flanked by a talented brother named Bob (hence "Bob 1" and "Bob 2"), not to mention yet a third Bob, surname Lewis—prime mover of the devolution concept—and they decide to form a band. But Devo, as much as anyone, has sought for alternate universes and none have yet been identified. It didn't happen in another place or another time. As the sci-fi movie poster of its origin story might read: "It Came from Ohio!"

This, then, is the tale of the long prehistory of what finally reached mainstream America's consciousness via the 1980 MTV pop hit "Whip It." The five men who appeared in that song's iconic video, dressed in matching black uniforms and topped with the distinctive energy domes—the Mothersbaugh and Casale brother-sets and drummer Alan Myers—were all born in Northeast Ohio between 1948 and 1954. As postwar children of the Baby Boom, they ingested a televised diet of the Beatles on *Ed Sullivan*, John F. Kennedy's assassination, Mr. Potato Head commercials, and idealized fictions of the American Dream.

Time and place have everything to do with the aesthetic and ideology. But what matters most is that the two leaders—Mark Mothersbaugh and Jerry Casale—as well as founding influence Bob Lewis, were artists in the truest sense. They actively and incisively observed their surroundings and used that information to try to create something meaningful. Ohio provided both the resources and limitations that would shape the message.

As they came of age, the group's members received radio signals from WMMS, a freeform Cleveland FM station that played the likes of the Velvet Underground and Captain Beefheart before evolving (or devolving) into a commercial behemoth that at turns ignored and mocked the fervent local New Wave underground, even as it was becoming recognized internationally as "the Akron sound." They happened onto a Kent State campus which, in the late 1960s and early '70s, represented an unlikely cultural oasis between New York and Chicago. Its resident and visiting faculty fostered and encouraged the sprawling ambition of "Art Devo."

The concept of de-evolution—the notion that humans are evolving in reverse—was informed by a bibliography culled in great part from local bookstores and thrift shops. It includes a bizarre volume of quack anthropology called *The Beginning Was the End*, which posits that human intelligence came about because cannibalistic apes ate one another's brains, leading to accelerated intellectual development but also the inevitable demise of the species. It includes a 1948 Wonder Woman comic that featured a De-evolution machine. It includes an obscure religious pamphlet published in Roger, Ohio, titled "Jocko-Homo Heavenbound."

In Northeast Ohio, the group was surrounded by a community of equally iconoclastic and driven musicians—art-rock adventurers and punk pioneers. When their multiform conceptual art project finally became a proper rock band, Ohio provided Devo a stage—the Crypt, a former rubber workers' watering hole widely recognized as the first American punk venue outside New York City. And, finally, as it did for scores of young Rust Belters with talent and ambition, Ohio provided the impetus to leave.

For all the richness of material Devo found in its homeland, it found little in the way of acceptance. Perhaps a hundred people cheered them as a local band. Far more were baffled, repulsed, and outright angered by Devo's visual and musical experimentation. Upon their departure, they were fawned over and abetted by the artistic likes of Bowie, Iggy Pop, Brian Eno, and Neil Young, and nearly pulled asunder by a music industry bidding war.

In one sense, they couldn't have become Devo without Ohio. In another, they couldn't have become Devo without leaving.

* * *

So now it can be told. This is the story of the sprawling Ohio beginnings of a band that was often misunderstood, that sometimes shot itself in the foot, and that manipulated the System as much as the System manipulated it. Is this the truth about de-evolution? Only if you understand one of the group's founding concepts, that of *plastic reality*, the notion that objective truth does not exist. If it was a joke, it was meant to be taken seriously. And if it was serious, it was meant to be laughed at.

For Devo, the idea of truth was literally incomplete. Their spelling of the word "true" was "tru." Look them up in the online version of *Encyclopaedia Britannica*: "Biographical information on the group's members was withheld by Devo to reinforce its mechanistic image."

"You ask band members the same question, you're going to get four completely different answers if they're not in the same room," Jerry Casale once said. "You'd read something Bob 1 said, something I said, something Mark said about the same concert, and you wouldn't believe that it could possibly even be the same planet. That was the idea."

But, as faithfully as facts will allow, this is a story of five spuds from an industrial wasteland with big ideas. It never should have happened. But it did. And in its wake, it leaves a parable.

Eventually, the band would ease backward. Its commercial peak—"Whip It" in the *Billboard* Top 20—represents the end of its ascendency. The music would become less interesting. Drugs would interfere. Lawsuits. Pressure for another hit. The drummer would leave. Bad choices would be made—recording lyrics by John Hinckley Jr. and the theme song to *Doctor Detroit*. The industry would cast them into exile. Machines would take over. The idea would not advance.

In the end, Devo was a microcosm of their own highly defined idea. Devo devolved. Devo ate their own brain. And who could blame them? It was one of the most delicious brains in rock history.

Chapter 1
1966

Gerald Vincent Casale walks into the Commuter's Cafeteria, in a far corner of the Kent State University student union. He is wearing a clingy fabric shirt with pirate sleeves, mod trousers with a slight flare at the bottom, and a pageboy haircut. He is neat. He is composed. He is sure of himself, even as he is surrounded by fatigued and paint-splattered beatniks, artists, and poets. He is one of them, and yet he seems different somehow. He appears to know the answer to a question that has not yet been asked.

There is a young man at one of the tables, tapping away at his portable typewriter. A woman smoking a cigarette. A few people talking. Down the hall, in the "Hub," jocks and frat boys and other assorted "straights" are eating burgers and fries. They want nothing to do with these Commuter's Cafeteria weirdos. Behind this room at the farthest end of the union is a set of glass doors that overlooks the student commons, a grassy area where, four years later, history would begin and all of this end.

The Commuter's Cafeteria has become a center of intellectual activity on a campus that is quickly maturing as an unlikely Mecca of sexy intellectualism, drugs, and rock and roll. LSD and low-grade pot are cheap and easy to score. There's an established beatnik culture: young people in fatigue jackets

Jerry Casale and Bobbie Watson, Kent State Honors College. *Photography by Joseph Horning*

and peacoats, people who write poetry and talk about art and revolution in that *particular* way. Some wear berets. A guy named Joe Walsh is playing with a local band called the Measles, one of the many blues and rock bands growing like magic mushrooms down on Water Street, the main bar strip.

Kent is in Northeast Ohio, twenty minutes from Akron, forty-five minutes from Cleveland. More importantly, it lies in the pathway of east-to-west—New York to Chicago; Los Angeles to New York. Kent is, to Jerry Casale's mind, the middle of nowhere. But that's not exactly true. It is in the middle of somewhere. But nobody knows where that is yet. That's the question that has not yet been asked.

The highest compliment you can get from Jerry is a laugh. If you can make him laugh, you have hit on something. His square-cut bangs form a lintel over a heavy brow. His eyes are dark, but when his face breaks into its smile, there is something wild and incisive. Almost immediately, and not by accident, he becomes a dominant force at the Commuter's Cafeteria. The cafeteria has five tables; two or three are informally reserved for this clique. Any time of day, they are occupied. Jerry becomes a regular.

The young man at the typewriter has a huge mustache and thick, curly hair. He is wearing bell-bottoms. His name is Bob Lewis. He is cool. He drives a Madeira red 1965 Chevy Biscayne 283 cubic inch V-8 with three-on-the-tree. He loves his car. He, too, is a leader. Like Jerry, he's remarkably smart, born and bred in this corner of Ohio, but seeming like he should have come from somewhere else. Bob is on a National Merit scholarship; Jerry is in the honors college. Bob is studying anthropology; Jerry is studying graphic design. Which seems about right. Bob watches people and tries to understand them. Jerry is clean and ordered. He understands how to distill a message. If you say something about a complex subject that seems to drive its nail, you can get Jerry to laugh.

There's something sinister behind that laugh sometimes. Maybe it's just the way he is. He was always different, always up to something.

* * *

Bob Lewis probably didn't belong in Kent. He had attended Cuyahoga Falls High School, where he was an outstanding student. He had won a National Merit Scholarship and had been accepted at the University of Chicago and Princeton. His counselor, whom Bob describes as a "slightly brain-damaged" wrestling coach, had neglected to mention that Pepperdine, another school that had accepted him, was in Malibu. So, while he could have been learning to surf, he instead chose to go to a state university twenty minutes from home. The reason for his choice was honorable enough. He was in love. His girlfriend of three years had enrolled at Kent State. Bob followed but was dumped by his lady for a frat boy halfway through the first semester. So he turned his attention to the culture around him. Bob already had a certain style. As early as ninth grade, he had accompanied his older brother to a Cleveland venue called the Jazz Temple to see John Coltrane and Cannonball Adderley.

So it seems obvious that he would become a key figure in the Commuter's Cafeteria crowd. A young woman named Bobbie Watson, a local homecoming queen on a scholarship, developed a crush on him. He had the bell-bottoms, the hair, and the youthful sophistication.

"I didn't know him really," she said, "but sensed that if I did, the world would make more sense to me. I was right—big questions about what it's all about were answered."

The group that congealed there in the bowels of the Kent student union began to discuss the world, what seemed right about it and, more importantly, what seemed wrong. Jerry Casale was especially good at pinpointing what seemed wrong.

* * *

"Biology is destiny," Jerry once said. "I was born Devo." This may be true. But let's stick for the moment to the literal: he was born Gerald Vincent Pizzute at 12:53 p.m. on July 28, 1948, at Robinson Memorial Hospital in Ravenna, just a few miles from the Kent State campus. The birth came almost nine months to the day from the wedding of Patrick and Catherine Pizzute. According to the family's account, his mother's labor was induced by the trauma of seeing her sister suffer a violent epileptic fit. Jerry came six weeks premature.

As will become clear, the notion of de-evolution can be applied to most things, including the family name. Jerry's father, a tool and die man at the Colonial Machine Co. in Kent, had been born Robert Edward Casale in Cleveland to unwed parents. In 1946, he had his name legally changed to Pasquale (anglicized to Patrick) Pizzute, adopting the surname of his foster parents. Then, in 1952, he changed names again, back to Robert Edward Casale. Amid the name changes came joy and tragedy for the young couple. A pair of twins was born twelve minutes apart in 1951; neither survived. The following year, on July 14, Robert Edward Casale Jr. was born. (In the family tradition of name changes, he would eventually become Bob 2.)

The family grew, with younger siblings trailing behind the two brothers. One after another, they entered the eight-classroom St. Patrick's School in the shadow of a Gothic church on Portage Street in Kent. There were nuns

Gerald Vincent Casale, Class of 1966,
Roosevelt High School, Kent, Ohio.
Courtesy of Roosevelt High School

in the shadowy hallways, kids crying and puking. When a student threw up, the janitor followed behind, spreading a pungent green-and-orange sawdust material to soak it up. Jerry, to keep from gagging, would walk down the hall with his head tilted upward. It was through this process that he became aware of—and eventually fascinated by—the Art Deco light fixtures, which looked like round upside-down pyramids. These ziggurats, and the experience they recalled, made an impression that would stick.

Jerry has carefully controlled the details of his personal story through the years and admits outright that many of the answers he's given are fictionalized to support the purpose of image manipulation. But when asked by an Australian radio interviewer about a recurring theme in lyrics like "Break your momma's back," and "Slap your mammy," Jerry half-heartedly confessed, "You've discovered a central problem. Devo was never loved by their mothers."

Following a show billed as Devo's "Homecoming Concert" at the Akron Civic Theatre on January 4, 1979, he went so far as to say he wished he'd never known his mother and referred to his aunts, uncles, and other attending relatives as the entire "spud gene pool."

"It's like you're born to your parents by accident," he said in a 1980 interview. "Maybe you're not the kind of person they would associate with if you didn't happen to be blood. So here they are forced to be nice to somebody that maybe they wouldn't even want to know. It goes the other way around. So there you are, stuck. I wish no one knew their parents. It's a burden."

Maybe Jerry was loved by his mother. But he grew into the kind of person who would say he was not.

"I don't really know what his home life was like," next-door neighbor and later bandmate Rod Reisman recalled. "I don't know how he and his mother got along. I don't know how he and his father got along, but Jerry was not a normal person. Of course, that doesn't make him a bad person or a weirdo. I just think there were certain aspects of his personality that he let come out. Somebody else might repress them, while Jerry would say, 'This is a crazy idea. Check this out.'"

At St. Patrick's, the subversive, nonconformist Jerry began to emerge. He would hide out of sight of the nuns, making faces and gesticulating to make the other kids laugh. As early as fifth grade, it was evident to classmates that Jerry was a gifted artist. As his boyhood friend Tim DeFrange recalled, "If drawing was a way of seeing, Jerry had 20-20 vision."

One of the nuns organized a poster-making competition. The theme was forest fire prevention, and young Jerry's illustration of two frolicking squirrels with the caption, "Save Our Friends!" took second place. But it was the hands-down popular favorite.

Soon, this technical facility began to merge with a growing perspective on the world. Jerry began to define targets.

"I never had a good time because of how horrible people were," he would later say. "The kids in my class, the teachers, the local scene. [You never knew] what you might get beat up for. You'd try to leave school, and the greasers would stand on the corner with a bicycle chain or something and make you pay them a nickel to pass. And you always felt uneasy."

He told a story later, most probably false, about how, at age sixteen, he had his teeth knocked out by a "subhuman delinquent" nicknamed Baby Huey. Once again, the notion of the picked-on outsider became an important part of the Jerry Casale—and Devo—myth. What Jerry claims is often more telling than actual fact. There is a certain kind of truth in his fabrications. Jerry was learning how to groom an entire class of misfits and nerds (the vast majority of most student populations) into his own coterie of followers. Sure, Jerry may not have had his teeth knocked out by a bully. Most of us didn't. But we can certainly relate to the idea and are willing to rally around an artist who seems to be speaking for all the persecuted souls.

Jerry made the switch from Catholic to public school at the beginning of the 1960s, when he entered Davey Junior High. The school was named after the prominent family that founded the Davey Tree Company. In their honor, Kent is nicknamed Tree City. (The small town even has its own arborist.) At Davey, Jerry's personality really took hold.

"Jerry was punk before punk was cool," his friend and later musical collaborator Peter Gregg recalled. "Before he knew what it was going to be, he was it. I knew it from the first time I saw him in the halls of the school. Jerry was the evil good boy from Day One. Walking elderly women across the street only to find out where their daughters would be later that night. No one had their guards up. Who knew? This was Ohio, for God's sake. We grow sweet corn. Jerry was always up to badness in the Midwest, Catholic, frat-boy-gone-bad way. He did pass at a glance from a distance to the unsuspecting; however, any skirt he was seriously trolling knew he was threatening. If not, her friends would quickly swoop in and set her straight. That's why predators have such a large territory."

Jerry and Peter, two years his junior, quickly became friends. Jerry, passing Peter's study hall one afternoon, spotted his pal and began gesturing through the doorway. Peter tried to contain his laughter but finally gave in. Both boys dug the rawer edge of the British invasion—the Yardbirds and the Rolling Stones. Jerry began calling his friend "Peter Noone," after the Herman's Hermits singer. They were both wild but in different ways. Peter would do crazy James Brown moves at school dances. They understood one another, which was good. Because, even then, they were growing away from the usual course of life in Tree City.

"Jerry knew Devo from the earliest," Peter said. "It was not a college art project for the masses, rather an attempt to save lives—his and some others. My guess for the starting point from which Jerry drove down the Devo road is St. Pat's in Kent, Ohio. [And it began] probably in the sixth grade. Somewhere in between the sisters driving nails through his palms and ankles at every chance and the girl across the row from him running up to tell the sisters what Jerry had just asked her to do in the dark and private cloak room."

* * *

For a teenager in Kent, life was distilled into a series of pictures and half-understood ideas. Something was happening on Friday nights down on Water Street, but that was a distant and exotic realm. Life instead trickled from record players and TV sets. Cleveland was the region's media center, offering three television networks corralled by rabbit ears and roof antennae. In 1963, a strange set of waves crossed those antennae. A Cleveland TV announcer named Ernie Anderson had been asked to host a late-night horror-movie show. He didn't want to do it. So, to preserve some modicum of dignity, he pulled a fright wig over his head, taped a cheesy Van Dyke beard to his chin, slipped into a lab coat and became Ghoulardi. He walked onto the set of Cleveland's WJW-Channel 8 and, introduced by Duane Eddy's "The Desert Rat," launched into a cool beatnik spiel, sitting on a stool smoking a cigarette, with cheap lighting effects to make him look "spooky."

"Hey, group," he'd begin at 11:20 p.m., in his sultry, back-alley voice. "Would ya believe, tonight we've got Vincent Price in *The House on Haunted Hill*. This movie is so bad, you cats should just go to bed."

The show was called *Shock Theater*. It debuted on January 18, 1963, and almost overnight (and to the surprise and partial dismay of Anderson), became a regional sensation. Friday nights became Ghoulardi nights, as he wrapped his act around movies like *Attack of the 50 Foot Woman*, *The Return of Dr. X*, and, most importantly to the future members of Devo, *Island of Lost Souls*, an adaptation of an H. G. Wells novel about genetic manipulation. One of the technological "innovations" Ghoulardi employed was to insert himself into the films through the use of a blank blue background, overlaying his image into the on-screen action. He would shrink in feigned horror from the 50 Foot Woman or pretend to tickle one of the characters. In the background, he played novelty songs and surf and garage rock—tunes like the Baskerville Hounds' "Space Rock, Parts One and Two." He used his popularity as a shield to run roughshod over station management. He lit firecrackers in the studio and rode a motorcycle through the hallways. All of these things landed directly in Devo's bag of tricks.

"The interesting aspect, I believe, was the willingness of locals to put out what they thought was funny or entertaining, coming up with what was really a new art form," Bob Lewis observed. "The irreverent humor of Northeast Ohio was also evidenced by... the famous Mad Daddy (Pete Myers, thrown off WHK radio in Akron for announcing 'The One-Eyed One Horned Flying Purple Peter Eater'). Myers was a radio phenomenon who hosted shows and had a fabulous spiel—'Let the Mellow Jello Flow!'... This all contributed to the particular kind of humor which helped form Devo's black humor."

Mad Daddy Myers had also previously hosted a B-movie program, but with nowhere near the success of Anderson. The Ghoulardi catch phrases— "stay sick," "turn blue," and "purple knif" ("fink" spelled backwards)—would become part of the native tongue among people of a certain age.

Shock Theater lasted only until 1966, when Anderson left for a successful career as a Los Angeles voice-over artist. He became the voice of ABC— that was him crooning the syllables of *The Loooove Boat*. But at the height of his Cleveland reign, an estimated 80 percent of the televisions turned on in Northeast Ohio were tuned to Ghoulardi.

Ghoulardi would have an endearing and enduring effect on this most important generation of Northeast Ohio rockers. Erick Purkhiser, who grew up in Stow, right next to Kent, would soak up the B-movie kitsch and spew it out as Lux Interior, his alter ego as lead singer for the Cramps. The Cramps' album *Stay Sick!* is a direct homage to Ghoulardi. (And the song "Mad Daddy" gave props to Pete Myers.) More than a generation later, the Akron-born Black Keys would continue the tradition with their 2014 album *Turn Blue*.

Lesser-known bands did the same. The Easter Monkeys, an 80s-era, post-punk garage band whose lineup included Pere Ubu's Jim Jones, soaked up the horror-show mystique, writing a song that included the lyrics, "Stay sick, turn blue, Ghoulardi's been waiting up for you." A tall, lumbering Akron scenester who went by the stage name "Orbit" moved to California and formed a band called Orbit and the Purple Knifs. A surf-rockabilly band in New York (via Akron) was called Purple Knif. And Michael Weldon, publisher of *Psychotronic* magazine and one of the foremost authorities on B-movie culture (and Ghoulardi), was also a player in three of Cleveland's most important pre-punk bands—the Mirrors, Styrenes and Ex-Blank-Ex. Filmmaker Jim Jarmusch was watching, too, from his home in Cuyahoga Falls, not far from where Mark Mothersbaugh and his brothers were growing up. In his early films *Stranger Than Paradise* and *Down by Law*, Jarmusch's black-and-white vision of an otherworldly America captured on film what others were spewing onto audiotape.

"We were the Ghoulardi kids," said Pere Ubu singer David Thomas. "It's been suggested by any number of us that the Cleveland/Akron (musical) event of the early '70s was attributable in large part to his influence. I was ten in 1963 when he went on air and thirteen when he left Cleveland in 1966. After him I believe that I could only have perceived the nature of media and the possibilities of the narrative voice in particular ways. Describing how he devastated the authority of the media, and of the Great and the Good, how he turned the world upside down, would take too long and would be too hard to translate—a dumb slogan or two, some primitive blue screen technique, and a couple firecrackers for 90 minutes on the TV every Friday night, how unsafe could that be? You have no idea. He was the Flibberty Jib Man."

The Ghoulardi aesthetic seemed to capture a much broader and more significant notion: Akron and Cleveland *were* a noirish sci-fi movie. In Cleveland, it was steel. In Akron, rubber. But both places were defined by aging brick factories with round chimneys that breathed fire and smoke. In Akron, housewives went out in the morning after their tire-building husbands had departed for the first shift and swept black "snow" from the doorstep. The powder was the ubiquitous carbon black that settled from the air. Otherworldly zeppelins and blimps lolled in the gray sky, as if this were Bela Lugosi's dream.

In Akron, a man who wore a hat and had a job and brought home the bacon could wake up at a house in Goodyear Heights, settle into a car with Goodyear tires, drive down Goodyear Boulevard to the Goodyear factory, grab a quick haircut at the Goodyear barbershop before clocking in at the Goodyear plant, then drive home later with the Goodyear blimp watching from above.

The windows in the Akron rubber factories were painted green, giving an eerie haze to the light inside. In the labs alongside them, rubber and polymer scientists worked with beakers and test tubes to create a new synthetic America. "Polymer Love" would be one of Jerry Casale's first significant artistic statements, a treatise on sex and technology that wallowed delightfully through the symbolism of his surroundings. He had an eye for these things, tuned in part by Ghoulardi.

The industrial landscape "worked as an art-directed backdrop for this kind of music we were making," Jerry said years later. "It had this hellish, depressing patina, this kind of dirty latex layer that fills the air, and the people in Akron seemed—their spirits were depressed; they were desperate; their kids were kind of like the characters in *Island of Lost Souls* that rebelled in the pit. In other words, they were just ready to go over the edge at any moment. They were so beaten down that they were gonna freak out. And it fit in with the early twentieth-century art movements—Expressionism, Dada, and others that were influenced by those kinds of environments in Germany and England. We had our very own backyard version of it. A rubber version."

This stuff wormed through Jerry's brain as he attended Kent's Roosevelt High School, beginning in 1962. He became active in theater and was a member of the Drama Guild and National Thespians. He was vice president of the Christian Hi-Y club and art editor for his senior yearbook, the 1966

Jerry playing harmonica in his RHS senior yearbook.
Courtesy of Roosevelt High School

Rough Rider. But he was still Jerry, dirtied up by the Yardbirds and the Rolling Stones. So, as yearbook committee members were mulling over which pictures of the track team and cheerleading squad to include, Jerry convinced them to publish a photograph of him playing harmonica, Dylan-style.

It has been widely suggested that Devo began with the 1970 Kent State shootings.

"Wrong," Peter Gregg responded. "It's true that the events of May 4, 1970, and their aftermath cemented Jerry's anger and focused his belief that human dignity is a feeble thing. But those ideas already had a strong foundation.

"The event moved Jerry more than I know," Gregg continued, "but then again, the prom moved Jerry more than I know. He and I spoke about that event at the time and (have) over the years, and the event was not the start."

Baby Huey won round one, figuratively knocking out Jerry's teeth. But Jerry was learning how to work the body. His sense of how to infiltrate an audience was forming; his talent for mockery, manipulation, and dark mischief was sharpening. He was going to mess with the spuds, and they were gonna like it. The Class of '66 gathered in the Roosevelt gymnasium for seniors day. Jerry got up on the stage and led the group in a rousing rendition of Bob Dylan's "Rainy Day Women #12 & 35," with its subversive "everybody must get stoned" chorus. Jocks sang; straight-arrow kids sang; even some of the teachers sang. There was power in this, a subversive power that Jerry was learning and teaching at the same time.

"Obviously, [high school] was a horrible and disgusting experience," Jerry reflected. "The people who were held up to you as model students—three years later they were fat and married. The teachers were either incompetents or had real personality disorders. You had to be an alien—just observing."

He put a band together and started playing Rolling Stones, Muddy Waters, and John Lee Hooker covers. Jerry was becoming a hoochie-coochie man. The band was called The Satisfied Mind, a name that seems at once mod, rocker and very, very Jerry.

Chapter 2

Little Mark Mothersbaugh got a Mr. Potato Head. It was his seventh birthday, and there is ancient 8-millimeter film of this event. In the jumpy home movie, Mark is holding up the toy kit for his father's camera while his kid brother Bobby screams in the background. Mr. Potato Head was different back then. In the 1950s, you opened up the box to find a plastic body with a spike neck to hold a real potato. You made the faces by piercing the vegetable's skin with eyes and ears and big cartoon smiles. There was a mustache and a pipe, eyeglasses and a hat. No toy before or since has made such significant use of root vegetables.

Hasbro offered children the opportunity to create their own postwar nuclear family from a sack of spuds. In 1953, Mr. Potato Head married Mrs. Potato Head, and they began producing offspring. Products called Brother Spud and Sister Yam came along a short time later. Hasbro outfitted the growing family with cars and appliances, even a boat. The Potato Heads were able to live the American dream.

Hasbro claims Mr. Potato Head was the first children's toy ever advertised on television. Mattel disputes this, insisting its Mickey Mouse guitar preceded it. Such corporate squabbling aside, it seems perfect that the first two toy commercials little Mark could have seen were for a guitar and a spud.

With that early Mr. Potato Head, every face was different, because every potato is different. This made quite an impression on young Mark. There was something human about the creative process, which transformed a child into a mad scientist-cum-plastic surgeon. Mark and Bobby were fond of making their potatoes fight. Stirred by the battle, they took bites out of their characters. "I still like the taste of raw potatoes," Mark would later observe.

That year, 1957, was an important one for Mark. In addition to Mr. Potato Head, he got his first pair of eyeglasses. Until then, his severe nearsightedness led adults to believe he was an unruly child. He got in people's faces when they spoke to him. He sat directly in front of the television. He was distracted in school, never seemed to pay any attention to the chalkboard. As a result, he was often punished. Finally, it occurred to someone at the school to have Mark's eyes tested. They discovered he was legally blind; he couldn't see more than a few inches in front of him. The day he left the optometrist's office, Mark's world changed. Through those Coke-bottle lenses, suddenly, he could see trees, clouds, chimneys, birds. "Gee, dad," he said walking outside for the first time with glasses, "is that what a jet stream is?"

Until then, when Mark drew pictures, images were of what people told him things looked like. He had never had any direct sense of artistic representation. There was a filter on everything. After he got his glasses, he began to draw trees. No other child in his class could understand why this act was so precious to him. He drew them over and over. His teacher, Mrs. Avery, said, "Why, Mark, you draw trees better than me." Mark began to dream of being an artist. At the time, he thought that being a great artist meant drawing trees better than anyone else, even the teacher. What he didn't realize was that not being able to see the trees for seven years probably affected his artistic vision more profoundly than anything else. His later interest in surrealism had a root in his early nearsighted existence.

Ed Barger, a Devo friend, patron, and sound man, later wrote and recorded a song with Mark called "Lost at Home."

"I wrote it thinking about Mark being a baby and not able to see," Barger said. "I'm lost at home / Crawled through all the rooms / I fit in none…"

Like all the best Devo music, this song blends a childlike vision with cynicism. The primal and the intelligent, constantly moving forward and back.

Mark Allen Mothersbaugh, Class of 1968—
Woodridge High School, Peninsula, Ohio.
Courtesy of Woodridge Local School District

* * *

Mark Allen Mothersbaugh was born May 18, 1950, at Akron City Hospital. He grew up in Cuyahoga Falls, a small city of less than 50,000 that borders Akron. His father, Robert Mothersbaugh, had served in World War II and attended college after his discharge, studying electronics before switching to social science. After college, Robert Mothersbaugh spent a year vagabonding in Mexico. But there was a girl back home in Akron who he couldn't get out of his mind. Her name was Mary Margaret Ratzer, a secretary who played piano for her church Sunday school department.

"It was either, 'Go home and marry her, or let her marry someone else,'" Robert recalled. "I decided I wanted to get married." He left his wandering shoes in Mexico and returned to Ohio, where he took a job as a regional sales rep for Life Savers Candy Company. Robert and Mary honeymooned in Windsor, Canada. They had planned to wait a couple of years before starting a family, but romance intervened. Mark was born nine months after the honeymoon.

The family grew. Robert Leroy Mothersbaugh Jr. (later Bob 1) was born August 11, 1952. James Michael Mothersbaugh came along in January 1954, and their sisters Sue and Amy followed. While their mother was busy with diapers and baby food, their father moved through a succession of sales jobs, leaving Life Savers to work for a book company, then a fire equipment company. He had a strong work ethic and a regard for positive thinking, honed through sales seminars and common sense. While the song "Whip It" is commonly regarded as a paean to masturbation and/or sado-masochism, it is actually derived from Mr. Mothersbaugh's maxims. "If a problem comes along, you must whip it." Self-reliance as the way to salvation.

The Mothersbaughs, helped out by Robert's GI Bill money, bought a house in Cuyahoga Falls. As they furnished it, Robert decided to include a keyboard and bought a Hammond Spinet organ. Mary played in the evenings with the kids, banging out church songs and old standards. As the kids grew older, a woman named Mrs. Fox was hired to come to the house once a week to teach piano. One after another, the children each sat down for a half-hour lesson, with Mrs. Fox patiently positioning their fingers on the keys. It took a good two hours to get through the brood. Mark played for his parents—church hymns and "Autumn Leaves," "Ebb Tide," and "Row, Row, Row Your Boat."

"I hated it," Mark said. "I thought music was a punishment to keep me from playing with my friends. That's how it felt until I was watching *The Ed Sullivan Show* and the Beatles came on. It was like someone took a gun and aimed an information bullet and shot it into my head."

He was thirteen at the time, with about seven years of bad organ experience.

"I thought, 'This is what I want to do.' So my friend Ronnie [Weizyncki] and I bought *A Hard Day's Night* music book. We sat around this tiny organ in my parents' living room. He had this accordion, and we were reading sheet music: 'It's been a hard day's night and I've been working.' We thought, 'This doesn't sound right.' After a week, we came to this horrible realization that we had learned the wrong instruments all this time. We were depressed, but it all came clear about a week later.

"I hear Ed Sullivan go, 'Back by popular demand, the Beatles!' All of a sudden, there is John Lennon sitting down behind a little portable organ, a Vox Continental. They played 'Help' and 'I'm Down.' He's playing with his elbow, up and down the keys. I'm going, 'Oh my God—I finally figured it out.'"

Little Mark had to get his hands on a Beatles record. So he scratched together his pennies and asked his dad to take him to the music store to buy the latest release by the insects from Liverpool. They went to the store, and there it was—the album cover with the four shadow-lit figures in black turtlenecks and shag haircuts. "I Want to Hold Your Hand" was printed in orange above the photo. "The Original Liverpool Sound" was printed below. Mark rushed home, pulled the record from the sleeve, carefully placed it on the turntable, dropped the needle and...something wasn't right. This did not sound like the band on *Ed Sullivan*. Mark picked up the cover.

The Beetle Beat. He read closer. This wasn't the Beatles. It was some knock-off called the Buggs, with intentionally deceiving packaging. Mark would carry the frustrating memory of this fake band; more than ten years later, he would write a song called "U Got Me Bugged."

Undaunted and still inspired, Mark began looking for people to form a band with. Of course, he already had two built-in recruits. Bobby had a general idea that he wanted to rock, but he had a little learning to do. First, he asked his parents for a sitar. So they bought him a sitar. Then he stripped all but six strings to try to make it into a guitar. His parents were kind enough to correct the mistake by giving him a real guitar. He was left-handed, but when he taught himself to play, using the bits of theory he'd learned in his organ lessons, he came out as a right-handed guitarist. Jim, recognizing the natural order in this, soon requested a drum set for his birthday.

"It just so happened that one of my best friends owned a music store in Cuyahoga Falls," their father recalled. "So that helped. I'm not talking like

I had money to throw out left and right, don't get me wrong. I had to measure all these investments. All of a sudden, we had three kids in the basement that were a trio—a group, and they were kicking it around with some music, and other kids were showing up."

Bob began picking out Chuck Berry and Rolling Stones bits on his guitar. Very soon, he began putting rock swagger into his repertoire. He learned how to mimic Pete Townshend's windmill arm sweep, a far more important discovery than anything in those years of Mrs. Fox's piano theory.

"You know, I think we always just expected it was gonna happen ever since we were little kids," Jim Mothersbaugh recalled. "I don't think Mark had a real job until he started getting involved in music. So, I mean, we took it really seriously. We spent a lot of time looking at everything about music and studying different musicians. We didn't quite know what would happen with Devo, but we knew something was there and it was worth the attention."

Actually, Mark did have at least one "real" job. When he was in grade school, his father went down to the local hardware store—one of his favorite places—and cut a little deal. He told the owners that if they hired Mark, he would pay all his son's wages out of his own pocket. He wanted Mark to learn the work ethic that was so important to him.

"He would go to the hardware store, and go to work," Robert Mothersbaugh said. "He was very proud, and I was kind of bragging him up to everybody else [the younger siblings]. 'You know, Mark's doing it, and you know, one of these days, you'll get a job.' They were never on an allowance. There was always work to do."

The household was taking on an increasingly eclectic tone. Rock in the rec room, "pull yourself up by the bootstraps" aphorisms around the dining room table. Potato fights. And animals. The family had a menagerie of odd pets. There were crows that had their tongues split to allow them a further range of sounds. The crows tried to talk, and the kids tried to understand them. There were flying squirrels. There was a monkey. All of these things were being absorbed into Mark's fertile mind—especially the monkey. He would later start wearing an ape mask as part of his everyday wardrobe, and monkeys would populate his song lyrics and artistic imagery.

As he played around with various musicians, Mark began to broaden his tastes and his chops. In high school he took some basic lessons on jazz improvisation, which further cracked open the possibilities. Around this time, he befriended a girl from nearby Firestone High School in Akron, really pretty, but also kind of hardened despite her young age. She was way into rock and R&B. She wanted to front a band, but she was so shy at the time that everyone would have to play in the next room while she sang, sitting on top of the washing machine. A few years later, as she came out of her shell, everyone who'd listen would get to hear about how she was planning to be a rock star. Well, of course, why not? They were all, in some aspect, planning to be rock stars. Otherwise, why would Bobby have learned how to strike his guitar strings as his arm swung an arc through the air? The girl's name was Chris Hynde, the younger sister of a sax player named Terry, who would soon crack into the Kent music scene. She was slender, with a brown shag haircut. She liked to hang out in downtown Akron, which she perceived as a romantic and slightly dangerous place. She loved the train station. It seemed like those trains might lead to London or Paris, and maybe one day she would board one of them. Eventually she did get out of town, settling in London, where her band the Pretenders did finally make her a star.

Mark and Chris had a band called Sat Sun Mat (after a movie theater ad for weekend matinees). It didn't last long, but it was an early star-crossing in a series of such encounters that would continue for both of them.

Meanwhile, Mark honed his technical skill in art. By the time he entered Woodridge High School in 1964, his teachers were encouraging him to focus on this talent. One teacher in particular, Nancy Brown Fidler, became a mentor. Mark studied painting and sculpture, commercial art, printmaking, and anatomy. At his high school graduation in 1968, he was awarded a ribbon for his artistic accomplishments and was recognized in the *Oriflame* yearbook as "Outstanding Senior in Art."

Mrs. Fidler "probably helped save my life by making me think about going to college, and by getting me nominated for a partial scholarship," Mark said. Even so, he had not yet figured out exactly what art could mean in his life. "I was really frightened that I was going to be a school-teacher,

Mark misuses the cutlery at a high school dinner function. *Courtesy of Woodridge Local School District*

that I was going to teach art at school. I was really worried about that. I knew, at the time, that I really didn't have enough maturity to be able to teach kids."

But he could grow hair. Boy, could he grow hair. The growing of hair became a chief pursuit for the teenager who still couldn't get that image of a wild John Lennon flailing on his little Vox keyboard out of his head.

"I'd see pictures in *Life* magazine of hippie kids," Mark recalled. "In Akron, Ohio, I was getting beat in school if my hair touched two fingers above my collar. I'd see guys with hair down to their toenails, and I'd think, 'Man, that's wild!'"

As Mark's wavy locks grew increasingly longer, he began trying out the fashions he saw on the backs of album covers. He was sent home from school one day for wearing a pair of madras trousers. He was threatened with expulsion if he didn't cut his hair. Reluctantly, he complied. But in his "Senior Last Will" printed in the May 28, 1968, issue of the Woodarian student newspaper, he bequeathed "seven years bad luck" to "any teacher who ever had a part in my compulsory haircut!" After high school, the hair grew and grew, down his back and all the way to his booty.

There's a picture that was snapped a few years later of Mark sitting on the Easter bunny's lap in an oversized wicker chair at one of those mall booths. Jerry Casale had dragged Mark to Chapel Hill Mall—the "friendliest mall of all" in Akron—where parents stood in line with their children to get a portrait in the Easter fantasyland built on a plywood platform over the fountain in the mall's concourse. Mark, wearing a tight red T-shirt, pegged jeans with the cuffs rolled and an audacious pair of two-tone, black-and-white wingtips, has wavy brown locks flowing well beyond his shoulders. Through his ever-present eyeglasses, he looks happy. The Easter bunny, with big blank eyes and floppy ears, looks like something out of Mark's skewed imagination.

Independent of Jerry Casale, Mark was forming his own reaction to the ideology of Ohio, a place, he later told *Billboard*, where "people grow up and become big babies." Although he was from Cuyahoga Falls, Akron, right next door, was what passed for a culture center, a magnet for Mark's sense of self-identification. It's no accident that he once observed that "Akron" sounds like the name of a planet. There was science fiction in his reality.

"The whole band's from Akron, Ohio, where the rubber meets the road," he once said. "It's the rubber capital of the world. There's a lot of potatoes in Akron. Akron's a big potato city. There's potatoes that drive cars and have families and jobs and take bad drugs and beat their wives and stuff. So I just spend most of my time dodging them. Mostly just trying to figure out what the hell was going on on the planet and trying to avoid the spuds that were driving around."

Mark enrolled at Kent State University in the fall of 1968. He was going to study art. He feared he was doomed to be a teacher.

Chapter 3

By early 1970, Jerry Casale had been in Kent, Ohio, for twenty-one years. He had already absorbed and processed the notion of "beautiful people." They didn't appeal to him. The notion of human antagonism? Didn't like that, except when it suited his purpose. The atmosphere of industry? "A hellish, depressing patina." As an art major, he was soaking in the curvy mutations of Dadaism and the jagged, heavy darkness of German Expressionism. As a music fan, he was careening between Captain Beefheart and the Yardbirds. He was scanning across the high points of the things he didn't like and the things he did like and beginning to see how they fit into some notion of art.

As a human being, he was surrounded by a set of people who were interacting like cells in a petri dish, forming a new culture. The Commuter's Cafeteria in the Kent State student union had solidified into a crack unit of young spuds. Bob Lewis and Bobbie Watson had become a couple. A guy named Gary Jackett, nicknamed "the General" for the decorations on his coat, had joined the fray. A musician from Cleveland, another unusually sharp wit named Chris Butler, was on campus. He would later play in an important local band called Tin Huey, then achieve greater commercial success with his New Wave brainchild, the Waitresses. And Jerry's old school friend, Peter Gregg, the wild James Brown dancer, had remained. He wasn't a Kent State student, but he hung around the crowd.

Every day, Bob drove his '65 Chevy onto campus and parked at a set of meters adjacent to the student union. Every evening, there was a parking ticket on his windshield. He would crumple it up, throw it into the back seat, and drive home.

Bob and Jerry whiled away the hours talking about the lectures of Professor Eric Mottram, a visiting scholar at Kent in the fall of 1968. Mottram was a strongly political socialist, who talked about the working class as a base for the production of all the arts. He was quite taken with Jerry and Bob, and they with him. Bob had also become a favorite of a poetry professor named Robert Bertholf, an ex-hockey player who had studied under Kingsley Weatherhead. A little later, Edward Dorn arrived, a nationally prominent poet whose "Gunslinger" series and fascination for America's westward expansion had earned him a reputation as "the Clint Eastwood of American poetry." A colorful figure willing to sip tequila and smoke pot with his protégés, Dorn would forge a friendship with these eager, off-the-beaten-path students. Bob and Dorn would remain pen pals for years.

And then there was an art historian named Charles Swanson.

"He was really intellectual," Jerry said of Swanson, "but a guy that had flipped his wig. I mean, really gone all the way. He was like Professor Erwin Corey. You'd go to his house, in any given room was a corridor (just) wide enough for a normal human to walk through. Other than that, every square inch of the house was stacked with objects, junk, magazines, and clippings. He was a pack rat collector, and just liked really heavy stuff—really incredible stuff. Then he started doing drugs late in life. He decided he was tired of talking about art; he was going to make art."

Jerry, Bob, General Jackett, and others who joined these discussions were finding an education not available in the classroom. They were in the position of being able to try out their harebrained notions on adults. And not just adults, but professors. They were being encouraged. Jerry had continued playing bass, working through the standard blues scales and notions toward something that better suited his emerging Idea. He had begun jamming with Bob Lewis and Peter Gregg. Bob had an apartment that he shared with two roommates above a barbershop called Haircut City, just off campus. The three of them would get together and play around with music.

Peter was an especially good guitarist with an especially sad biography. As Bob Lewis recounted, he came from a household of six rambunctious brothers. Around the time he started high school, his father died of a heart attack. About two years later, his mother, partially paralyzed from a water-skiing accident, committed suicide. So, by his middle teens, he was in need of a new family. He found it on Water Street.

"The Kent music community, including Joe Walsh and people in the Measles, kind of embraced and adopted him," Bob Lewis said. "He was a real good dancer, and was at all the clubs. On guitar, Pete was kind of an idiot savant. He could play really funky or soulful guitar, and perhaps most importantly for us, Pete had an incredible knack for coming up with riveting licks."

So they would sit in the apartment, hammering on an idea. It might be a hook or a goofy lyrical phrase. They'd run through a few different things, and then Jerry would laugh. That meant they were onto something. They'd keep going for hours. Pete usually provided the musical idea, with Jerry smoothing it out, keeping it simple with his bass. Bob would play slide guitar, often smearing it into unusual places. It was purposely monotonous, the simplicity of repetition allowing form to emerge. The early song "I Need a Chick" emerged from that pattern, with an almost nursery-rhyme pattern (despite its profanity). Short lines with an A-A/B-B/C-C rhyme scheme and an adolescent boys' instinct driving the content, starting with "I need a chick / to suck my dick" and devolving from there.

It also was often purposely stupid. In a sense, this reflected the teachings of Eric Mottram. There was intellectual depth to the process, but no desire whatsoever to keep a safe distance from the most common adolescent humor. Devo, later, would always mix up—and sometimes struggle with—the balance between high and low. Someone would inevitably ask them to justify how a silly, horny blowjob song was supposed to be art. But if it had made Jerry laugh initially, there was most likely something behind it.

* * *

By the spring of 1970, Jerry had entered into a casual relationship with Kent State's Students for a Democratic Society. The SDS was a national collective of campus radicals opposed to the ongoing war in Vietnam. Jerry didn't necessarily buy into the whole thing, but he was attracted to the group's general notions of revolution and subversive tactics. The local SDS chapter often held meetings in an old Victorian house on a Kent hilltop that had become known in the neighborhood as "the haunted house." This informal headquarters shared a driveway with the Casale family home. So Jerry didn't have to fall far from the nest. He used his training in graphic arts to help make posters and other propaganda for the SDS, but he was also smart enough to sort through their rhetoric. In some instances, the mindset struck him as naïve.

"They were thinking too Marxist," he said. "They didn't trust me because I wasn't a true politico. I definitely shared a lot of their sensibility about social justice, and about the corruption of the system. I knew that. All the information was there, people just didn't read. SDS would reprint blatant admissions by the Government.... They would get internal memos and reprint them, and everybody said it was propaganda. But it was the real thing, and nobody would believe it."

To Jerry, the government seemed even more dangerous than the SDS believed. He had a lot of people on campus to discuss these notions with. Two friends, Allison Krause and Jeffrey Miller, were also opposed to the war and interested in the ideas, if not all the tactics, of the SDS. Miller, who had come to Kent from New York, had dabbled musically with Chris Butler and was especially strong in his feeling that the war was wrong.

The most hardcore element of the campus radicals, a very small segment, had produced entire treatises on how to mess with The Man. "The night is your friend," one how-to newsletter began. "Dropping into a bush or clump of trees is often better than running. Don't move to [sic] soon. Invariably a curious dog (not a police dog) will pick up your trail and track you. Wait until dog is 3 feet away (don't move). Open your mouth as if you were going to say 'out,' and move your tongue to the rear of your mouth cavity. Then make a hissing sound as loud as you can."

There was information on the use of subsonic frequency generators, supposedly developed in secret by the government, that were capable of producing a sound that would cause a person to lose control of his body functions. To Jerry, immersed in the world of sound, this was especially intriguing, partly because it also seemed a little ridiculous.

The Vietnam War protesters wanted to change the world. Among the most radical of them, anarchy was a favorite tool. They embraced mischief and outright dangerous sabotage. They studied how to disable phone systems and experimented with ammonia-filled balloons. Would they put LSD in the water supply? There were plenty in the government who believed they would. But Kent was still a Midwestern state college; most of these extreme ideas remained somewhere else. In terms of student unrest, Kent wasn't even on the radar. Who needed to know the proper technique for hiding in the bushes? You could just say your piece, then go down to Water Street to see Joe Walsh play with the James Gang.

* * *

On Thursday, April 30, 1970, President Richard Nixon announced that the United States was escalating the war by invading Cambodia. The next day, a protest was held on the Kent State campus, sponsored by The World Historians Opposed to Racism and Exploitation (WHORE). It was a relatively peaceful affair, unfolding on a sunny day that found about five hundred students in jeans and headbands chanting slogans. Some of the history majors buried a copy of the Constitution. Friday's events carried over into the warm weekend night down on the Water Street strip. JB's and the Kove, the two most popular spots for live music, were packed, and talk of politics merged with the usual conversation about parties and classes, girlfriends and boyfriends. But as the beer took hold, so did the outrage about the course of Nixon's war. And soon, trouble spilled over into the street. A bonfire was set in the middle of Water Street. Students threw beer bottles at police cars, and a mob moved toward the center of town. People threw rocks and bottles through the windows of banks and utility companies.

Mark's younger brother Bobby, still in high school but playing hooky, was on campus and in the center of the action that day. As he recalled, "I was taking acid at the headquarters of the Kent chapter of SDS the Friday that the riots started and looked out a window and saw riot police beating hippies senseless." So, apparently unbeknownst to his parents, the teenager returned to Kent on Saturday.

Saturday dawned with hangovers, a downtown littered with debris, and an angry mayor. A dusk-to-dawn curfew was declared, and students were restricted to campus. A rumor began spreading that the campus ROTC building was to be the next target of the protesters. So, late in the day, Leroy Satrom, the mayor of Kent, contacted the Ohio National Guard. Around dark, a group of about six hundred students gathered on the student Commons, just outside the glass doors of the Commuter's Cafeteria. There were informal speeches, slogans, and fist-pumping. The swell began to move across campus, with other students spilling out from the dorms to join in. The group that arrived at the small, wooden ROTC building on the commons numbered more than a thousand—and Bob Mothersbaugh was amongst them.

Around eight p.m., students began throwing rocks. A wastebasket went through a window, then a couple of flares. Someone dipped a rag into the gas tank of a nearby motorcycle, lit it on fire, and threw it into the building, which caught fire. According to Bob, "I returned to Kent to join in the protests and was photographed by the FBI helping to burn an American flag." As he recalls, "[it was that American flag] which somehow burned down the ROTC building on campus."

When the fire department arrived, protesters yanked on their hoses and jabbed holes in them with knives. Police drove away the crowd with tear gas. The National Guard arrived on the scene to assist with the dispersal. Some of the soldiers were hit by rocks as the building burned to the ground.

And then came Sunday. Another demonstration. That night students blocked an intersection and, surrounded by police and guard troops with a police helicopter hovering overhead, they presented a written list of demands. These ranged from the immediate (that the guard withdraw from campus) to the long term (lowering of tuition for all students). After a bullhorn announcement that curfew had been tightened, from one a.m. to eleven p.m., anger erupted. In the scuffle that followed, two students were bayoneted. Fifty-one were arrested. That night, as police and National Guardsmen rounded up curfew violators, they stopped one of Bob Lewis' roommates, Bob Webb, on the stairs that led up to the Haircut City apartment. They arrested him.

And finally came Monday, May 4, 1970. Around 11:30 that morning, students began to gather on the Commons, some ringing the campus bell to attract a crowd. Chris Butler and Jeffrey Miller arrived together. Miller was wearing a cowboy shirt and a pair of jeans. Butler's drum set was at Miller's house.

Jerry arrived, along with other members of the group of friends. Peter Gregg was there, along with Fred Weber, Bob's other roommate, who sang with the Measles. Like most of the students, they just wanted to see what all the ruckus was about.

More arrived, upwards of 1,500. At around 11:50, the National Guard troops borrowed a bullhorn from the campus police and made an announcement to disperse. The crowd chanted, "Fuck you!" Another announcement was made. The chant evolved to "Power to the people; fuck the pigs!" A third call, a third response: "One, two, three, four; we don't want your fucking war!"

Some of the students did move on. Gregg and Weber retreated back onto the Commons, away from the guard's advance. Others continued taunting and throwing rocks and other objects. Like most students, Jerry was somewhere in the middle, attracted in part by curiosity and in part by a sense of outrage. He wasn't a rock-thrower, but neither was he a disinterested observer.

The guard, a little more than one hundred strong, formed a skirmish line and moved across the Commons, away from the student union, over a rise called Blanket Hill, and down to a practice football field. Tear gas canisters flew back and forth, almost in a game of catch. Guardsmen fired canisters at the students; the students threw them back. The guard huddled at the football field for about ten minutes, then began moving up Blanket Hill again, back in the direction from which they had come. More rocks, more taunting.

At the top of a hill, near a small pagoda, a group of the soldiers suddenly stopped, turned, and began firing. In thirteen seconds, at least fifty-four shots were fired. A crude audiotape, made from a dormitory window, sounds like a brick of firecrackers going off. For one fleeting moment, the crowd wondered what the sound was. Blanks? Warning shots?

Then the bodies began to drop. Sandra Scheuer, a student who had been walking to class, fell dead, shot in the neck. William Schroeder, an ROTC candidate who had paused to watch the commotion, was killed, shot in the back while he lay prone on the ground. Jeffrey Miller, who had earlier made an obscene gesture at the soldiers, fell dead, shot through the mouth. Allison Krause, who had cursed at the guardsmen, fell dead, shot in the side. Nine others were wounded. All the rest were stunned, angry and sad.

Jerry ran to Allison Krause's side. "I saw the huge M-16 exit wound in Allison's back. I almost passed out."

The standard line goes that the confusion of those thirteen seconds has never ended. Decades later, even in the face of a massive investigation, depositions, photographs, 8-millimeter film of the incident, interviews—a grinding quest for answers—the event remains as ambiguous as it was on that sunny May afternoon. But all those questions didn't matter to Jerry Casale. He was one of the few who found an answer that day.

Many times, Jerry has repeated the gravity of the effect. "I would not have started the idea of Devo unless this had happened. It was just the defining moment. Until then, I might've left my hair long and been a hippie. When you start to see the real way everything works, and the insidious nature of power, corruption, injustice, brute force, you realize it's just all primate behavior."

Bob Lewis' collection of unpaid parking tickets became irrelevant. A general amnesty on library and parking fines followed the shootings, saving him $700. The FBI impounded Chris Butler's drum set from Jeffrey Miller's apartment. He never got it back. That too was irrelevant. But what those

DEVO adorned in orange "Don't Shoot—I Am a Man" hunting vests, c. 1977. *Courtesy of Bobbie Watson Whitaker*

things represented—casual jamming without a sense of direction; countless afternoons in the forum of the Commuter's Cafeteria—came to an end.

"The life of the cafeteria effectively ended on May 4, 1970," Bob said. "Following the dispersal of students, immediately thereafter. The new union was built, and things were never the same. It, like Camelot, flowered, shimmered, and disappeared."

Chapter 4

Almost immediately after the Kent State shootings, James Michener came to town. He was going to write a book about an American tragedy. He interviewed student after student, everyone he could find who might have something to offer. He sent researchers out among the people. Michener was on the same fact-finding mission as much of the country in that spring, summer, and beyond. Of course, many facts would be found. But the truth would not. If there ever was a plastic reality, this was it.

And so it came to pass that James Michener, famous author, got himself invited over to Chris Butler's apartment to eat brown rice and pick some brains. But, of course, these were no ordinary brains. Jerry was there, keeping a sardonic smile from his face as the conversation began. Michener asked them about Kent, about May 4, about what they saw, how they felt. It was an engaging exchange.

Twenty minutes into the interview, there was a furious pounding at the door. Jerry jumped up and answered it. Bob Lewis was standing there with a 12-gauge shotgun. Wild-eyed, he pumped a shell into the chamber and yelled, "There's pigs all around, man! This is the revolution!" Michener nearly upchucked his brown rice.

This had all been planned in advance. It was not just a prank. It was a statement. It was, in fact, an artistic statement. A performance. Much of Kent was wrapped in sadness and anger and earnest reaction to the campus tragedy. This group was no different. But a specific decision was made to turn those feelings into a fairly elaborate, subversive statement about human stupidity. This was the new manifestation of the theories Jerry, Bob, and their friends had been tossing around. It was a turning point.

Jerry, in a more earnest attempt to commemorate the shootings, designed a graphic, a silhouetted figure falling backward, with four drops of blood. The image appeared on buttons that found their way onto tattered denim jackets and tie-dyed T-shirts. But Jerry was quickly moving beyond simple memorial gestures. The elaborate ideas of his college years were coming into focus.

* * *

By 1971, a significant cross section of the established and burgeoning local music scene became concentrated in four apartments over an electronics repair shop called DayHo Electric, with an adjoining pizza place called Guido's. Jerry lived in Apartment 1 with his girlfriend Nancy Neal. Chris Butler lived with his girlfriend in Apartment 2. Apartment 3 rotated between Peter Gregg, Joe Walsh, and their friend Bruce Hensal. And Apartment 4 was home to Terry Hynde, the sax player for 15-60-75, a group that came to be known as the Numbers Band and proved to be a glue for the local scene. More than fifty years later, the Numbers Band was still playing its sophisticated beatnik blues. Terry's kid sister Chrissie often crashed there on weekends.

Jerry decorated his apartment with a wall-size cardboard mural from Akron Provision, the butcher shop where Bob worked. The bottom half had a red brick pattern, and the top was a pastoral scene, with cows, a barn, and a windmill.

"Jerry lived down the hall from Bob and I," Bobbie Watson recalled. "He would come over every night, and so they compared their days. And they would exchange information that they had gotten during the day. Most of the talks didn't begin until real late at night. Most of the talks didn't end until two o'clock or three o'clock in the morning. I would use 'rap session' to describe them. Exploration."

Invariably, the smell of baking pizza would waft up from Guido's. They ate a lot of pizza.

There was some recording equipment downstairs at DayHo Electric, and the loose collective of musicians convinced the owner, Dave Metz, to record them. Jerry and the others had been experimenting with all kinds of sounds—windshield wipers and telephone busy signals, a washing machine. So they hauled their gear down to DayHo and laid down crude recordings of "I Need a Chick," "Rope Song," "Might Not Live Forever," and others.

"Clearly the first punk recording," Peter Gregg observed. "No matter whatever some NYC band and MTV may say about them doing the first punk recording. Not true. Jerry was way first."

Bob stuck an index card on the shop's bulletin board, announcing his desire to buy a used Fender Telecaster. A sales rep from the guitar company saw the note and told Bob he could get him a brand-new one for $150. Bob gave him the cash, and a few weeks later he was the proud owner of a blonde Telecaster with a maple neck.

* * *

Around the same time, Mark Mothersbaugh moved into a house on Balch Street, in a working-class neighborhood of West Akron. The house was rented by three friends—Marty Reymann, Ed Barger, and Dale McGough—who had grown up together in Akron's working-class Firestone Park neighborhood. Reymann and Barger had taken an interest in this sensitive, energetic young artist and allowed Mark to live there rent-free. They fed him and encouraged his ideas. He was writing and making music and visual art, supported by this hippie-style patronage.

Every day, Mark wrote. He filled notebook after notebook with observations, ideas, fragments of song lyrics and drawings, with ever-growing confi-

Booji Boy didn't mean to do it. Devo photographed at Goodyear's World of Rubber exhibit. *Courtesy of Bobbie Watson Whitaker*

dence. This eventually was published as *My Struggle*, a treatise of the wry, incisive, and sometimes vulnerable Mark Mothersbaugh. He held nothing back. There was something to offend everybody, beginning with the title's allusion to Adolph Hitler's *Mein Kampf*. The early draft of the manuscript had the working title, "The sad story of a very dead man.... My Struggle, or life in the Rubber City." At this point, the writing was a rather secret activity. Bobbie even admitted she was afraid to see it, worried it might reveal too much about the workings of her friend's mind. This version of the book had Mark A. Mothersbaugh listed as the author, but when it was published several years later, it was under the pseudonym Booji Boy, Mark's key onstage alter ego.

Despite his reticence, Mark asked his friends to contribute to the book. When few complied, he attributed some of his own writing and drawings to them. Meanwhile, he was also working on silkscreen prints and decals at the Balch Street house.

"Mark was still at college when we were living together," Ed Barger recalled. "We would go out to Kent State to shoot the negatives for his decals and burn the screens. Mark was pure, entertaining, and funny. I remember Mark left the decal paper out one night, and cockroaches ate the glue off the paper. I was like Andy Warhol's assistant, and even made a few of my own decals. I certainly gained an understanding of the creative process, and Mark was a great artist."

Mark had been introduced to Reymann and Barger by a drummer who lived behind them, a guy named Mike Powell. Mark and Powell had begun playing together in Flossy Bobbit, a two-man band that was sort of a cross between Emerson, Lake & Palmer and Suicide—high concept keyboard arpeggios with a raw, violent edge. Mark had become interested in the innovative compositions of Harry Partch and the electronic experimentation of John Cage and Morton Subotnick. He could not have known about the Fluxus activities of Czech "broken music" pioneer Milan Knížák, or heard scarce recordings of his fragmented, burned, and collaged "record-objects" dating back to 1963, as they characteristically dismantled the turntable. Yet, Mark shared his affinity (and that of the German artist Gustav Metzger) for the creative potential of Auto-Destructive Art.

"I used to take my brother's Pink Floyd records and my sister's Bee Gees records and I would destroy them," Mark later recalled. "I put scratches in them, so I could get them to skip. Because I was looking for new ways of making music."

Powell, meanwhile, had a different set of interests.

"He used to say to me, 'You know, I just sit around with my gun and say, should I blow my head off or should I go rob a gas station. Uh, I'll go rob another gas station!'" Reymann recalled. "He did six in a month or so. He had real long blonde hair at that point. He'd take any drug you gave him. You'd just hand it to him, and he'd take it! He was one heck of a drummer when he was semi-straight, but he was terrible when he was wasted. He would just go off like a damned kamikaze."

Jerry concurred: "Mike Powell was a scary, scary guy. He was about six four, thin, hyper, speed freak, blonde hair, big bugged-out kind of eyes that looked like he needed his thyroid regulated. [He was] an amazing, way too busy drummer—like if there could be one beat, he'd put in four."

Mark takes an unintended trip. *Courtesy of Bobbie Watson Whitaker*

This unlikely duo was getting gigs around the Akron area, often to the surprise and dismay of bar owners. They reached their peak one night in the lounge of Bowl-a-Rama Bowling Lanes. They had picked up a guitarist named Dane Griffin and, according to some accounts, had changed the name of the band for this gig to GOD. As Michael Powell's old friend Bill Storage remembered it: "I recall being present when Mike announced that they would use the name GOD in front of his father, and one of his father's friends named Adrian Trachel. Adrian's style was very dry, and he made some comment about the stupid name. Mike explained that it stood for 'Guitar, Organ, Drums.' Adrian responded that since Mike was obviously the brains (and the drummer) of this outfit, he should take more credit and instead use the name DOG."

"I heard GOD perform," Storage continued. "They did some incredibly bad covers, partially due to Mike's vocal contributions, including 'It's So

Easy to Fall in Love' (Buddy Holly)." In the center of the stage was an old 1950s television set filled with tomato juice. The finale was a song called "Man vs. TV." At the climactic moment, Powell jumped from behind the drum set, picked up a sledgehammer, and smashed it into the television, spewing "blood" everywhere.

This was clearly bad form for league night in Akron, the home of the Professional Bowlers Association. The bouncer chewed out GOD, but Barger was inspired. He and Reymann had been interested in fostering some kind of musical project. Reymann had some money to invest, and Barger knew production.

"We initially backed Dane Griffin," Reymann said. "We bought him a Les Paul. We took him up to the 16-track studio in Cleveland with three Black girls who were backup singers, and Mark and Mike Powell played on the recordings. When we listened to the tapes, we knew right away that we were wasting our time with Dane and decided to make Mark our next project. It was obvious he was far more talented than the rest. We put a bunch of bands together with Mark Mothersbaugh. I put up the money to back the whole thing."

Barger and Reymann bought Mark a Hammond BV organ that was converted to a Hammond B3, and three Leslie speaker cabinets that Barger had customized by Harrington's in Chicago. McGough, who worked at the post office, borrowed $4,000 from his credit union, enough for a $3,000 Mellotron analog synthesizer and some PA equipment, purchased from Staff Music in Akron. He believed, as his friends did, that this was an investment that might pay off someday. Marty also put up the cash for a Mini Moog, which Mark played with the casing removed, exposing the electronic guts in what surely was an attempt to intensify the machine's visual presence. Perhaps not surprisingly, Mark would be the only Mellotron player listed in the 1974 Directory of the American Federation of Musicians' Akron chapter.

"We spent close to twenty grand on this band," Barger said, "and that's not counting the sound system; a reel-to-reel video system; two cameras and a switcher which Marty and I owned."

One day, Mike Powell decided to pull a little prank on Mark. He slipped LSD into his friend's peanut butter and jelly sandwich. It freaked Mark out.

He wrote about it in one of his notebooks. Someday, this might be useful information.

*　*　*

Over in Kent, the collective above the pizza shop solidified. They were making music together, watching television together, swapping books and writing poems. Almost everything that passed through their atmosphere was captured like a small bird, inspected, tagged, and allowed to fly again.

Someone spotted a November 12, 1971, headline in the *Youngstown Vindicator*: "Speeding Auto Leaves Bodies Strewn on W. Federal." The article reported: "At least three persons were killed, and at least 13 were injured shortly before noon today when a car rolled along the sidewalk on Federal Street . . . sending bodies flying into the air. . . . Horrified passersby stood by helplessly as the car mowed down its victims."

Hence came one of the earliest Devo songs, "Auto Modown": "Auto Mo-down, down in Youngstown, bodies got the blues / Auto Mowdown, noon in downtown, bodies with no shoes."

"We would watch pro football," Bob Lewis recalled, "and take Ed Podolak [Raiders] and Otis Taylor [Chiefs] and turn them into [to the tune of 'Heartbreak Hotel'], 'My mother was a Negro / my father was a Pole / My name is Otis Podolak / Let me shove it in your hole.' [Once, we were] watching an end zone display where the receiving end scored a touchdown, flopped on his back, waving arms and legs in celebration, which became, [in 'Praying Hands'], 'Assume the position, go into doggy submission.'"

They got into the music of Bob Marley, channeling the loose concentration of simple beats, straightforward lyrics, and the notion of an artist fighting for liberation. All of these things were connecting.

There was another news item that also led to a song. But this one hit closer to home. In late summer of 1971, Jerry got a job as a cashier at the Adult Physiological Studies Center in downtown Akron, a coy code name for a place most people recognized as "the porno shop." In the pre-video era, this was where men in raincoats went to watch movies with titles like *Diary of a Nymph* and *School for Sex*.

Jerry smiled his bad Catholic schoolboy smile as he took the wrinkled bills from men who averted their eyes as they went to sit in the dark. He brought home pornography in which he found equal parts disgust, titillation, and humor. He'd show it to Bob Lewis, and they would get the joke. Unfortunately, Jerry had bad timing. He was serving as assistant manager in the fall of an election year, when some of the local politicians decided to make a media splash by cracking down on illicit activity. So they targeted the Adult Physiological Studies Center. There was a series of busts at the shop on obscenity charges. In one instance, police went in and arrested all the employees. Later in the same afternoon, they returned to discover the film projector back up and running, and they made another series of arrests.

So Jerry was in rather dangerous territory. On September 8, 1971, the cops walked in during a showing of *School for Sex*. They arrested Jerry for operating a theater without a license and hauled him off to jail. One friend, Jennifer Licitri, recalls that he gave a false name at the time of his arrest to avoid being identified in the newspaper—Jerry Casanova. It didn't work. The next day, the *Akron Beacon Journal* headline announced, "*School for Sex* Is Closed" and the story included Jerry's real name and address.

The experience may have been traumatic for him, but it did not go to waste. Jerry recalled it in a song called "I Been Refused," which included the line, "Judge said you're the porno king, go to jail for awhile."

* * *

In that winter of 1971, Bobbie Watson's sister Norma gave her a stack of comic books. Bobbie was a big comics fan; she had learned to read from Huey, Louie, and Dewey word balloons. She began sifting through the books. Among them was the "all-girl" issue of *Adventure Comics* #416, which included a reprint of the March–April 1948 Golden Age *Wonder Woman* (issue #28). The story focused on Professor Zool's laboratory, where he was experimenting with transforming monkeys into other animals. According to Bobbie, she showed the comic to her boyfriend Bob, who was immediately drawn to page sixty-four, to this peculiar machine invented by Professor Zool.

Booji Boy behind the wheel of the McLaren M16B that won the 1972 Indianapolis 500 at the Goodyear Tire & Rubber Co.—World of Rubber Museum in Akron. *Courtesy of Bobbie Watson Whitaker*

It was called an Evolution Machine. It was a box with a lever and some dials on the front. At the top of the lever was the word "Evolution." At the bottom, "Devolution." Zool put a monkey into the machine. When he pulled the lever downward, the monkey became a prehistoric tree fox. Devolution in action.

This was a concept that had been emerging from all those stoned, highbrow discussions and had been supported by the life they were observing around them. Bob got very excited. That night, when Jerry stopped over as usual, Bob showed him the comic book.

"My memory is a visual one," Bobbie said. "I see their animated faces and remember the energy in the room."

Like many of the key moments in Devo's history, this one has several versions. Bobbie has said in a sworn deposition that she got the comic book from her sister. She later recalled that it might have come from a thrift-store excursion. The silliness of such an argument over a *Wonder Woman* comic (and the fact that it became part of a court record) is pure Devo—and pure plastic reality. But it became as important as the discussion that followed, as Bob and Jerry played around with the term "devolution":

Devolution.

De-evolution.

The avant-garde had marched art forward, with Art Nouveau and Art Deco. What happened when all this was outdated, and art retreated?

You'd have a De-evolutionary Army.

Art De*vo*.

Devo.

That was it. A four-letter word said it all. But exactly who first uttered that word remains disputed to this day.

Chapter 5

Jerry was depressed. His longtime girlfriend, Nancy Neal, had left him. When they had met, he was a freshman, and she was a graduate student in psychology who rode a Harley. They had been together through all those important years, and now she was gone. So maybe his eye was tuned toward dark and ugly things one day when, poking around a junk store with Bobbie and Bob, he discovered an old mask. It was a leather ski mask that covered the whole head, with holes for the eyes and mouth. It was warped from being soaked with water. "Fantastically hideous," Jerry recalled. He bought it.

He loved that mask. It just seemed to capture some part of how he was feeling. He put it on and looked in the mirror. Gorj. That would be the name of the monster inside this mask. Gorj: "He who is not always thus." He wrote what Bob Lewis called a "valium prayer to the god of depression" and had a color process print made. On one side was the prayer; on the other was a picture of him wearing the mask inside his kid brother Roger's toy space helmet. He called it the Gorj card.

Jerry put together a costume to go with the mask, a butcher's jacket with an enema bag bandolier strapped over his shoulder. It was a frightening sight, hard to look at, but hard to ignore. And he began to think about what it all meant.

"Gorj was a flawed human character that had gone through some sort of psychic torture," he explained. "It was pre-De-Evolution devolution. It was performance art, but we didn't have a name for it. Obviously, the imagery we were going for, [or] stealing from, were all monsters, mutants, psychopathic killers and, you know, the underside of society. This is what basically everybody tries to ignore.

"They're so close to it themselves. It's a condition all humans find themselves in—they're all mutants. They're mutated apes, and they're psychotic, and as a species they are destroying every other species on the planet. They are basically full of shit. They have turned the world upside down, and [still] believe that they're at the top of the evolution chain. We saw through that, especially when they cease being honest about the fact that they have a dark side—when they cease having a conscience. They are capable of horror. So, freaks and mutants provide the mirror—what they seek to avoid, the vanity and folly of hip, straight people."

Gorj definitely had this dark side down pat. Jerry began to make appearances at the Kent State art school wearing the Gorj outfit, with his friend Jim Bubbi literally in tow. Jerry would have Bubbi on a leash, dressed in a Mexican wrestling mask, gym shorts, and high-top wrestling shoes. Bubbi's character was called Pootman. Pootman wasn't allowed to stand up. He stayed on all fours as he and Gorj toured the exhibits in the art school. Gorj had his enema bag filled with milk. The pair would stop at an exhibit, give it a look, and Gorj would point at it.

"Pootman!"

Pootman would wiggle his ass and hold his nose like it stunk. Then he would get his reward, a milk feeding from the enema tube. "Teachers and critics all dance the poot." That lesson from the song "Jocko Homo" came from Pootman and Gorj.

* * *

Jerry found another girl, and he became infatuated with her almost immediately. She said her maiden name was Tamara Cora Landamore, but she went by Cora Hall, indicating her marriage to an Englishman named Roger Hall. She was British, though some initially doubted her accent. And she claimed to have come from some sort of aristocratic background, but that, too seemed dubious.

"When Jerry first met her, she was ill and dressed in rags because all of her belongings were elsewhere," Bobbie Watson recalled. "She had outrageous stories of things that had just happened to her. Jerry was condescending to her, instructing her about clothes to wear, disbelieving her many stories. She was really sick and weak, and her stories of a grander life seemed to be a fiction—until her trunks arrived and we all saw that her belongings showed more sophistication than Jerry was wishing for. She changed her straggly hair into a cut that was a trademark look for her. She sewed up some little dresses from the Vogue pattern book."

She was, apparently, for real. As Bob Lewis recalled, her father was English, and her mother was Swedish; they were high-end professionals who lived at a posh address in Kensington. Then, when her mother ran off with a Swedish ballet dancer, and her father died, she was left at an orphanage. She came to the United States with her husband, Roger Hall, who had been a student of Eric Mottram.

For a time, as Jerry pursued her, Cora was the beauty and Gorj was the beast. But finally, Gorj won her blue-blooded heart.

* * *

In May 1972, as the spring quarter ended, Jerry and Cora flew to California. Bob and Bobbie followed in the red Chevy Biscayne, making their first cross-country trip. Their professor, Eric Mottram, published a poem the following year in the magazine *Sixpack*, dedicated to Bob and Jerry, titled "Left for California: The Slow Awakening."

Their friend Gary Jackett—the "General"—had moved out there the year before. He was living in Laguna Beach, in a mostly Hispanic neighborhood about an hour south of Los Angeles and a short walk from a beautifully calm beach. He was doing artwork for *The Staff*, a free "hippie, drug,

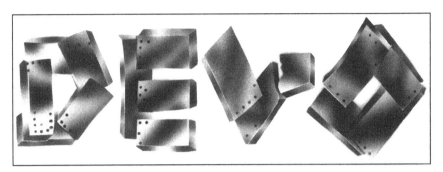

General Jackett's airbrushed "D-E-V-O" lettering to accompany *The Staff* articles. *Courtesy of Gary Jackett*

music, political paper." He had been sending dispatches from out West back to his friends in Kent, and they decided to join him. Jackett said he could get them jobs writing for the paper.

Shortly before their arrival, there was a little incident in *The Staff* newsroom. Jackett hadn't been paid for a couple of weeks. He went in to see the editor and demanded his money. The editor pulled a gun from his desk drawer and pointed it at Jackett.

"Get back to work! I'll pay you when I can," he said.

Jackett shook his head, gathered his belongings, and quit. Next thing he knew, here came the Kent contingent. Jackett was renting a duplex, and he set them up with a place to stay in the garage. Although things had turned decidedly sour at *The Staff*, Jerry and Bob still managed to get in the door.

"The editor was absolutely crazy," Jerry said. "But, you know, we drove up one week to L.A. and begged this guy to let us do something. He gave us, I think, four pages."

That was all they needed. Jerry and Bob had poured all their intellectual noodlings of the past several years into music and poetry, artwork, and stuff like Gorj. Now it was time to bring it into focus. Jerry wrote a piece called "Polymer Love." Bob wrote a piece called "Readers Vs. Breeders." These would be published on July 14, 1972, in what became referred to as *The Staff*'s "Devo issue."

"Readers Vs. Breeders" drew heavily from Eric Mottram's course syllabus, making references to *The Technological Society*, by Jacques Ellul, and *Laws of Form*, by G. Spencer Brown. Mottram, who had written an essay titled "Entropy and The Choice of Inertia" in 1970, had given a lecture at Kent State that is widely credited as one of the seminal moments in the formation of the Devo philosophy.

In "Readers Vs. Breeders," Bob wrote that technology was forcing humans to become machines, "and imperfect ones at that." Exploring the tension between technology and the organic world, he realized, "What we seek then, is that transcendent state most fully engendered by Fred Flintstone—technologically sophisticated caveman."

He continued: "The de-evolutionaries, devolutionaries, or Devo-tees, as it were, have developed as their basic premises the concepts of cathonic progress and fluid catharsis. Cathonic progress is essentially the idea of going up by going down.... The concepts of Devo are aimed at two kinds of people, those who should know but don't, and those who don't know but should."

The first group are the readers; the second are the breeders. In the face of an increasingly, artificially sanitized world, "the devolutionaries seek to remind (technocrats) of the belch, fart and belly laugh."

"If you find this explanation and presentation stimulating, or repulsive," he concluded, "contact DEVO thru the magazine. The whereabouts of the Devotees is known."

Jerry began "Polymer Love" by defining the ambiguity of the word "plastic": "On the one hand (oooh) plastic is a vituperative scream hurled against the straight world for its rigidity, negation of process, and fear of death. Conversely, plastic connotes superiority over natural forces. It is nonbiodegradable, nearly unlimited in its capacity to be transmuted in form and function; the archetype of the New Way."

He then romped through an anecdote about a couple, "Ken" and "Barbie," whose sexual encounters are sanitized and robotic, "space-age neophytes (who) know they've got to cover up."

Jerry concluded: "Like they been askin' for years: 'Does it make more sense to understand man as a biological phenomenon with all that implies, or to try to fit human behavior to the prediction-generalization model of 19th-century physics?' The man who scratches his head at that question is in trouble. To explore is divine, but to ignore is Devo."

These essays, which explicitly hammered down the foundation of the Devo Idea, were written in the California sun as the smell of the ocean carried over the rooftops. It was, potentially, an idyllic summer. Jerry and Bob were proud of their work. Jerry went so far as to mail an inscribed copy of *The Staff* to Eric Mottram in England.

As Jerry and Bob worked on the paper, Bobbie and Cora took jobs as waitresses to help with the rent, dressing in black go-go boots and miniskirts, and they all lived together in the garage. But there was plenty of tension, mostly stemming from Cora's presence. She and Jerry had frequent, bitter fights. She liked men with money, and Jerry didn't have any. Living in a garage was not something she was accustomed to. And Cora didn't necessarily endear herself to Bobbie, either.

"She kept taking my dress out of my suitcase and putting it in her suitcase, completely visible to me when I would walk to their side of the garage," Bobbie recalled. "I would retrieve it, saying nothing, and she would take it back, again and again."

That summer, as Jerry and Bob sat in the yard writing their essays, General Jackett worked alongside them, spray painting a set of letters on 17 x 24 poster board. Too big to ignore, they spelled out the word.

D-E-V-O.

Chapter 6

Although there is a variety of potato called "Early Ohio," Northeast Ohio is not known as particularly fertile spud country. It's much better known for its sweet corn. Even so, Jerry and Mark each, independently of one another, developed a fascination for the potato as an art medium. Mark's seminal Mr. Potato Head experiments help explain his side of things. But Jerry found meaning there, too. So it would only make devolved sense that one of the first interactions between these two involved potatoes.

Mark discovered some of Jerry's cut-and-paste constructions in the Kent State art department. "Jerry had blown up pictures out of his high school yearbook of especially good-looking people, and had these little potatoes hanging all over their heads, faces and stuff," he said. "(Potatoes hanging) off this kid's ear, looking like he's reading a book."

Mark, meanwhile, had been doing artwork of scientists and astronauts holding potatoes, studying them. Probably not surprisingly, each of the young artists had given deep thought to the lowly spud.

"We created our own slang, partially to entertain ourselves because we were bored," Mark said. "So we made potatoes part of the Devo philosophy and called ourselves 'spuds,' both pejoratively and as a compliment." Potatoes, he said, are "the dirty hard workers of the earth," rather than "the aristocratic, above-ground fruits of the world." Once again, the no-nonsense work ethic of Mark's father was showing up in his own philosophy.

Jerry was equally adept at breaking down the potato ethos. "The potato is a staple that keeps us alive," he said. "It is totally unglamorous and underrated. It is also a conductor of electricity. You know that they teach you in science class how to make potato transmitters and potato radio receivers. They have all eyes around... (and) the potato is a symbol of our humble beginnings."

Mark and Jerry's paths began to cross through Kent's art and music circles in the early 1970s. They became friends around 1972. Jerry recalls that the first time Mark saw him, Jerry was doing the Gorj shtick. This certainly seems appropriate. Not only did the whole band later embrace masks and costumes, but the sheer mutated ugliness of Gorj is exactly the sort of thing Mark would latch onto. Mark had been making a lot of art from found images. He took pictures from medical books, drawing himself into them and manipulating holy cards. He used a lot of idealistic '50s images. There's a drawing of a peppy-looking, uniformed service station attendant filling a vaguely erotic fur-lined woman's boot with his hose. There's what appears to be a schoolbook image of a father and son gazing cheerfully toward the night sky. The father has one hand on the son's shoulder as the son points toward the starry heavens. The caption has been edited to read, "When viewing divine creation, a parent should seize." A set of three small boxing diagrams appear above the picture, so it looks as if the boy is pointing toward them.

"Look son—Uranus!!" Mark's handwritten dialogue bubble reads. "(Little lower Johnny—lower—uh—and to the right.)"

"Oh Dad—look," the son responds. "Muhammud [sic] Ali vs. Joe Frazier. (Careful pa—I'm 'nude' to this fascist jazz.)"

✶ ✶ ✶

After his return from California, Jerry enrolled in an experimental art class at Kent State. Mark, who had continued playing in Flossy Bobbit, had also enrolled, along with General Jackett (who did a lot of traveling to and from Kent), a film student named Chuck Statler and some of the art school's best graduate students. Taught by a professor named Robert Culley, the class was called M-A-T-E-R, an acronym for something like Materials, Art, Technology, Energy, and Research.

"Man, did it produce some great stuff," Jerry recalled. The class was held in an old warehouse in downtown Kent, about a half-mile from the university. Kent State's enrollment had boomed in the 1960s, and the art department got squeezed by more "traditional" academics.

Nevertheless, the avant-garde class thrived outside of the campus mainstream. Jerry used the opportunity to hone Gorj; M-A-T-E-R was custom-made for his burgeoning performance art. Jackett and another student named John Zabrucky got some big square glass mirrors and constructed a time/space tunnel. Viewers crawled through about twelve feet of tunnel, reflected from all sides. Shortly thereafter, Zabrucky moved to Los Angeles and started a successful movie prop house called Modern Props.

Jerry's most memorable class project was called The American Dream. He got a roll of artificial grass carpeting and spread it out on the floor. Then he brought in a short-wave radio, tuned it to some horrible static, and set up a barbecue grill. He stood there cooking hot dogs in a sort of living exhibit. This was the kind of imagery Mark had been working with and that would carry throughout Devo's career—a totally recognizable, yet thoroughly mutated vision of American iconography and idealism.

* * *

The exact reason Bob Kidney decided to name his band 15-60-75 is not clear. What did happen, though, in those heady days on Water Street, is that the loose bunch of hippies and beatniks in their audience took it upon themselves to rename the band. "Going to see the Numbers tonight?" they'd ask. And so they became the Numbers Band. The group was led by the powerfully dark Kidney, who was steeped in the blues, but eventually developed his own kind of poetic take. He was tall and cast a commanding eye over his audiences. As the Numbers Band continued playing through the seventies, eighties, nineties, and well into the following century, Kidney, his brother/multi-instrumentalist Jack, and saxophonist Terry Hynde evolved through an intriguing river of artsy, minimalist, roots-inflected rock, dismantling the blues and reassembling them to suit Kidney's head. The low-key, sometimes sullen Kidney would contribute to the rotating membership of the Golden Palominos in the 1980s and would remain an important link in the Northeast Ohio rock scene, eventually being awarded the 2012 Cleveland Arts Prize for Lifetime Achievement.

Back in the early '70s, Kidney was already a discriminating band leader. Jerry's friend Rod Reisman had been playing drums, but Reisman eventually fell out of grace. It happened at closing time one night. The band was still playing, but Reisman was exhausted, so he decided to close down the set with a flourish, Keith Moon-style.

"I started kicking my drums off the stage, off my little platform! This is with a band that says they play blues and jazz, right? So, Kidney calls me over to the piano. He's playing piano in those days too. Calls me over and asks, 'Why'd you do that?'

"I said, 'Bob, I was done. I had nothing left.' I didn't want to look at him and say I really just wanted to go the fuck home. But truly, I said, 'I had nothing left. That was it, all I could do.' And he says, 'Well I don't like it. It's been done by every rock band in town.' Like a rock band was a bad thing."

So Reisman quit, and his buddy Jerry got the gig. Jerry was still on the cusp between his blues upbringing and his highly developed sense of art and subversion. Jerry was a tight, extremely simple drummer who held the band together. But Kidney soon decided he liked Jerry's bass playing better and moved him out from behind the drums.

"Everybody did exactly what (Bob Kidney) told them, where he told them, how many notes, everything. He was the General," Jerry said. "Personally, I think that was the Numbers Band that I liked the best as far as the sound went. Everybody was so good sounding in that band. It was a band I don't think ever sounded as...aggressive or edgy after that. It really got people moving back then. And Kidney, like, pulled back because he thought it was too rock and roll. I mean, I had talked him into doing a couple Hound Dog Taylor songs and things like that."

Another friend of Jerry's, a high school classmate named Tim Maglione, was playing sax with the Numbers Band at the time. He observed the push and pull between Jerry's old-school blues sensibility and his growing sense of the modern world.

"His ego often conflicted with the even larger ego of bandleader Bob Kidney," Maglione recalled. "Even at that time, Jerry's ideas about what the band should be doing musically were kind of bizarre. 15-60-75 was doing mostly 'solid' Chicago-style blues, but Jerry would frequently argue that we should be writing music that incorporated McDonald's commercials because that's what people could most identify with. We were all inundated by television commercials. He also thought the music should sound 'mechanical and industrial' because, once again, we were all in 'the industrial age' and inside we could most appreciate a sense of 'mechanical-ness,' or 'robot-like' music."

This all came to a head one evening when Jerry could no longer suppress his theater of the absurd. The band was playing Bo Diddley's "Who Do You Love," always a big highlight of the set. The dance floor was packed; people were really into it. Jerry pulled out a chimpanzee mask he'd been hiding. (His accounts of this have been contradictory; in some versions it's a Colonel Sanders mask. Either way, his point was about to become clear.) He pulled it over his head and continued playing. Halfway through the song, Kidney realized that people were laughing and pointing over to his left. He looked over and saw what was happening. "He...lost it. Just fucking lost it," Jerry recalled.

Jerry was kicked out of the Numbers Band, essentially, for devolving into an ape. It seemed like he could see where his future lay.

One night, Jerry went to see Mark's band at JB's. Mark was wearing a weird silver suit. He still had the long hair and the prog-rock leanings, but he was definitely headed in the same direction as Jerry. Jerry decided that this was the musician he needed. It was time for what soon would become infamous as "the important sound of things falling apart."

Chapter 7

In early 1973, Kent State professors Robert Bertholf and Edward Dorn were given the task of putting together an arts festival. They wanted poetry and music, performance and visual art. By then, both professors had become important influences on Bob Lewis and Jerry. They had been listening to the bright students' discussions of devolutionary theory for a year or more and had been chipping in their own ideas. Dorn, especially, had been giving considerable thought to the ironies of "progress" and wondering if civilization might indeed be moving in reverse.

"Dorn," Bertholf recalled, "was going to write a play called *Crank It Back, A Play for The Country on Its Bicentennial*, which was a review of the transportation system in 1876 as compared with 1976. And it was proposed that the 1876 transportation system, mainly built on railroads and waterways, was more efficient than a highway. Time goes forward, but culture does not necessarily go forward at the same increments of progress.

"There was talk about a lot of things. There was talk about writing a poetic line that was totally boring. [The goal of the poem] was to remove all characteristics of any high rhetorical art. And the same was talked about with music: "…Someplace I have poems by Jerry that are so awful they would have to be devolution."

Dorn and the boys had discussed a television nature program that described both the "sea mouse" and a particular species of snake that had returned from living on land to living in the sea, reversing the expected evolutionary process. He, Bertholf and a few others had become valuable sounding boards. Bertholf found both the thought and the music to be significantly unconventional.

"Originally [devolution] could be found in various ways, in various sources," Bertholf said later. "The point was that in 1971 these two people [Bob and Jerry] together brought that idea into a new contention and redefined it...made it an active medium for understanding. First, it was a socio-political situation. And then finally a whole procedure of persistently de-classical music.

"I remember in May-June of 1972, [Bob] had just bought a white electric guitar, which to me was a fairly outrageous act. Bob was playing in the evening. They were not plugged in. They were not using their amplifiers. They were just playing, but it was what I later recognized as...like Mozart. It was the same sort of driven monotonous rhythmic base that is the inverse of Mozart. Again, it was a Mozart melody that I later recognized when I heard the music that Devo was producing...the beginning of a rhythmic structure. It was distinctive enough that when I heard Devo in concert, I [could] remember the white guitar being played and that music...the determined boring chords. They were non-melodic."

Bertholf's colleague Ed Dorn was a member of the Black Mountain school, which also included Charles Olson, Robert Creeley, and Robert Duncan. A native of Illinois, Dorn arrived at Kent shortly after the campus shootings, at the invitation of Bertholf. In the 1993 preface to his *Recollection to Gran Apacheria*, a verse study of the Apache Indian tribe, he recalled his early impressions of Kent, where this Apache poem was the basis for his course in the literature of the far West.

"The atmosphere and mood among students and townspeople were disturbingly vindictive," Dorn wrote. "Graduate students, when you encountered them in the hallway, would stay you from appointments, like ancient mariners. The checkout women at Safeway held you in thrall, like a Gestapo slowly perusing your papers.

"Two members of the percipient Devo [Bob Lewis and Jerry Casale] were in that seminar," he continued. "The atmosphere was laden with innuendo. I came to see the Apache—which was the subject I'd assigned myself—as the students, 'the irreconcilables,' and the enemy, Ravenna and Kent, as the ranks of General Miles and the Cavalry. Whatever the relevance of the metastrophe, there was a heavy charge in the environment."

Jerry was one of the conductors—and receivers—of that charge. "Kent wasn't then like it is today," Jerry said. "There was some just inexplicable kind of spontaneous combustion in that area that didn't make sense really. [Of course], we didn't know that. We were taking it for granted that this was the way college should be. This is the way it always will be. At that time, Kent had a really progressive faculty.... They were responsible for bringing most of the interesting young filmmakers, sculptors and artists from the East Coast. [The faculty] brought them in as guest lecturers, poets, and musicians.

"Morton Subotnick was there doing workshops in the basement. It just was incredible. You know, Mark Rudd came and spoke—Abbie Hoffman, Norman Mailer, and Harlan Ellison. They would bring in the New York Film Festival winners, and show us all these films by, like, the Kuchar Brothers and all these underground films like *Babo 73*. We were just taking this kind of stuff for granted, that this was the way it was."

Whether they appreciated it or not, the members of the Devo circle were steeped in a culture that fed and nurtured their decidedly outsider notions. So when Bertholf and Dorn began planning the Creative Arts Festival in earnest, Bob asked them if it might be possible for him and his friends to play some music. They agreed. Of course, even they were probably not certain what they'd agreed to. A date was set for the concert—April 18, 1973—and Bob and Jerry began figuring out how to pull it off. Although they and Pete Gregg had been making music together, they had never put together a full band. But it was a given that Jerry would play bass and Bob would play guitar. For the rest of the band, they began looking around them. This was the chance Jerry had been looking for to get together with Mark. They definitely wanted him to be part of it. Rod Reisman, a townie from Kent, was a great drummer. They'd ask him to play. And Jerry's brother Bob was a decent guitarist. They could probably talk him into it. But who would sing?

Bob suggested his roommate, Fred Weber. Weber was a talented vocalist, having fronted Joe Walsh's former band, the Measles, and another big local band, Lace Wing. But he was also totally traditional. He sang pop, rock, and blues covers and originals that sounded like pop, rock, and blues covers. He hadn't been part of all these highbrow discussions of evolutionary theory, of human absurdity, of Dadaism and what their business cards would soon identify as "Chinese computer rock'n'roll." He was a bar band guy. But he was also Bob's roommate, and a really good guy. So when they asked him, he said, yeah, he'd do it.

The next hurdle was material. The group didn't have a set, per se. They had recorded some stuff, but that was before Mark had come into the mix, and it would all change with his keyboards.

And what about a name? The word "Devo" had stuck, but they wanted to give it more intellectual punch. So they settled on Sextet Devo, a moniker that somehow seemed befitting of the academic nature of the festival and the Kent State University Recital Hall where the performance was to be staged. In that same vein, and perhaps at the expense of the more polished Fred, they listed the singer as "Chas. Frederick Weber III."

By the time all this was settled, they had three days to practice. They worked on half a dozen or so songs and rehearsed diligently. They wanted to put on some kind of a "show" and decided, in keeping with the simplicity and monotony of the music, that each member would dress in a different, single color, kind of like the Olympic rings. For their newspaper advertisement for the show, they used a picture Bob had clipped from the September 1954 issue of *National Geographic*. The photograph, taken in semidarkness with infrared film, captured a group of schoolchildren sitting in a movie theater, literally frightened out of their seats. The actual source of their terror was a highly climactic moment in a documentary film of a bird and snake in a fight to the death. But the band replaced that caption with the line, "A typical Sextet Devo audience."

The picture seemed just right. Sextet Devo's music was calculated to both attract and repel. The group wanted to be heard, but it also wanted to challenge and provoke. One song they had worked on, "River Run," included a long segue into Mark's interpretive reworking of the fourth movement

```
SEXTET DEVO
GERALD CASALE, ROBERT CASALE,
ROBERT L E W I S, MARK
MOTHERSBAUGH, ROD REISMAN,
CHARLES FREDERICK WEBER, 3RD
PRESENTS




POLYRYTHMIC TONE EXERCISES IN
DE-EVOLUTION
1)PRIVATE SECRETARY
2)WIGGLE WORM
3)BEEHIVE/FLASH, WHAT GOES
AROUND COMES AROUND
4)SUBHUMAN WOMAN
5)RIVERRUN
6)SUN COME UP MOON GO DOWN
```

The Sextet Devo debut 1973 KSU Creative Arts Festival program. *Courtesy of Bobbie Watson Whitaker*

of Brahms' First Symphony. "We weren't very good musicians except for Mark at the time," Bob said, "but we were clever. In fact, maybe a little too clever. It took a long time for the audience to kind of catch up."

Meanwhile, the members of the SDS, from whom Jerry had distanced himself after the shootings, were working up some kind of a response to the Creative Arts Festival. In a communiqué to members that proposed a "Radical Arts Project," the SDS suggested, "developing a broad and coherent methodology for organizing work around the arts...maybe a critique written concerning the upcoming Creative Arts Festival." Or perhaps better, they continued, "an Action could be done around it." In the end, they seemed content to suggest, "maybe we could put out a pamphlet about 'What is Radical Arts Project, Anyway?'"

Whether such an "Action" materialized is unknown, but Sextet Devo was about to give a musical version.

The evening of the show arrived. The group, scheduled for seven p.m., was billed as "Sextet Devo: six on six" and described in the program as "polyrhythmic tone exercises in de-evolution." Bob Casale, the budding radiologist, was wearing a set of scrubs. Reisman was dressed in black to match his drum kit. Jerry was wearing a butcher's coat copped from Akron Provision. Bob Lewis had a monkey mask over his head. And Mark was dressed in a doctor's robe, a pair of Converse Chuck Taylors, and an ape mask.

The audience was rather sparse. Mark walked onto the stage alone and took his place at the keyboards, stage left. At full volume, he began to play, beginning with a mutated romp through "Here Comes Peter Cottontail," a version that would have made Mrs. Fox's skin crawl. In a twisted voice, he began with the familiar lyrics before devolving into improvisation: "There's a nurse for Uncle Johnny and a boat for sister Sue, there's a douche sack for my mommy and a box of bunny poo..."

With the band still waiting to emerge, this led to what had become known as "the headache solo." Bob Lewis described it this way: "Ka- Twinnnng (downward sliding note), Ka-Twinnng, Ka-Twinnnggg, Ka-Twing... Ker-Plannng (upward sliding note), Ker-Plannng, Ker-Plannnng, Ker-Plannnnng... Ka-Twinnng, Ka-Twinnnng, Ka-Twinnngg, Ka-Twinnng Ker-Plannng, Ker-Plannnnng, Ker-Plannnnnng, KerPlannnng This went on for 15–20 minutes, while Mark scurried about the stage, seeming to be unable to control the sound, reacting every time the cycle changed, holding his head with both hands as if beset by an horrific migraine."

The tableau was set, and the rest of the band came out, picked up their instruments, and began to build on this unsettling foundation. Their set included the songs "Private Secretary," "Wiggle Worm," "Beehive Flash," "What Comes Around Goes Around," "Subhuman Woman," "River Run," and "Sun Come Up Moon Go Down." There was a vague sense of the traditional sound of a rock band, but with Mark's keyboard squealing and squawking over the top and Jerry's sense of intentional monotony running underneath. Poor Fred Weber, dressed in a turtleneck sweater, stood sideways, holding his microphone uncertainly, as if caught between a desire to try to pick up his musical cues and a desire not to be seen in the middle of all this.

The performance was captured on primitive, black-and-white half-inch portapak video. At one point, Mark played the theme song to *Mr. Jingeling*, a local, low-tech television segment that resurfaced every Christmas season. (Mr. Jingeling, sponsored by Halle's department store in Cleveland, was a sort of full-grown elf who was the keeper of the keys to the North Pole. Every afternoon he appeared, whipping the children of Northeast Ohio into a frenzy of commercial wonder.) The band devolved from this recognizable jingle into a throbbing, monotonous, tortured blues. A single note carried the rhythm, with a thin, repetitive guitar lead over the top. Mark, adding weird keyboard noises, occasionally swung his arms, ape-like, bobbing back and forth in a decidedly un-funky groove.

In this moment, the band captured Jerry's notion of a completely devolved blues. And in fact, this earliest musical foray revealed what would become a Devo trademark: the ability to remove "soul" from the mix of pop expectations and to replace it with something else, usually gray matter. Even in this primitive performance, even with a group that didn't fully mesh musically, Sextet Devo succeeded intellectually. They managed to make their postmodern statement by giving musical "commentary" within the context of their own music. Their business cards would soon declare this "Chinese computer rock 'n' roll, scientific music + vis. arts…for beautiful mutants." This group was the opposite of, say, the Numbers Band, which fully explored the inner workings of the blues, tuning it like a supremely talented mechanic. Sextet Devo went into the same engine with a pipe wrench and sledgehammer and turned the thing into a spaceship that was bound to crash.

The performance continued, with Weber being a good soldier, lending his talented pipes to songs like "River Run," the title of which comes from the first and last words of a James Joyce novel.

The crude video of this evening shows an audience, if not frightened out of its seats, at least intrigued. There had been discussion among the band of only filming the audience, training the cameras toward the seats to record, not action, but reaction. In the audience footage that does exist, a young woman appears to whisper in the ear of her companion, half-pointing toward the stage; a young man stares in almost transparent confusion, suggesting he wants to get it, but he seems unsure how to accomplish that goal. Finally, at least one segment of the audience decided to go with the groove. "River Run" was the last song and included Mark's long Brahms solo, leading into a bossa nova of sorts. Harvey Bialy, a poet who was one of the guests at the arts festival, was accompanied by some California-style hippie chicks with long hair, beads, and fringe skirts. They got up from their seats during the instrumental interlude and began to dance, just as they might have done to the Grateful Dead.

And then it was over. Marty Reymann, who served as the band's roadie that night, helped tear down equipment and loaded the gear into his van. Reisman, who had played on the condition that he be paid, got his money and departed. He hadn't necessarily disliked the experience, but he was sure he'd had enough. Sextet Devo didn't have any more performances scheduled, and he wasn't interested in staying involved with something that didn't seem to have much future.

As for Weber: "I enjoyed goofing around with them," he said, "but after that initial performance, I knew that was it for me. It was all too strange. I don't think it necessarily had anything to do with that appearance, but I pretty much stopped performing with bands and moved to Virginia within about a month of the Sextet Devo debut."

That left the Casale brothers, Bob Lewis, and Mark Mothersbaugh to consider what they had wrought. Mark, in almost painful sincerity, reflected on the experience in *My Struggle*.

"I want people to be able to look at me and say, 'There goes a responsible man,' or, 'There goes a respectable guy,' or even both," he wrote. "Somehow though, I always end up being the clown at the fish pond, or the monkey on stage.

"My band finally gets a chance to perform at the Creative Arts Festival at Kent State University...a real intellectually pretentious affair!!! Virtual orgasm for the I.Q. conscious Spud; and, how do I walk out on stage? In a doctor's robe with a monkey mask on, standing at an organ playing 'Here comes Peter Cottontail'...and all the other guys just stood there in the wings for a full five minutes, while my face turned bright red, under the mask! Not at all the way I wanted to see it!"

Chapter 8

Mark was getting sharper and sharper at taking things out of context. He had continued a search-and-destroy mission with textbook pictures, old catalog photos, happy-homemaker advertising images, and the like, cutting them up and manipulating them. A father running into the kitchen, cat attached to one leg, little boy clinging happily to his side, is carrying a dismembered woman's nude torso like a side of beef. "Poppa's got the vittles," the caption begins. His startled wife drops her cups and saucers.

Mark found these images all around him. He rifled through the stacks at flea markets, thrift shops, and used bookstores. He knew what he liked. So it was with a highly trained eye, not long after the Sextet Devo show, that he came across an old religious pamphlet with a brown cover. The title was *Jocko-Homo Heavenbound*. The cover showed a man pushing himself out of the body of an ape, with an angel standing behind, raising her finger skyward. The writer's name was Dr. B. H. Shadduck, author of *Puddle to Paradise* and *The Toadstool Among the Tombs*.

The pamphlet had been published in Roger, Ohio, in 1924. As Mark leafed through the pages, he discovered the book's only illustration, of a devil with big wings, horns and a pitchfork, and the word "DEVOLUTION"

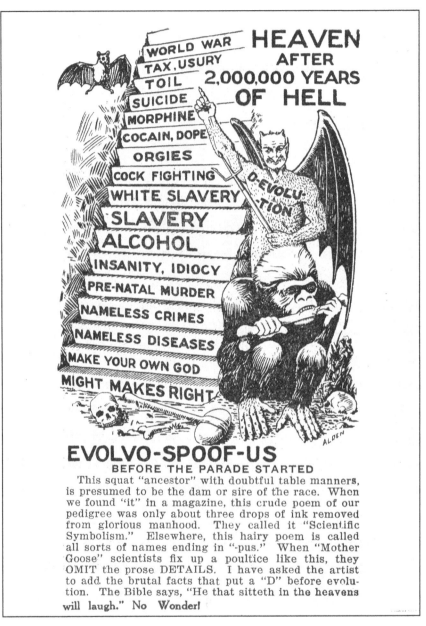

Alden's illustration of the Devil with a "D" before evolution in the 1924 B. H. Shadduck publication

written across his chest. The devil is standing behind a gruesome-looking ape gnawing on a bone and gesturing toward a flight of stairs. A bat flits by for effect; bones and a skull are scattered below. Each of the steps on this stairway to hell is labeled with sins. A whole litany of them: world war, tax, usury, toil, suicide, morphine, cocain [sic], dope, orgies, cock fighting, white slavery, slavery, alcohol, insanity, idiocy, pre-natal murder, nameless crimes, nameless diseases, make your own god, and might makes right.

With a few obvious exceptions, this could have been the backstage shenanigans at an early '70s rock concert. The good Dr. Shadduck, of course, couldn't have made that connection as he wrote fifty years earlier. But he also, based on his commentary, would not have been surprised by how quickly such activity had become romanticized by youth culture.

Shadduck clearly had a bone to pick with the state of humanity. Mark did, too. So the young art student read on. Shadduck was a staunch opponent of Darwinian evolutionism; this was one of several pamphlets he wrote on the subject. Monkey-man—literally Jocko-Homo—was at the bottom of the ladder, not the top, he argued. "God made man," Shadduck wrote, "but he used a monkey to gather the dirt." His editorial-style sermon goes on for forty pages, ending with the genteel suggestion, "Reader, if this little book seems worthwhile to you, why not send a copy to the boy in college?"

Mission accomplished. Mark found the little book incredibly worthwhile. Author Donna Kossy, in her book *Strange Creations*, referred to *Jocko-Homo Heavenbound* as the Devo "Old Testament." The book's title and ideas would later be applied to the group's musical manifesto, "Jocko Homo," a song that says pretty much everything one needs to know about the band's philosophy. Mark showed his discovery to his friends, and they recognized it as a significant entry to this bibliography they'd been compiling.

"It really pleased us to have that book," Jerry said in a 1995 magazine interview with Kossy. "[We were] building more of a reservoir...a storehouse of quack information."

Jerry and Mark, if they didn't share Shadduck's Calvinist views, were at least sympathetic to his notion of human corruption. Jerry, echoing his own reactions to the Kent State shootings, paraphrased Shadduck's thesis statement by asking, "... [H]ow can people who are responsible for so much pain, suffering and moral hypocrisy think that they are ascending into Heaven, when really, they're twisted and sick and what they think is 'good' is 'bad?'"

The book also gave ammunition to a growing notion of *plastic reality*, the concept that truth is often contradictory and impossible to nail down. "You ask band members the same question, you're going to get four completely different answers if they're not in the same room," Jerry once explained. "You'd read something Bob 1 said, something I said, something Mark said about the same concert, and you wouldn't believe that it could possibly even be the same planet. That was the idea. In other words, it would start to become clear how each level of reality was working independent of the other one, sometimes together, sometimes causing horrible conflicts. We were into that."

"Devo," he said another time, "knows everything is based on inconsistency." In Shadduck, they found moral affirmation of this. "In every false teaching," Shadduck wrote, "there is an element of truth."

With this important piece of information in hand, they continued their music-making, albeit at a casual pace. Although the Sextet Devo performance had been seen by some as a grand success, the group did not appear in public again until a full year later, at the second Creative Arts Festival. Bertholf began planning the event months in advance. In a December 1973 letter to Ed Dorn, he wrote, "Talk of the spring Arts Festival has come up again. In fact, there is a lot of pressure from far corners to change the thing around, which means, now that people see it is a good thing, they want part of the action."

Devo, having dropped the "Sextet" from its name, would be part of that action. As with the 1973 festival, Bertholf invited a number of notable poets. Robert Creeley, one of the most important figures in the Black Mountain school, was to attend. Dorn, who had left the university, would be back as a featured poet, along with Holbrook Teter and Joanne Kyger. Devo would be in heady company.

The group's lineup would require some significant retooling. The singer and drummer were gone. Jerry would at last get to move up to the microphone and handle most of the lead vocals, and Mark suggested that his brother Jim, who had been playing drums in bar bands with their other brother Bob, might be interested in joining. The Mothersbaugh siblings were fairly tight; Bob, in fact, shared an Akron apartment with his sister Sue, who was working as a receptionist. So Jim was an obvious choice, but also an intriguing one. Jim had been tinkering with a set of homemade electronic drums, attaching guitar pickups to rubber practice pads. But the gigs he was playing as part of groups like Sneaky Pete and The Mothersbaugh Band didn't exactly lend themselves to this kind of experimentation.

"My brother Bob and I were off doing the rock'n'roll thing, and getting tired of it," Jim recalled. "We realized that in the little bars in Akron nobody was going to walk up and say, 'Man, you write great music! We're gonna give you a record deal!' We had been coming to that realization, you know. We had figured out fifty different ways to play 'Smoke on The Water'—from polka versions to classical versions. And so, the Devo thing…I think Bob and I both didn't understand where it was coming from really. I don't even know if Mark and Jerry did back then. I think I was sort of an emergency fill-in when I was brought into Devo to be the drummer. It just sort of worked out because I was a willing participant for a long time, [and] they…put up with my electronics. It was a mutual arrangement."

The new version of Devo worked up a considerably different set of material. The group was scheduled to perform on April 23, 1974, in the brand-new Kent State University Governance Chambers, a room that looked like a miniature United Nations and would later be the setting for a significant scene in Devo's seminal film, *The Beginning Was the End: The Truth About De-Evolution*.

Somebody must have been smitten by the previous year's gig. The day of the performance, the *Daily Kent Stater*, the campus newspaper, waxed ecstatic: "Devo makes a triumphant return to the site of last year's spectacle.… This is your chance. This year's performance will degenerate in the Governance Chambers (as is altogether fitting). Seats will be at a premium, so get there early. Don't miss 'Private Secretary,' 'I Been Refused,' 'Sub-human Woman,' 'The Rope Song,' 'Pigs Waddle,' 'Be Stiff,' 'Androgyny,' 'O No,' and 'All of Us' as performed by Gerald and Robert Casale, Robert Lewis and James and Mark Mothersbaugh…the incredible Devo."

At seven o'clock that Tuesday evening, Devo took the stage. As with the previous year, the music was primitive, with weird keyboard splashes and droning robotic structures. Jim Mothersbaugh's drum kit cemented the mechanical intent, sounding more like something out of a tire factory than a music store. There were blips and beeps from Mark and staccato punches from Jerry's bass. They were continuing to deconstruct the idea of a rock band and to construct the grand idea that had been worming its way through all the art they were making.

After the show, Bertholf hosted a party at his home to close down another successful festival. The members of the Devo crowd attended, as did Robert Creeley. The famed poet's most distinctive physical characteristic was the patch that covered his missing left eye, giving him a somewhat gruesome presence. He looked like a pirate. After a night of drinking, the Devo musicians found themselves on Bertholf's front porch, engaged in an intellectual discussion with Creeley, who was also rather drunk. As Bob Lewis recalled, Jerry appeared, wearing his Gorj mask and putting on the whole act that went along with it. As Mark sat watching, Gorj sidled up to the famous poet and intoned, "I was not always thus."

Creeley, not missing a beat, turned to Gorj, flipped up his eye patch to reveal the ugly hole underneath, and responded. "No shit? Me neither."

Mark screamed in horror. Or was it delight?

* * *

A month after the second Creative Arts Festival, Bob Casale got married. The twenty-one-year-old, who was working as an X-ray technician, was wed to a secretary named Sherry Lynn Stringer, who had been Bob's high school sweetheart.

Their lives were moving forward. Although he would not graduate, Mark was pretty much finished with college, and Jerry, having earned degrees in both twentieth-century literature and drawing and design at Kent State, was ready to try his hand at teaching. In the spring semester of 1974, he got a job as a part-time art instructor at The University of Akron, hoping this might be the beginning of the course of his life. He had become friends with some of The University of Akron art faculty; Don Harvey, whose reputation was growing, invited Jerry to talk to his classes about the Devo multimedia concept and attended Devo performances in Kent. The job was going well, and Jerry liked doing it. Unfortunately, Mark unintentionally derailed his friend's teaching career.

Jerry had his students keep sketchbooks. The idea was to teach them that they didn't have to suddenly create a masterpiece, that the process of art was incremental, and by keeping a daily art journal, they could develop their creativity and style.

"Whatever you want to do in them, I don't care," Jerry told the class. "If you want to, cut things out of magazines, paste them in there and draw funny additions to them."

Art can be funny, he explained. There are no rules. But you still have to work at it. The questions in response were inevitable: "What's it supposed to look like? What do you expect us to do?"

"They want to know exactly what was going to get them a grade," Jerry recalled. "Pathetic. And I go, 'No, you don't understand. No two should even be alike.' Well, that even bummed them out more."

So the diligent teacher brought in sketchbooks by his artist friends to provide examples of how others had done them. Most of the friends had been in the M-A-T-E-R class. One of those artists was Mark Mothersbaugh.

"[Mark] did these really frightening scatological drawings and tracings out of medical books... but then he would draw himself as the doctor," Jerry said. "I only showed... the kids the funny stuff like... a face just barfing on the moon, and things like that. [I presented them with] ridiculous drawings... a little baby's body... [with] an old man's head on it and he'd have him saying something. I thought, 'Well, they'll think this is funny and they'll see that they can be funny.'

"Well, other stuff in that book, you couldn't possibly show it at a state university, and I knew it. So, I had just marked the pages of everybody's books that I wanted to show the class, and I hired an AV guy with an overhead projector. Then I would just show those pages of the book. We were about halfway looking through sketchbooks when a mandatory break came up, with a bell that rings. The books were under the shelf on the overhead projector cart, and the light came on and everybody leaves the classroom. I go to the teacher's lounge.

"Pretty soon I get a teacher coming in going, 'Jerry, will you step outside?'"

"What's going on?" Jerry asked.

"Well, you know, Stacey's down with Dean so-and-so and she's still crying; she's hysterical.

"She had gone back into the classroom early before the break was over, grabbed Mark's book and started flipping through it," Jerry continued. "And [she] saw—it's like this complete medical diagram of a baby being pulled out of a woman, breech birth. Mark has drawn himself in with a phone company tool belt on and a big grin on his face. Just really, really—just nasty shock-value creepy. And that did it."

The images were from a series of 1972 cards titled "Parlour Games" that also would appear in *My Struggle*. Each illustration manipulated a medical-book drawing of the birthing process, with Mark adding chainsaws, hammers, and other disturbing elements. In one picture, Dr. Mark Mothersbaugh is holding a baby that has been cut in half.

"So, I go to the Dean's office and it was just like out of a good bad movie. I walk in and the girl won't look at me. She's got all red eyes, and she stands up and leaves. [The dean] tells me to sit down and he's holding the book. And he goes, 'Well, Mr. Casale, is this your idea of an art education at Akron University?' He just turns it around, and shoves it at me open to that page. I tried to explain myself, but it didn't cut any ice. He said, 'You can finish out the semester, but you better go look for another job.'"

* * *

Two months after the Creative Arts Festival, *Time* magazine published a review of an odd book that had been making waves in Europe. It was called *The Beginning Was the End* by Oscar Kiss Maerth. The red cover, with a hollow-eyed, almost skull-like image of a man's face, bore this brief explanation of what lay inside: "How man came into being through cannibalism—intelligence can be eaten."

The basic premise of the book is that the human species was an accident of evolution. That cannibalistic apes began eating brains because it increased their sexual desire and intelligence. This brain consumption led to a sort of hyper-evolution, which led to man. But that process had also led to an oversized brain too big for the human skull to accommodate, and a resultant mental illness that triggered a perverse sense of progress, bound to lead to human demise. Maerth believed the primates had been able to communicate by ESP, but that their brain eating had destroyed this power.

"Man is a newcomer on the earth," the book begins. "He can remember neither the hour of his birth nor his origin. For a long time he fancied himself the centre of the world as he imagined it, and by God's will its appointed master. He placed himself at the apex of an imaginary self-constructed pyramid, and he has had to climb down from it step by step in the course of the last two thousand years. He stands at present on the lowest step, but he must now retreat even from there. He must learn the truth concerning his origin and himself."

The truth about de-evolution, in other words. As soon as the Devo members learned of this book, they carried the *Time* magazine review with them as proof such a book existed and became obsessed with finding a copy. Bob Lewis wrote Ed Dorn asking for help in tracking it down. They knew it would be important to them. Like *Jocko-Homo Heavenbound*, this strange piece of scholarship placed Man on the final step of his downward climb.

The Beginning Was the End was rumored to be a bestseller in Europe. "Oscar Kiss Maerth" was thought to be a pseudonym, a pun on "Oscar Kiss My Ass." The author was alleged by some to be a former Nazi hiding out in South America. According to both his widow and his close friend Klaus Schleusener, who provided editing advice, Maerth was not a Nazi or Nazi sympathizer. Even so, he clearly supported the eugenics movement for improving society, i.e. those with the best genes should be encouraged to procreate, and those with inferior genes should be prevented from breeding.

Time seemed not to take the book very seriously. The reviewer, R. Z. Sheppard, wrote that it, "bears all the markings of pristine eccentricity: a big theme, a closed system of self-perpetuating logic, a disdain for accepted thought, no specific scientific references, no index, and no bibliography."

The book, impossible to find in Kent or Akron, appeared to be a masterpiece of plastic reality, not to mention a treasure trove of devolution. Although it would take more than a year before Jerry and Bob Lewis found a copy in a New York City bookstore, it would become, in Donna Kossy's words, the Devo "New Testament."

Photo-booth images of Bobbie Watson and Bob Lewis, 1975. *Courtesy of Bobbie Watson Whitaker*

Jocko Homo: Heavenbound pamphlet by Dr. B. H. Shadduck

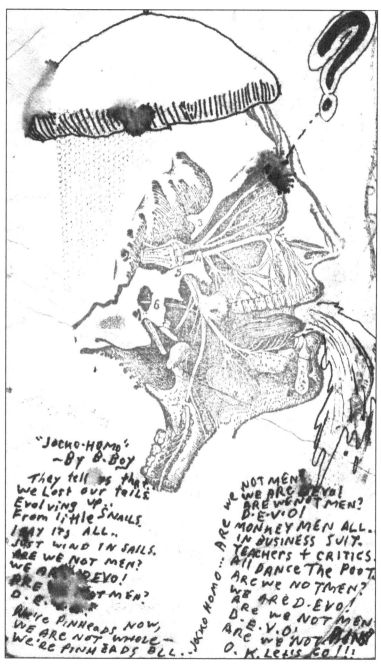

Original c. 1974 lyrics sent by Booji Boy to KSU art professor Ian Short in thanks for the inspirational pamphlet. *Courtesy of Bobbie Watson Whitaker*

Chapter 9

"What is the law?"

Dr. Moreau, standing at the edge of the House of Pain, is trying to restore order among the half-men he has surgically created from beasts. This is his domain, the Island of Lost Souls, in the creepy 1932 film adaptation of H. G. Wells' novel *The Island of Dr. Moreau*. Charles Laughton, as Moreau, cracks a whip and casts a menacing eye over his throng of mutants. Bela Lugosi, face covered with hair, gives the rote response.

"Not to run on all fours—that is the law." He addresses his fellow mutants: "Are we not men?"

"Are we not men?" they grunt in unison. The call-and-response goes on. Laughton: "What is the law?"

Lugosi: "Not to eat meat—that is the law. Are we not men?" Mutants: "Are we not men?"

Laughton: "What is the law?"

Lugosi: "Not to spill blood—that is the law. Are we not men?" Mutants: "Are we not men?"

Nearly a century later, this scene still sends shivers.

"His is the hand that makes," the congregation continues. "His is the hand that heals. His is the House of Pain."

An early outdoor performance in front of KSU's Johnson Hall. *Courtesy of Bobbie Watson Whitaker*

When the film was first released, it was widely banned, so disturbing was the notion of a scientist twisting God's work. But *Island of Lost Souls* did eventually find an audience, and forty years after its release, it had become a touchstone for young people in Northeast Ohio, thanks to Ghoulardi and his long-running successor and protégé, Chuck Schodowski. "Big Chuck" teamed up with a TV weatherman named Bob "Hoolihan" Wells. Patching together their nicknames, Hoolihan and Big Chuck continued the tradition of airing old horror movies on late-night television, amid schlocky skits and "certain ethnic" (read: Polish) jokes. *Island of Lost Souls* was a classic staple, and it burned itself into formative brains.

"It was one of those films that just scared the shit out of me as a kid," Bob Lewis recalled. Jerry, too, held a special place in his heart for the film, which he found equally frightening but also somehow sincere. And Mark had an epiphany as he made a connection between the on-screen horror and the conditions of his own existence.

"I remember watching *Island of Lost Souls*," he said, "and there's this scene near the end where there's a revolt, where the subhumans, the failed experiments—or as they called themselves [imitating a horror-movie voice] 'Not men, not beasts—THINGS!' are rebelling. They lit the jungle on fire and you see them running—at night, the fire is reflecting their shadows on the House of Pain as they run through the jungle, and you don't really see them; you see their shadows. These hunched-over creatures, hobbling in pain and terror and chaos, just trudging by this House of Pain. And I remember at that moment feeling a camaraderie, and feeling like, 'I've been there.'"

To him, Akron, with its landscape of smoke-stained factories, seemed to reflect the House of Pain. Akron was the nation's second-cloudiest city, after Seattle. It's not hard to dwell on darkness there. Mark and Jerry shared a certain disdain for a place where great numbers of young people had no future outside those hot, grimy rubber factories.

At some point, Bob Lewis copied down dialogue from the movie, recognizing its alignment with the Devo philosophy. The film's key line—"Are we not men?"—seemed to capture so much of what Devo was about and would become a key phrase in their vocabulary. The line evoked the darkness of evolutionary misdeeds, which had become a staple of the Big Idea. It also captured, with odd poignancy, the feeling of being an outsider. And it suggested the question invoked by the Kent State tragedy—the worth of a human life. Devo were brave nerds, and that line could just as easily be uttered in a jock-nerd confrontation. "Am I not a man?" a brave nerd might utter as the jock grabs him by the shirt-front. Of course, the jock would probably just screw up his face for a moment, trying to figure it out, before popping him one anyway. Still, the idea of the put-upon outsider rebelling against his conditions had an important resonance.

* * *

Devo still didn't think of themselves as a working band, or even, necessarily, a band. The core members were making art of all sorts, and music happened to be one medium. But it was also an increasingly obvious one. Perhaps even the strange music of these art students could find a niche. If a message was to be spread, a stage in a bar was better than a highbrow zine or an art journal.

In Kent, that connection was especially obvious. The college town's music scene had continued to thrive. The James Gang had broken out, and Joe Walsh, former scenester, had become a bona fide rock star. When the James Gang opened for the Who in Pittsburgh in 1969, Pete Townshend called Walsh "the greatest living guitarist." Walsh, even as he grew more famous, remained a touchstone for the musicians back in Kent. Others, including Glass Harp's Phil Keaggy, had also gotten attention. Keaggy was an unusually talented guitarist. He was reputedly one of the few guitarists Jimi Hendrix ever allowed into Electric Ladyland studios. There had been nights, not so long before, when one could go see both guitarists playing in local bars next door to one another.

Back home, the Numbers Band remained a rock of the foundation, holding court at JB's, the Kove, Walter's Café, and other clubs. So, after the second Creative Arts Festival, Jerry asked Bob Kidney if his group might be able to open for the Numbers Band. Kidney, despite the previous tension with Jerry, agreed.

Jerry immediately got busy designing his stage costume. He obtained a butcher's coat and spent countless hours dipping the ends of a couple hundred tampons into liquid latex primary colors—red, yellow and blue. He had a girlfriend help him sew the tampons onto the coat. When it was finished, it looked like a fringe jacket, which was the desired effect. It worked as a commentary on the whole Woodstock aesthetic: Roger Daltrey looked good in fringe. Sly Stone looked good in fringe. Jerry looked mutated in fringe.

The coat is described in Booji Boy's *My Struggle*, complete with a diagram for painting the tampons. This "simple experiment involving the phenomena of dreams" came with a warning: "This experiment should not be performed by children, without adult supervision."

The show was at the Kove. Jerry had asked his friend, Pete Gregg, to sit in with the band on a few songs—"I Need a Chick," which Pete had co-written, "Auto Modown," and "I Been Refused," the song inspired by the Adult Physiological Studies Center affair of a few years before. Jerry donned his outrageous coat of many tampons and took the stage. Jaws dropped. These were Numbers Band fans, after all. They had come to boogie. Jerry and company had come with a completely different agenda. There was a certain sense of convention even in a bohemian college town and Devo, from its very beginnings, was finding friction at nearly every turn. The experiment had succeeded in the safe haven on the Creative Arts Festival. Now it was time to carry the word out to the masses.

"Am I not a man?" the coat seemed to scream.

The band began playing, anchored by Jim Mothersbaugh's electronic drums. Jim had been working steadily on improving this kit. It was impressive not only for its innovation—one of the first of its kind—but also for its sheer visual effect. He had gone to a local Midas muffler shop and had pieces of tailpipe bent and plated with chrome. The kit, with a white-noise generator for a high hat and pads triggered by humbucker guitar pickups, was hooked to a synthesizer that sometimes took on a life of its own. The operation, Jim recalled, was still very crude. "I mean, sometimes we'd be on stage and these things would just lose control and start making their own sounds and noises," he said. "We'd have to stop and get the stage quiet from vibrating, so we could get 'em fixed and get going from there."

To Jerry, the drums were the instrumental equivalent of the tampon coat. "God, those homemade electronic drums sure looked impressive," he said. "Incredible, frightening looking. Everything was made from scratch. It's like if the Little Rascals said, 'I could make some drums.' The welded base alone, it opened up into a V, it weighed something like seventy pounds. We'd set that up for a gig. People would just look and go, 'What the fuck?' They would just be horrified. And then the sound that came out was completely unmusical. It was just like amplified trashcans. Made it sound great though."

The drum machine was a rarity. Sly Stone had pioneered its use, including one on his 1971 hit, "Family Affair." But the last place one would expect to find such a kit was behind a struggling local band in Kent, Ohio.

Recollections vary on the band's lineup that night. Bob Casale probably didn't play, and Bob Lewis probably did. Regardless, everyone and everything on the stage—even Jim's drum set—took a backseat to Jerry's coat. He would turn sharply, and the tampons would fly about from his sleeves and body. He would pull them off and throw them into the crowd. His effort at performance art was met with bewilderment.

Midway through the set, Jerry invited Gregg to join in. This had been his main musical partner at the beginning of this experiment. Gregg was a talented guitarist, but uncomfortable playing before a crowd. So, suffering from a combination of stage fright and what he later described as a "home medication accident," stoned and dumbfounded, he spent his whole time on stage tuning his guitar. Confused barflies probably assumed it was part of the show. At least he wasn't pelting them with feminine products in the name of art.

* * *

Bob Lewis was growing more serious about Devo's possibilities. In a letter to Ed Dorn, he wrote, "Up until now, the stuff that has been put together is a poor joke, with the punch line being that there was lacking one rather crucial factor, i.e., the sheer physical dexterity necessary for any successful assay into the world of musical performance. This, with time, has been somewhat alleviated, and it begins to progress more rapidly. Will send cassette when possible and congruent with ego pre-requisites."

The band had continued recording sporadically. Marty Reymann and Ed Barger had been so enthusiastic about Mark's future that they decided to build a studio specifically for him. Behind a car wash Marty's brother owned in Norton, near Akron, they built a small concrete-block building. Mark came up with its name. He dubbed it Man Ray Studios, a play on Reymann's surname that also directly referenced the famous French Dada-Surrealist, Man Ray.

"Marty and I built Man Ray Studio from the ground up," Barger said. "We owned the building and equipment, while Marty's brother Dennis owned the land and car wash. I designed the studio, and it was made of cement blocks. I even had the slabs soundproofed from the walls, so when

The band at Kent State on May 13, 1977. *Courtesy of Bobbie Watson Whitaker*

the trucks rumbled by you wouldn't hear them. The control room slab was separate from the studio. The sound from the studio was separate from the control room. This was not some converted garage, but carefully planned and built as a recording studio. I had an all-tube Ampex four-track—just like the machine with which The Beatles recorded Sgt. Pepper."

The band soon began to rehearse there, which, Mark recalled, came with a rather unusual set of conditions.

"It cost us 50 cents every time we rehearsed because we had to drive through a car wash to get to our bunker," he said. "In the winter...our car would just be covered in a sheet of ice."

Even as Man Ray was emerging as a home base, Devo ventured into Audio Recording, a state-of-the-art 16-track studio in Cleveland, to cut a demo. Playing on those sessions were Jerry and the three Mothersbaugh brothers. Their friend Bruce Hensal, who had been touring with Joe Walsh, went with them to help produce.

"We were freaking the engineer out because he was used to working with Grand Funk Railroad," Hensal said, "and we kept asking him if he could make the guitar a little smaller, a little thinner. He was like, 'What?'"

Not to mention this crazy set of electronic drums. Bob Lewis remembers that the material recorded in Cleveland included "Mechanical Man" and "Smart Patrol."

Devo had also produced some tapes at an Akron studio called Krieger-Field, named after a St. Bernard. The growing archive of increasingly proficient material had yielded a respectable demo tape, and Bob decided to try to move the matter forward. A friend from the early college days, Patrick Cullie, had moved out West at the urging of Hensal. Bob and Cullie, along with Fred Weber and a few others, had gone to Woodstock together and had both been students of Bertholf's. In 1970, right after the shootings, Hensal had gotten a job working for famed promoter and rock impresario Bill Graham, running sound at the Fillmore West in San Francisco. Hensal hired Cullie who, in part through his friendship with Joe Walsh, had gotten into the record business. But he had still maintained his Kent friendships. This led to an almost surrealistic moment on May 4, 1970.

"The day of the shooting," Cullie recalled, "I was riding in a limo to Ann Arbor with Rod Stewart and the Faces, heading for a photo shoot when it came on the radio. I was freaked because all my friends, lovers and both my sisters were there."

Bob and Cullie had remained close. So in the summer of 1974, Bob and an old Commuter's Cafeteria friend named Peggy Freemon set off for California to find him.

"Bob wanted to get advice on how to market a rock group, because that is what Cullie was doing, and very successfully," Bertholf recalled. "He was trying to get information from a person who was experienced in the field. How do we approach the act of making it and how to find a studio in California that would make a master tape, or whatever the technical term is."

Bertholf, at the time, had "serious doubts" about whether Devo had any chance of succeeding. But Cullie had seen Devo during his visits back to

Kent and had been especially impressed with Mark. "I saw then the genius of this kid I had been hearing about," he said.

Cullie had also seen the tampon coat, which helped lead him to believe Devo was "a performance art project, not really a commercial entity."

Bob did find Cullie in California. They talked. Cullie offered what advice he could and agreed to accept the 16-track demos Bob had brought along. He would see if he could open any doors. Through these same connections, Bob also managed to get the tapes into the hands of Irving Azoff, "a young self-made millionaire via the Eagles, Joe Walsh, Minnie [Ripperton], etc."

Cullie shared Devo's art-school sensibilities, but he worked in the music business mainstream, and recognized these tapes might be hard on the ears of his associates. He promised to do what he could.

* * *

Meanwhile, the more Devo gelled into a band, the more tension there was between the members. Jerry argued with Jim. Mark argued with Jerry. Bob Lewis, who also argued with Jerry, was being eased out. Marty Reymann and Ed Barger, Mark's patrons, didn't get along with Jerry. There was not yet a stable lineup, yet even the core group seemed unstable. At one point, everyone except Mark and Jerry had quit the band. Bob Casale stayed away through 1974 and much of 1975. "The important sound of things falling apart"—adopted as the band's slogan—was as fitting a description for the personnel as for the music.

Bobbie Watson recalled that a lot of Jerry and Bob's ongoing conversations focused on "how frustrated they were about the band moving forward and Mark not directing his energies the way Jerry would like him to. During that period there was a lot of hostility between Jerry and Mark, and Bob [Lewis] was the mediator. Mark was resistant to anything directly from Jerry."

Jim also found himself a subject of Jerry's criticism.

"Jerry realized he could run Jim off," Barger said. "He would do things that the others would scratch their heads and wonder about. Jerry was very sophisticated, and would plan years ahead. The other band members would go along with Jerry, not knowing that these deeds would come back to bite them later. I think he was also looking ahead to whoever would be the drummer. He knew whoever replaced Jim would eventually hate him too. Everyone would eventually."

Jerry was, indeed, a dominant personality. He was ambitious and confident, and these characteristics inevitably earned him some enemies. Reymann, who had invested considerable money, time, and goodwill in Mark, was frustrated with the direction of Mark's career, and especially blunt about Jerry's involvement. "Since the beginning, we kept on telling [Mark] to get rid of this dud. I've disliked Jerry Casale since the moment I met him. We told Mark so many times to throw that jerk out of the band."

But Devo clearly needed Jerry. He was the engine that kept the thing driving forward.

* * *

The band recorded some more material in the fall of 1974. At Krieger-Field Studio in Akron, Devo put down versions of "Be Stiff" and "Can You Take It?" The music, in the studio anyway, was becoming more polished and coherent, even as the live shows continued to confound and occasionally inflame audiences. According to the band's official Devo Rap Sheet, membership at the time included all three Bobs—Lewis, Casale, and Mothersbaugh.

As the Krieger-Field sessions continued, Devo was booked to play a benefit at JB's for *Shelly's*, a homespun literary magazine produced by Shelly's Book Bar in Kent. As described the following year in Kent State's Chestnut Burr yearbook, Shelly's was a "dingy dimly-lit bookshop where, since October 1973, a group of poets and assorted interesteds have been meeting weekly in an atmosphere both argumentative and appreciative.... Shelly's is the kind of slice of life depicted in Norman Rockwell paintings. The faded green walls and the aisles are lined mostly with used paperbacks, and there is that inevitable scent of mustiness found in all bookstores worth their salt.... Many of those who participated in Shelly's from the start were originally associated with the *Human Issue*, the university-sponsored literary magazine.... In an obscure

Jerry and Bob1 perform in stockings, Gurkha pants and custom "Huboon" T-shirts. *Courtesy of Bobbie Watson Whitaker*

Call-and-response with audience. *Courtesy of Bobbie Watson Whitaker*

Mark fronts the band from offstage. *Courtesy of Bobbie Watson Whitaker*

little store in a mostly obscure town, a refreshing and intense experience takes place regularly that receives no prizes and is accorded little acclaim."

The magazine's first issue, in October 1974, included song lyrics by Jerry, poetry by Bob, and illustrations by Mark. Jerry's lyrics to "All of Us," which would later be reworked into the song "Going Under," include a quintessential verse about a place where "dreams are crushed" and "hopes are smashed."

"All you stupids anyway," it continues, "We're all going to die some-day..." Mark's illustrations continue his twisted-doctor motif. The magazine printed a two-panel image he'd been producing on decals. In one of the panels, a man in glasses and a lab coat stands before a man in an armchair, reading a newspaper printed with "ALL OF US." The doctor is holding a pitchfork with what look like testicles dangling from the end, aiming the tines toward the man's head. A child holding a tire appears to be falling from above, toward the seated man. These panels would later be published in *My Struggle*.

Bob Lewis wrote a poem about May 4, titled "Tree City #1." After describing the dawn, Bob writes,

> Mid day, mid day the fourth day of May a calm unreality in the airs above the Commons, the guard ranged across the open…fire in the streets!
> fire on the green!
> Anarchy / Revolt / Alarum terror sweeps the velveeta people.
> …gas…gas…it's a gasssss

Devo supported this literary venture by playing the JB's benefit. Bob had set up the show, which proved to further a growing trend. Audiences were repelled by the group, and Devo's response was to heap on more revulsion. As long as they were on stage, they could crack Dr. Moreau's whip. The lessons Jerry had learned goading his high school assembly to sing "everybody must get stoned" were finding a real-world application. He found a thrill in this.

"I remember playing [JB's in the fall of '74]," Jerry said. "We were doing 'Last Time I Saw St. Louis' and songs like that. 'Oh No,' 'You Go Home,' and all those really obnoxious kinds of things. We'd go, 'Here's one by Bad Company!' and we'd play 'Can You Take It.' People are going, 'What the fuck?' Losing it."

Although Bob Lewis had booked the show and remained dedicated to helping Devo progress, this gig proved to be a turning point. It was his last time on stage as a regular member of the band.

Maybe this was inevitable. Bob Mothersbaugh, clearly a more accomplished guitarist, was becoming a regular member of the lineup. Additionally, there was tension between Bob Lewis and Jerry. It stemmed from the proto-Devo days, right through Bob's insistence on Fred Weber as the Sextet Devo vocalist and continued through his inability to make headway with Patrick Cullie and the California music industry. So maybe Bob saw a split coming, but that didn't make him feel any better about it.

DEVO at JB's at a benefit show for Shelly's literary journal, 1977. *Courtesy of Bobbie Watson Whitaker*

DEVO at JB's at a benefit show for Shelly's literary journal, 1977. *Courtesy of Bobbie Watson Whitaker*

Chapter 10

In January of 1975, Bob Lewis wrote a letter to Ed Dorn and his wife Jennifer.

> With the equinox comes the spring issue of *Shelly's*, which will follow shortly, and which promises to be hot stuff. It appears that Messrs. Casale, Mothersbaugh and myself will be able to affect at least a temporary overthrow of portions of La Charity's godson, at least long enough to get in a couple of shots, and there is talk of having various local personae 'lecture' to freshman classes, (We already have in our possession a number of grad assistant types who require the magazine for their courses), and I can just see Jerry talking to various assembled concerning potato love and the genetic imperative.

"La Charity" is a reference to the owner of Shelly's Book Bar. The store and its literary magazine were providing a much-needed platform. Bob, as editor of the third issue of *Shelly's* magazine, found a nonmusical venue for a philosophy that had by then been festering for years. He used the magazine to reprint Jerry's "Polymer Love," and his "Readers Vs. Breeders" from *The Staff*. He also included artwork by General Jackett—a dark illustration of a woman in bondage, bending over from behind, with a train barreling toward her bare buttocks. In a separate, inset panel, the same train is making its exit.

The band consults with Bob Lewis in the apartment dining room at 103 S. Portage Path in Akron. *Courtesy of Bobbie Watson Whitaker*

The issue was published shortly after the fifth anniversary of the May 4 shootings. As Bob's poem from the October issue attests, the event still resonated sharply. In the issue edited by Bob, Mark wrote his own May 4 poem. Written in four numbered stanzas, it includes a passage about Allison Krause from the perspective of her lover. "Allison—sweet Allison.... We were to be wed in June," it says, going on to sketch the shootings in vivid minimalist style.

Among Jerry's contributions was a form letter for the breakup of a relationship. The letter, attributed to "Lt. Jerry Casanova," seems generic, with fill-in-the-blank spaces where the names should be. It begins, "It isn't that I've tried to avoid you but I have decided that we shouldn't see each other anymore." But it also includes the line, "I'm going to Jamaica for awhile with friends." Cora Hall, having toyed around with Jerry's heart (and filched his favorite pair of sunglasses) had, several months before, traveled to Jamaica to house-sit for friends.

Bob reported this news in a letter to Ed and Jennifer Dorn: "As you may already know, Cora is at this moment in time located in England. You see, after visiting Jerry in L.A., making $100 worth of long-distance calls around the globe, and ripping-off his most prized sunglasses, she went off to Jamaica on a little jaunt. On the way back to the Coast, she met some guy in Vegas who was flying to England the next day, so she wangled an invite, and wound up on the sceptered isle. Well, England bummed her, so she called Jerry trans-Atlantically and asked him to front the ca$h for her flying back to the Coast; well now, my man Jerry is often a turkey, but not this close to Thanksgiving, and he politely declined to get suckered that way."

So maybe the letter was real, and maybe it wasn't. But Jerry Casanova was behind in the count.

*　*　*

With the band in a state of relative confusion and near-limbo, Mark continued diligently working on his art. In February of 1975, he scored a solo show at the Packard Gallery, an edgy venue by Akron standards, run by an owner dedicated primarily to bringing current New York artists to the Midwest. Ray Packard had brought Peter Max to town and trotted him out in front of an elementary school class. He regularly showed works by burgeoning artists from around the country. His gallery presented significant exhibitions by Andy Warhol and Louise Nevelson, among others. An outspoken critic of the local art scene, Packard once commented that, "If all the world were like Akron, art would die for lack of support."

So he was probably especially pleased to be able to support a homegrown talent like Mark. The show, which opened in February of 1975, featured a series of hand-stamped prints and lithographed postcards. The prints had the aspect of wrapping paper, with a series of small, repeated images, some from children's rubber stamp kits and some from old engravings from grocery store ads—things like soap boxes and tomato juice jars that evoked Warhol. The postcards recreated old magazine and book illustrations.

When the show opened, Mark was featured in an *Akron Beacon Journal* story, which described him as "good-natured and somewhat shy" and made special note of his eyeglasses and their yellow, green, and blue enameled frames. Perhaps to appease a mainstream audience, Mark told the reporter, "I've decided to quit being crazy and try to come up with something coherent. What I was doing before—things like silkscreens of disemboweled females—wasn't doing me any good. It was getting people mad at me." The article made no mention of Devo, and only passing reference to Mark being a "composer and performer of rock-oriented music for keyboard synthesizers."

Mark's pieces at the Packard Gallery were priced cheap—$20 or $30—but he had trouble selling them. He was finding the same frustration Packard had been stewing in. Mark had even gone so far as to place classified ads in *Rolling Stone* to sell his artworks but received little response.

"I remember my Uncle Gene came to one show," he recalled of another exhibit, "and he was the only person who bought a painting. He felt sorry for me."

Still, Mark did find a way to make a living using his art background. He rented a space in a downtown Akron mall, Quaker Square, in the converted former Quaker Oats factory. Marty Reymann says he put up some money to help get the venture started. Surrounded by historic artifacts—including advertisements for Quaker's "cereal shot from guns!"—Mark opened a shop called Unit Services, where he sold rubber stamps and printed T-shirts. Jerry joined him working the counter. The twelve-hour day was divided into two six-hour shifts, but they often spent long hours together in the store, talking.

Mark spent a good deal of time rummaging for materials. Although he made a lot of his own stamps, he also used discarded dies that he found at rummage sales, flea markets, antique stores, and the like. He was especially fond of shopping in novelty shops. Ed Barger accompanied him on some of these trips.

"He would always ask the owner if we could go into the back rooms," Barger said. "We would rummage through everything. Mark has this great novelty collection. Since I knew he liked them, I bought lots for him. And things I liked, he would buy for me. Mark was a generous person."

Mark in a Kalimba Bros. mask with Jerry at DEVO HQ in Akron. *Courtesy of Bobbie Watson Whitaker*

On one of these trips, Mark ventured into a shop in nearby Canton called Marsino's. Digging through the oddball goodies, Mark came across a rubber mask of a baby's head, with orange molded hair, rosy cheeks, and a round, open mouth. It was innocent-looking, but also kind of disturbing. Mark, who had been wearing his rubber ape mask on stage, was immediately drawn to this baby's head. He bought it and, as Jerry had done a few years before with the Gorj mask, he created a name and character to go with it: Boogie Boy, which would later be amended to Booji Boy, thereby distancing the character from the hippie, get-down music of the Water Street bar strip.

Booji Boy represented the infantile spirit of de-evolution. When Mark wore the mask, he spoke and sang in a high-pitched tone, unburdened by the realities of the world. "Oh, Dad—we're all De-vo!" Booji Boy would later exclaim to General Boy, who was Mark's real father.

Around the same time, and most likely at the same store, Jerry discovered a pair of "Chinese specs," novelty glasses with flesh-colored lenses and slanted eyes. These immediately suggested another character—the Chinaman.

"Chinaman was a persona I took on to dispense shocking, un-liberal, un-American-style wisdom and thought," Jerry said. "Dispense it as if you're, like, this philosophical Chinaman. You know, like Chinese philosopher say, 'Ha Ha, Fuck you!' It was partly...to attack Western ideology—Western mindset, and to be a foil to the infant spirit of Booji Boy....To be (like) Rowan and Martin from *Laugh In*—that kind of team. You know, Booji Boy and Chinaman would have made a good talk show....Booji Boy had a beautiful, full-headed mask, and had universal appeal. I mean, who doesn't like a baby?"

"The Chinaman" would eventually write the introduction to *My Struggle* and become a character in *The Truth About De-Evolution*. In that introduction, he would write that Booji Boy "wears his mask not to hide from justice, but to perform it."

Mark and Jerry began wearing masks most of their waking hours. This would seem strange anywhere, but Akron, especially, was not the kind of place to embrace these performance art ideals. There were practical concerns, as well. "It was hard to eat," Jerry explained. "Mark would always ask for a straw and order a milkshake."

* * *

Mark and Ed Barger had moved out of Marty's Balch Street house in 1973 and were living as roommates at the Beaven Apartments on Walnut Street, across from Harlan Hall, an apartment building Mark's father owned. But by late 1974, Ed Barger was spending most of his time at his girlfriend's place and could no longer justify paying rent for both him and Mark. So Robert Mothersbaugh Sr. offered his son a free apartment at Harlan Hall if Mark would agree to serve as manager. Mark accepted. He became responsible for this old, twenty-nine-unit brick building with Tudor accents, known as the first fireproof building in Akron. This would seem like an ideal setup, except that Mark was required to handle basic maintenance. "Oh, boy!" the senior Mothersbaugh recalled with a wry smile.

Mark may not have been adept at basic repairs, but he was very good at securing tenants. He would put Jerry up in unoccupied units, shuffling him around like a human shell game. Barger lived in the building for a time, as did a friend named Ward Welch, who would later adopt the stage name Rod Bent (and, still later, Rod Firestone) as the singer for the Rubber City Rebels. Bobbie Watson lived there, as did Mark's younger sister Sue. As with the Kent apartments above Guido's Pizza, the place became an enclave of music and art. This was great for them, but not so great for the other, more established tenants.

"All the tenants were scared out of their minds of me," Mark said. "One night, we were up making a tape. It was a torture routine and we were getting pretty carried away, shouting things like, 'No, not the punishment cone!'… This old lady knocks at the door at two in the morning, and I answer it in a dress and a hood. Jerry had this rubber chimp mask on and his hands were tied behind his back. That poor lady…"

Mark continued working on *My Struggle* while he lived at Harlan Hall. In it, he wrote about his job as apartment manager: "I don't need no doctor, in spite of what the tenants here at my fair old Harlan Hall say. They really love me, even that witch LePera. She writes a couple letters a day about lights in the building that need fixed, or bitching about her drain. Worst part about it is, she lives across the hall from Chatty, the little nurse down in 202 who is always letting us put things in her freezer, or some other good deed only a nurse should perform."

"Chatty" was a woman named Cathy Mirwin, whom Jerry had briefly taken up with after the breakup with Cora. Bobbie recalled that he urged her to cut her hair and dress like Cora, almost as an extension of the Pygmalion myth. But he also apparently was sneaking around with Marty Reymann's girlfriend, Jennifer Licitri. "I was tip-toeing around, and being a bad girl. It was pretty serious, and he wanted me to move to California with him," Licitri later recalled. "I have old letters from Jerry calling himself Chinaboy and calling me Chinagirl. I have poetry with his Chinaman face that he gave me as a break-up letter."

Mark, meanwhile, had begun living with a woman named Marie Yakubic, who also went by the name Marina. She was married to a musician who had played in the Mothersbaugh Band. Apparently her husband didn't care. Mark and Marina's relationship blossomed under tragic circumstances. According to Bob Lewis and Bobbie Watson, Marina had been raped at gunpoint by an intruder while still living with her husband. He did not visit her in the hospital, and Mark took pity on her and went to see her. After her release, he took her in.

"Their apartment at Harlan Hall was one room basically," Bobbie recalled, "mats on the floor for bedding. Wall-to-wall bed was all Marie wanted, with a little kitchen to warm her tea. Their body heat never left the room. She said the perfect day for her (days on end) would be for them to never leave that room and spend the day touching. Mark would invite others (over) and she was willing to keep Mark happy by being the gracious hostess—but it was not her choice. She resented Mark's activity with anything that took him away but was not vocal about it—she sighed deeply. She was gifted in touch and massage."

All in all, it was a pretty good setup, with days at Unit Services and nights at Harlan Hall. But Jerry and Mark were still convinced that something could happen in California. So they gathered up copies of their demos, the Booji Boy mask, and the Chinaman glasses, and headed west.

Chapter 11

Jerry and Mark hung a tape recorder from the rearview mirror as they set out for California. As they drove, Mark wore the Booji Boy mask and Jerry wore the Chinaman glasses. For twenty hours, the routine droned on—the cassette recorded them as the Chinaman asked philosophical questions about life and Booji Boy answered them in his innocent squeak.

"Booji Boy—what is meaning of life?"

"Gee, I don't know. But that sure is a pretty sky."

There was strange chemistry between these two, and their alter-egos seemed to capture it. Jerry was overtly intellectual and confrontational. Mark was in many ways pure and sincere. They needed each other—Jerry needed to be asking the questions, and Mark needed someone to ask them.

They had their demos in the car with them. The primal early recordings were becoming more sophisticated, with Mark's synthesizer emitting robotic, hypnotic (and occasionally erotic) discord. From his cartoon-drenched perspective, this was *The Jetsons Meets The Flintstones*. Their ultimate destination on this road trip was Joe Walsh's estate in Topanga Canyon. Despite the closer proximity of New York City, Devo was beginning to home in on California as their musical promised land, feeling the pull of the West just as Ed Dorn had. Much of the reason for that was the road paved by Walsh.

By now, his solo career was in full bloom, and he was on the verge of joining the Eagles. And despite the obvious chasm between every aspect of their aesthetics, he was someone who could do something for them. Bob Lewis had helped arrange the visit, again with a call to Patrick Cullie. Walsh had agreed to meet with Mark and Jerry.

Their old friend General Jackett had become an airbrush artist and was painting Walsh's stage T-shirts for him. He had been talking up Devo in the Walsh circle, telling people about this great Moog player and this really strange but intriguing sound. When Jerry and Mark arrived in Topanga Canyon, Walsh was ready for them. They sat and talked awhile, then pulled out the tapes.

Walsh listened to this band with clanky electronic drums; a singer who sometimes sounded like an alien; the rigid, minimalist guitars; the lyrics about potatoes, monkeys becoming men, and men becoming monkeys.

"It was a nice scene," Jerry recalled. "He swung on his swing, and went to the kitchen to make popcorn, and uh, he put his arms around us out by his eucalyptus trees and told us to listen to the hoot owl, and then he kind of drew us close to him and hugged us and said, 'This is how I really feel—come back when you got something.'"

Still scratching his head, Walsh later admitted to their mutual friend Peter Gregg that he couldn't tell if the tape was running backward or forward.

Even with the disappointment of this continuing rejection, Mark and Jerry kept scheming, with a healthy sense of dadaism. While they were still in California, they caught a show called *Help Thy Neighbor* on a public-access channel—a call-to-arms to help people in need. Mexican kids were interviewed saying that they were going to resort to a life of crime if they couldn't find jobs. They wanted to become gardeners, not gangsters. So the host would say, "You heard it folks, now let's... help thy neighbor!" Calls came in to the show with donations of gardening supplies.

A woman phoned in to say that the family's father had died recently at home in bed. The kids and other family members were upset about the mattress. Soon, bed donations came in from the audience.

Mark and Jerry looked at one another. What if they went on the show in wheelchairs, claiming to be Vietnam vets? "We've got a good attitude about life," they'd say, "but it's just so hard to get folks to listen to our music." Then they'd ask for a record deal. It was one of those "just might be crazy enough to work" ideas. But they didn't go through with it.

* * *

Jerry and Mark's trip included Thanksgiving dinner at the home of Peter Gregg, who, like Walsh, was living in Topanga Canyon. Mark brought a keyboard and Jerry brought his bass, and they sat around having a devolved, pre-supper hootenanny. Mark was wearing one of his masks—the Bluesman— a retro-racist caricature with curly white hair, big earrings, and thick lips. As Gregg's girlfriend worked in the kitchen, the three of them sat together in a spare bedroom, and Gregg played a version of a Keith Richards lick while Jerry sang, "I don't smoke, I don't drink, I don't know what I do do," over and over. They were having a good time. When dinner was ready, Gregg's girlfriend called everyone to the table. They all took their places, including Mark, now in his Booji Boy mask.

As he tried to eat through the mouth opening, Gregg's girlfriend began to get upset, thinking Mark was making fun of her carefully prepared meal. So Jerry, always the domineering force in these absurdist performances, told Mark to take off the mask, and the holiday meal proceeded.

They continued experimenting with their performance art as they explored the Los Angeles streets. With Jerry in his Chinaman get-up and Mark again as the Bluesman, they stood on the boulevard median in Hollywood. When traffic stopped for a red light, they would work their routine. Things got a little dicey when they wandered into a predominantly Black neighborhood, and the locals did not appreciate these two white kids flaunting racist stereotypes. When they stepped into a liquor store, Jerry, sensing the tension, removed the Chinaman glasses. But the Bluesman held his ground.

Mark and Jerry made the long drive back to Ohio, playing Booji Boy and Chinaman as they drove, and wondering if they were barking up the wrong tree. Obviously, Joe Walsh, the blues-drenched, folksy rocker, wasn't going to be Devo's guy. But he was all they had.

Bob Lewis, upon hearing about how they'd been received, wrote a letter to Ed Dorn: "Jerry continues to try and push our particular load of shit on the Coast, but he says that he is meeting with sales resistance, i.e., it's too REAL, and they don't want to hear about it."

Cullie, who had continued working hard to find his own place in the music business, was torn between his friendship with Devo and his understanding of industry dynamics. He still had the demos Bob had given him, but he just wasn't sure what to do with them.

"I thought it was funny, ironic, hip, all that stuff," Cullie recalled, "but I'm the first to admit, I didn't really see the commercial possibilities. It just seemed too weird to drive mainstream revenue. And maybe part of it was that since Devo and the entourage came from my backyard, I didn't give it the credence it deserved. I was looking to step out on my own and away from Irving (Azoff, the Eagles' manager), because he was a real prick. So, if I had felt that Devo was a project that I could get signed and manage and make money on, I would have done it on the spot. I just didn't see it."

So Cullie kept the tapes mostly to himself. He did eventually play them for a Capitol Records rep, and his instinct was confirmed: "The guy at Capitol, after hearing the demo, said, 'Patrick, I like you. You're a smart guy. And my advice, if you want a career in the music business, is don't play this for anyone else. It's terrible.'"

* * *

If Devo was looking for their niche, they certainly found a toehold in April of '75. The band was booked to play following a Kent screening of John Waters' new movie, *Pink Flamingos*, arranged by Kent State film professor Richard Myers, a significant underground filmmaker. Again, the little college town was getting exposed to something that normally wouldn't be expected in Ohio. Kent continued to be the beneficiary of an enlightened faculty.

Admission was $1; the film was billed as "the most disgusting movie ever made," and Devo's name in the advertising was followed by the commentary, "How LOW can you go?" This was more like it.

Bob Lewis, recognizing the opportunity, dashed off a letter to Ed Dorn. "Devo perform Friday before a special showing of *Pink Flamingos*," he wrote, "and at last perhaps will have its proper audience. The aficionados of Miss Divine are already well along the trail toward devolving. It's a little scary."

By now, the members of the band were being billed by their characters' names. This night would feature Boogie Boy (not yet evolved into "Booji"), Chinaman, Jungle Jim, and The Clown. This almost sounded like the cast of characters in a John Waters film. It's certainly hard to imagine a significant American artist more in tune with the Devo aesthetic. Waters used low humor with allegedly high ideals; the infamous scene where Divine, a drag queen, eats dog feces is the film equivalent of a song like "I Need a Chick." They loved kitsch, they loved laughing at American conventions they found stupid, and they loved to put on a show that would make audiences squirm.

"*Pink Flamingos* was our favorite film," Jerry said later. "We just couldn't believe he got it made. We thought this was incredible. We just wanted to meet John Waters, you know? Basically, he and his friends were the Devo of Baltimore. The same kind of transgressive, irreverent, kind of collage-like... 'let's rethink all this, folks.' People that are kind of blue-collar, but smart, and have no respect."

Even with what would seem a more sympathetic audience, Devo still struggled for acceptance that night. The band played two sets, after each of the film's showings. At one point, Mark walked onto the stage while the movie played and, pulling a trick from Ghoulardi's bag, used a long stick to point out various aspects of the film.

* * *

The encounter with Joe Walsh served to underscore a growing ideal in the Devo philosophy. Although they'd had no personal experience with stardom, or even acceptance, they bristled against the notion of the Rock Star. Even though punk rock didn't yet exist as a recognized genre, this notion of knocking idols off their pedestals was a cornerstone of the ethic, and Devo fully embraced it.

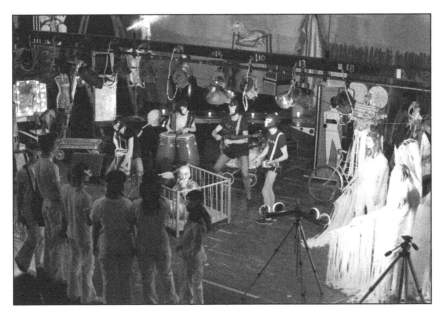

On the set with DEVO in wrestling masks playing bongos, guitar, and a portable space heater. *Courtesy of Bobbie Watson Whitaker*

"What we hated about rock and roll was stars," Mark said. "We watched Roxy Music, a band we like, slowly become Bryan Ferry and Roxy Music. If you got a band that's good, you bust it up and sell three times as many records."

Devo was an odd tangent of that concept, however. The band was elitist in many ways. Although the members would generally lump themselves in with the rest of the spuds (at least rhetorically), the simple act of pointing out dullards put them in a position of superiority. There were Readers, and there were Breeders, and it's safe to assume Devo didn't consider themselves Breeders.

Still, the band clung to a certain populism even as they distanced themselves from the populace. Some of this, no doubt, grew from the no-nonsense work ethic Mark had inherited from his father. Mark was a serious young man, and while he had not chosen anything close to his dad's career path—he vehemently resisted traditional day jobs—he did work hard on his art. He wrote in his journal; he made postcards and rubber-stamp prints; he practiced on his keyboard. He was a workman, but fully outside the traditional definition. Devo once described artists as good-looking people who can't hold down real jobs. This seemed to be a commentary on themselves, and to capture both a sense of self-denigration and self-realization.

And so it was that Devo went shopping for clothes. The band was scheduled to play at the third Creative Arts Festival in April. The crude, but structured accessorizing of the 1973 festival, when each of the members had worn a single color, had evolved. The fascination with masks and uniforms was growing. For this performance, they chose hard hats and blue workmen's jumpsuits. They were becoming spuds, Mark's "dirty hard workers of the earth." Completing the ensemble were matching clear plastic masks, which essentially erased the face. Mark still had his beloved long hair, but these masks were a conscious attempt to portray the anti-rock star. There would be no personalities; there would simply be personality.

By then, Kraftwerk's watershed 1974 album, *Autobahn*, had found its way to Ohio. Jerry loved this record. The early Kraftwerk recordings had been the work of two breakaway members of the progressive krautrock scene, with long, ponderous jams. They played in sweaters and leather jackets, experimenting with synthesizers and traditional instruments. But a growing fascination for robots and a desire to make the music an entire, controlled package led to the *Autobahn* aesthetic. The German band had sharpened its image, accomplishing the same things Devo was trying to do halfway across the world. *Autobahn* seemed to be the work of automatons: close-cropped hair, emotionless faces, minimalist graphics, and a growing refusal to divulge any personal details. Kraftwerk was, in a sense, becoming post-human. Devo recognized the possibilities in that.

* * *

Devo was trapped between two worlds, a point made even more clear when Joe Walsh came back to Ohio to play a concert with his Barnstorm Band. Although Mark, Jerry, and the others still clung to a hope that they might be able to make use of his coattails, they had a growing disdain for

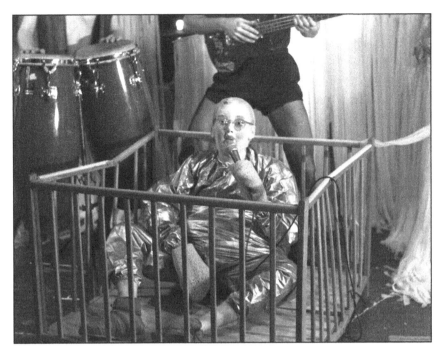

Booji Boy performs in his crib for a film project with KSU professor Richard Myers. *Courtesy of Bobbie Watson Whitaker*

Walsh's music, lifestyle, and audience. Mark showed up at the concert wearing the Booji Boy mask and left it on for the entire show.

Bruce Hensal remembers that the mask was especially distressing to the Barnstorm Band's piano player. "He started yelling at Mark because the mask was freaking him out," Hensal said. "The guy was shouting, 'Take that off! Take that off!'"

There was a party afterward at General Jackett's house, a place nicknamed the Headquarters, above a flower store. Walsh attended with his band and the rest of his entourage. Lots of drugs were consumed. So when Jerry and Mark—still wearing his rubber baby mask—arrived, there was some chemically enhanced confusion. Many of the partygoers thought the mask was actually Mark's face. Mark's girlfriend Marina had brought some raspberries to the party. As Booji Boy stuffed them in, red juice ran down his face, looking an awful lot like blood.

Chapter 12

If the Devo gigs were still few and far between, at least they were becoming more choice. Halloween 1975 found the band booked to open for Sun Ra at Cleveland's WHK Auditorium. The concert was a private Halloween party for Cleveland's top album-oriented rock station, WMMS FM. None of this really made sense.

Sun Ra, although a nationally significant figure, fell outside the station's heavy rotation of Rolling Stones, Bad Company, and Lynyrd Skynryd. And Devo—well, it's pretty certain none of the station's employees had even heard of them. Probably someone had suggested that the Akron band might be good for a Halloween joke without really explaining the punch line. Sun Ra was in residence at Cleveland's Smiling Dog Saloon from October 28 to November 9. Ed Barger worked there, so it's possible he had something to do with Devo being booked. However it came to pass, though, the night proved to be a defining moment in Devo's ability to use music as a weapon of mass destruction.

The WHK Auditorium dated to the 1930s, when it was built as a radio broadcast theater. Located on a stretch of Euclid Avenue between downtown and some of the city's worst neighborhoods, the "HK" was a perfect symbol

Mark sans yellow suit at WMMS-sponsored show. *Courtesy of Bobbie Watson Whitaker*

of a collapsing industrial giant. Once lovely and ornate, it had fallen into decadence; rock and rollers were gathering together the detritus of someone else's dream. Tuxedoed men and fashionable ladies had once enunciated into chromed microphones there. And now Devo had arrived to set up their gear.

Various members of the WMMS staff were milling about with their friends, dipping into a vat of tequila sunrise and inhaling nitrous oxide. WMMS was known as the "Home of the Buzzard," taking the nickname from an annual event in nearby Hinckley, where, once a year, turkey vultures came home to roost in Ohio's version of the San Juan Capistrano swallows. The station's logo, ubiquitous on T-shirts and bumper stickers, featured a cartoon buzzard, and had become a symbol of everything Devo thought was wrong about rock and roll. Mindless mass consumption of music programmed by clueless suits. There was an intensely blue-collar image to WMMS; Leo Travagliante, known by the handle "Kid Leo," closed each afternoon drive-time shift by announcing it was "time to wash up and punch out." Kid Leo would soon gain significant industry cred by championing a young New Jersey singer/songwriter named Bruce Springsteen. WMMS and Springsteen were made for each other—all denim-and-leather, no-nonsense, working-class rock. Widely credited as a key figure in breaking Springsteen, Kid Leo would eventually become a Columbia Records vice president. But before he left the station, his incessant claim that Cleveland was the "rock and roll capital of the world" would help land the Rock and Roll Hall of Fame and Museum on the shores of Lake Erie.

Back in 1975, though, Kid Leo was mostly concerned with celebrating at the big Halloween bash. Although the WHK Auditorium could seat 1,500 people, the crowd was relatively small, with select invited guests from Cleveland's rock elite. Murray Saul, one of the station's best-known personalities, was tapped to be master of ceremonies. Saul was known as "the get-down man" for his trademark bellowing of the catch phrase, "Gotta, gotta, gotta…GET…DOWN!"

Devo was dressed that night in the same blue Dickies work suits and clear masks they had worn at the Creative Arts Festival. Mark wore the baby mask. Once again, they were billed under their characters' names. Mark was Booji Boy, Jerry was the Chinaman, Bob Mothersbaugh was the Clown, and his brother Jim was Jungle Jim. Their appearance didn't raise a lot of eyebrows at first. Who knew they always dressed like this? It was Halloween, and everyone was wearing a costume, although most had opted for the traditional witches, gangsters, and hunchbacks.

Devo set up its gear, complete with the Halloween-ish electronic drum set, and Jerry called for Murray Saul to say a few words into the microphone, with the high-pitched Booji Boy piping in, "Murray—Murray." Saul ambled onto the stage and started spewing his husky, stoned-hipster radio spiel, stumbling through a thick-tongued commentary on Cleveland's new marijuana law.

"Aaaaahhh-ooohhh, such the easy life. It is what it is, and it is such the such," he said, making virtually no sense. He turned to the members of Devo, wishing them a happy Halloween.

"Good evening," Saul continued. "I thought you would at least come in, at least, real clothes instead of such out-*rage*-ous costumes."

"Tell it like it is, Murray," Booji Boy warbled.

"Dass right," Saul said. "You got da concept."

"He tells it like it is," the innocent Booji pointed out to the crowd.

Saul rambled on about the long-neglected auditorium and then broke suddenly into an almost belching, "Ooooohhh-Aaaahhhhhh! We have been goin' crazy, goin' nuts because IIIITTTTSSS FRIIIIDAYYYYY! FRIIIIDAYYYYY!! FRIIIIDAYYYYY!! [Unintelligible.] Yowza, howza whad-da-hodda-hodda."

Then, after a couple more hee-zas and yowzas, he explained that this would be a crazy party and, "We're gonna do it, cuz we GOTTA, GOTTA, GOTTA (followed by about ten more slurred gottas) GET DOWN!"

And finally the introduction: "Oh, we gotta go low with De-vo. What it is!" And then Saul stumbled off as Jim started plunking out a staccato rhythm on the drums, Mark following with a series of grating, repetitive mechanical screeches from his synthesizer. Once this musical hair shirt was sufficiently spread out, Jerry, in what was now a fully mutated version of his backwater blues, began howling, "My woman's subhuman…" It began to dawn on the audience that if this was a joke, it wasn't funny. And if it wasn't a joke, it had to end immediately. Drunken ghouls and witches began shouting at Devo. A beer can flew toward the stage. Then another, and another. The band's response was obvious. They didn't like it? Then we'll just give 'em more. They soldiered on, inspired by the confrontation.

They played "Bamboo Bimbo," an equally tortured—and torturous—blues variation. When it ended, there was an almost inaudible smattering of applause. Devo had some friends in the audience, which is probably the only reason

Bob 1 with wrestling headgear during "Mr. DNA" solo. *Courtesy of Bobbie Watson Whitaker*

they weren't killed that night. Marty Reymann had come with his brother, a tough, brawling Vietnam veteran, and some other guys from Akron's working-class Firestone Park neighborhood—guys who liked a good fight. They became de facto bodyguards for this bunch of skinny "performance artists" who seemed intent on ruining someone else's party.

"We're Devo—D-E-V-O—and we'll prove it right now," Jerry spat out. While a few members of the audience remained, perhaps hoping to kick some ass, the room was nearly evacuated. "You guys just can't take it," Jerry said. It was brutal. One of the band members took a bullwhip from a Halloween "dominatrix" and began cracking it at her, ordering her to submit. This had worked for Dr. Moreau, but it was having the opposite effect on the drunken audience.

Late in the set, the band debuted what would become its defining anthem, "Jocko Homo." The song went on and on and on, with the group repeating the call-and-response: "Are we not men? We are Devo!" Someone grabbed a microphone and screamed, "You're a buncha assholes!" prompting Jerry to begin taunting in a cracked voice, "Is he not a man? Is he not a man?... He is Devo... He is Devo," finally driving the offending figure from the room, with the band continuing to taunt as he left the building. "Jocko Homo" went on for six minutes but seemed three times that long. As it ended, Mark's synthesizer emitted a wash of noise over and over as Devo played "I Need a Chick," driving the final nails before the whole mess fell apart in white noise and confusion. "Why don't you get outta here?" someone yelled as the sound began to fade. "I'm telling you to get outta here!"

The battlefield was littered with beer cans and other debris. It wasn't clear who had won. Certainly not Sun Ra, who made his entrance to a nearly empty auditorium. As he opened his set with "25 Years to the 21st Century," the only people there to see him were Devo and their handful of friends.

This was as close as Devo would come to fulfilling one of its fantasies. Jerry, in his days with the SDS, had heard about subsonic frequency generators, which were capable of producing a noise outside the normal audible frequency, and to cause people to lose control of their body functions.

"I asked myself, 'What are the creative uses of those?'" Jerry once said. He and Mark often repeated their description of the ultimate Devo concert.

"We'd like to hand out diapers at the door at a concert of 10,000 people and then for the finale we'd turn on the subsonic frequency generators and cause spontaneous bowel movements!" they once explained in a joint interview. "And rather than being uptight about it they would love it! Like that's what they came for and they would be mad if they left without it! Rather than lighting matches for the Eagles—one mass infantile, pre-sexual eruption—all tense muscles going lax!"

In other descriptions of this hypothetical "perfect concert," Mark and Jerry envisioned these performances taking place all over the globe, with Devo controlling the music and—by virtue of subsonics—the audience, from afar. This carried another echo from Kraftwerk, who talked about having robots perform concerts around the globe simultaneously, as the members ran the show from their Düsseldorf studio.

If Devo hadn't succeeded in making the members of the WMMS Halloween audience shit themselves, they had used a wall of sound to drive them away, like the Pied Piper in reverse. This may not seem like a significant accomplishment, but it did serve to cement a piece of the Devo theory: It was open season on pinheads. The reaction of the audience, to Devo's mind, simply proved that the great masses were clueless spuds.

The night passed, with the four members of Devo and their few friends being treated to a private audience with Sun Ra.

That same night, not far away, another, equally confrontational local band made its debut. They were called Frankenstein, playing at a Cleveland bar called the Piccadilly Penthouse. The singer, Stiv Bators, got into a fight during the band's set, and Frankenstein broke up immediately. They would reform that winter and take a new name—the Dead Boys.

* * *

That Halloween of 1975 was riddled with bizarre turns for Devo. Mike Powell, the volatile drummer from Flossy Bobbit, had asked Jerry if he could borrow the Gorj mask for a costume party. Jerry didn't really want to part with it, but Powell was not the kind of guy you wanted to argue with. So Jerry handed it over, went off to play the WMMS gig, and Powell headed out for "devil's night" in Akron. Along the way, he stopped into a convenience store. Wearing that hideously twisted leather mask, he pulled out a gun and robbed the place. He would eventually be caught and charged with four counts of aggravated robbery for holding up beverage stores and a pizza shop. He was convicted and sent to prison. In the process, the Gorj mask was taken into evidence. Jerry never saw it again.

Gorj or no Gorj, Devo's visual image was becoming more provocative and cohesive. Even Mark fell into line with the others, allowing Marty's girlfriend (and Jerry's mistress) Jennifer Licitri to cut his beloved locks. Maybe this had something to do with the heat inside the Booji Boy mask, but now all Mark had to shake around was a set of unruly bangs.

Devo began doing some photo shoots. They gained access to Goodyear's "World of Rubber," a museum devoted to the wonderful science of tire

The band with Jim Mothersbaugh (standing in for brother Bob1) during photo shoot at the Goodyear World of Rubber Museum. *Courtesy of Bobbie Watson Whitaker*

making. The museum contained antique tires, part of a Corsair built in one of the company's Akron factories during World War II, diagrams of the tire production process, and one of Mario Andretti's race cars, poised for racing action on a set of Goodyears. Devo posed in this setting. It was perfect for them, a place where reality was crossed with Ghoulardi-like science fiction. They romped through a forest of fake rubber trees and sat behind the wheel of Andretti's car.

In the process, they further developed their oddball photogenicity. They had, early on, discussed the idea of Devo as a multimedia project. Music was becoming a means to that end, but, in those long days at Unit Services, Jerry and Mark began to discuss the other possibilities. This was an art project. What other media could they tap into?

They began to kick around the idea of making a film.

* * *

Variation on the promo photo theme. This time in their blue work suits. *Courtesy of Bobbie Watson Whitaker*

At this point, Jerry was outnumbered in Devo, three-to-one, by Mothersbaughs. His brother Bob, married and working as a radiologist, had lost interest in the project, and there was tension based on family dynamics. Several members of the Devo circle recall Jerry riding Jim Mothersbaugh hard, complaining about the technical bugs in his drum set and his inability to keep good time. And Jerry had begun lobbying his brother to rejoin the band.

By mid-1976, with the gigs continuing sporadically, Bob Casale finally decided to return and, after a show in Cleveland and another *Shelly's* magazine benefit in Kent, Jim finally decided he'd had enough.

"I think Jerry brought his brother Bob in because he was a little overwhelmed by the Mothersbaugh brothers," Gary Jackett said. "It was obvious that there were two different musical directions that Devo was trying to pursue. With Bob Casale [back] in the band, Jerry sort of had two votes. It wasn't long before Jim got sick of Jerry's routine. At a certain point, he just didn't want to do it anymore. Jerry could be a fun-loving, great guy, or he

Promo photograph for debut single co-release on Booji Boy & Stiff Records/UK. *Courtesy of Bobbie Watson Whitaker*

could be a total jerk. One day you loved the guy and had great fun with him, and the next day he'd be totally flipping out."

Without a drummer, the band was free to focus on some of its other goals. Early in 1976, they began working on a script that would help explain what, by then, was nearly a decade of discussion about de-evolution.

Chapter 13

After years of false starts and frustration, 1976 was Devo's turning point. It's hard to say precisely why it took so long for the group to sort itself out. They had talent and ambition and encouragement from people they respected. But they were also kind of a mess live, and the membership was always in flux. Still, maybe there was a whiff in the air that some sort of musical revolution was brewing in New York and London, or maybe there was just a maturity to the grand Idea. Whatever it was, Devo, in late 1975, started on the project that would change their lives.

Jerry had met a film student named Chuck Statler while attending Kent State. With a shared interest in arty and offbeat cinema—"everything from Buñuel to Russ Meyer," Statler recalled—they became fast friends, taking some of the same art classes together. Statler filmed the Sextet Devo concert in 1972 before graduating and relocating to Minneapolis to pursue a career in film.

Jerry and Mark, meanwhile, had discussed the idea of making films to go along with their songs. This was a novel idea at the time. Sure, the Beatles had done *A Hard Day's Night*, but aside from straightforward film clips of performance, there wasn't much of a precedent. Devo wanted to do shorter

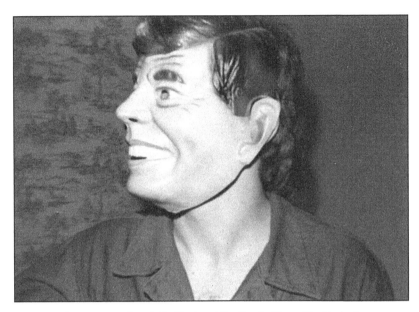

Jerry as John F. Kennedy while filming *The Truth About De-Evolution*. *Courtesy of Bobbie Watson Whitaker*

conceptual pieces, art films that used their music as a beginning point. After the glorious disaster of the WMMS Halloween show, the band realized they were getting nowhere playing local clubs. It was time for this different medium of attack.

Jerry and Statler reconnected when the young filmmaker was visiting home for the holidays in 1975. He and Jerry went to an all-night diner to talk. "And he was bemoaning the fact that... he doesn't think there's a lot of future to the band if they don't make a break in the near term," Statler said. "At which point, because I had enough equipment, I said, 'Before you do anything, I want to document Devo.' Because I knew what it was."

Statler returned to Minneapolis and the two began exchanging letters, working out the creative and production details. "Although we were visually inclined, we had no knowledge of filmmaking," Jerry said. "That's where Chuck came in." Statler gave them a sense of how a film was made, what it would cost, how to write a script and the like. "Neither one of us, Jerry and myself, had any thoughts about exactly what we were gonna do with it, but we both know it would be worthwhile to document this performance and this concept."

The first hurdle was the budget—around $2,000. Jerry and Mark had saved a little money from Unit Services. But they would need to borrow more. Kate Myers, a friend of the band, agreed to put up some cash. The Myers family was prominent in Akron; Kate's parents, Louis and Mary Myers, were major patrons of the arts and owned the largest private collection of modern art between New York and Chicago. And Kate was married to Sandy Cohen, whose parents owned Portage Broom & Brush—Jerry's employer. Sandy was something of an intellectual, and appreciated what Devo was trying to do.

Mark and Jerry knew they could save money on talent. They began enlisting their circle of friends, the "Devo-tees." And they began thinking about how they might want to present the "truth about de-evolution." The concept, as it had picked up steam, had become too far-reaching to be wrapped up in a neat entertainment package. Things like "Polymer Love" and "Readers Vs. Breeders" had helped broaden the idea, and now it needed to be brought back into focus. Certain elements had emerged since then that would clearly work in a short film. Booji Boy, for instance. That face and the voice behind it would be great in a movie. So they began writing a script.

Although Bob Lewis was no longer playing with the band, he remained close. On the back of a postcard to Ed and Jenny Dorn, postmarked April 9, 1976, he wrote, "Work on 'The Script' progresses slow. All Devo-tees pinned out. Rubber fumes everywhere. Bertholf requests Devolution lecture for Honors College Freshmen."

Unit Services became the central office for the film, with friends and band members popping in and out to discuss the progress. Quaker Square was a sprawling complex, with shops, restaurants, and displays about Akron history filling the former cereal factory. The old silos had been converted into a hotel, so every room had round walls. That winter, Jerry had met a young woman, Susan Massaro, who worked downstairs in Quaker Square's large restaurant. She and Jerry had their first date on Valentine's Day and quickly became a couple. Jerry wanted her to move in with him at Harlan

Hall, but Susan had a six-year-old daughter and didn't think it would be a very good environment for her. But she and Jerry became close, as she dropped into Unit Services a couple times a day on her breaks.

"I remember Bob [Lewis] coming into Unit Services and saying that he had got the Governance Chambers to film a portion of the movie," she said. "I helped him and Jerry set up a sheet that was to be mimeographed with lyrics to the songs that were going to be used in the movie, that was to be handed out."

The Governance Chambers in the Kent State student center had been the site of the second-ever Devo performance two years before. The band liked its official-looking setting, with rows of seats with desktops facing a stage. They knew they wanted some sort of *Dr. Strangelove* set, where the news of human decline could be properly conveyed. Similarly, they secured the "president's room" at a McDonald's restaurant near downtown Akron. The room had a long conference table, and its walls were lined with large, formal portraits of suit-and-tied white males. A fast-food restaurant may seem like a strange place for an executive dining room, but it made sense in Akron, where the white and blue-collar aspects of the tire industry were intertwined. This particular McDonald's was nestled between the world headquarters of the Goodyear, Firestone, Goodrich, General, and Mohawk tire companies, and also the aging factories that surrounded them. So presidents and punch-clock workers alike could dine there.

The rubber industry also provided another movie set, Goodyear's World of Rubber, where the previous photo shoot had taken place. The museum included rubber chemistry equipment, large vats with pipes and gauges that gave an aspect of retro-futurism. The scenes of the band playing would be shot on the stage at JB's in Kent.

And they knew of a great location for an outside establishing shot. Mark's father owned Great Falls Employment Agency at the time, in a century-old building in Cuyahoga Falls. A few years before, he had undertaken a restoration project to return the façade to its original appearance as a nineteenth-century dry goods store. But that was the front of the building. The side boasted a decidedly 1970s mural, painted on the brick by a group of high school students as part of a city project the previous summer. Lady Liberty's arm extended in from the right, holding a torch surrounded by the sun, with beams emitting across the side of the building. Over to the left were clumsy images of great Americans. And in the center, in huge block letters, was the slogan "Shine on America."

By late spring, the group was ready to begin production. They had decided to base the film on two songs—a twisted cover of Johnny Rivers' "Secret Agent Man" and "Jocko Homo," the song that served as Devo's thesis statement. These seemed like logical bookends for the movie. "Jocko Homo" explained de-evolution, and "Secret Agent Man," which turned the original spy-rock riff around backwards, showed it in action. Johnny Rivers' heroic, cloak-and-dagger protagonist became, in Devo's hands, a victim of mind control. This would be the only notable lead vocal appearance by Bob Mothersbaugh in the band's history, but in a world of Bobs that found him billed as "Bob 1," the key line, "They've given me a number, but they've taken away my name," took on an ironic and less valiant meaning. It was devolved.

And "Jocko Homo" said it all. The lyrics drew on years of intellectualizing and served as a refined collage of the elements that defined the truth about de-evolution, right down to the title, lifted from B. H. Shadduck's religious pamphlet. The song, filled with the quirky mechanics that had become the group's trademark, begins: "They tell us that we lost our tails / Evolving up from little snails / I say it's all / Just wind in sails…"

This is all that highbrow discussion with poets and professors summed up in twenty-one words. Then comes the chorus, "Are we not men? We are Devo." This defining statement came directly from *Island of Lost Souls*, the film that entertained, frightened, and helped define de-evolution. Then the second verse: "Monkey men all in business suit / Teachers and critics all dance the poot…"

Devo's intent was to take the stuffing out of pompous humans. "We're only smart monkeys, let's not get too snotty," Bob Lewis once explained. The poot, of course, was Jerry's dance from the early Gorj days, intended to ridicule someone else's creation. But, as always, Devo included themselves in the criticism: "We're pinheads all."

Mark recalled marrying the *Island of Lost Souls* atmosphere with his growing musical philosophy.

"The movie and the [Jocko Homo] pamphlet contributed equally along with Akron, Ohio, to the song.... It's all pretty easy to figure out from there. I was intent at the time, of differentiating Devo from pop music, thus the 7/4 timing that made novice dancers every other bar, dancing on the off beat, so it was very theatrical on purpose. The song [and Devo at that time] had a Fluxus feel, and any of the artists we met, even if we worked in different media, or even had different outlooks, we often felt a camaraderie with [them]."

The key players for the film were selected. Although Devo was in a state of flux, the departed Jim had agreed to play drums with Jerry and his brothers Mark and Bob. Ed Barger, General Jackett, and Jennifer Licitri were enlisted, as were the girlfriends—Marina, Susan, and Bobbie Watson, who was still with Bob Lewis. One of the Harlan Hall residents, Karen Freeman, who waitressed at a mall restaurant with Bobbie, was also talked into taking a role. (She was shy, but they promised she'd be wearing a mask, just like most of the other actors.) Even Susan's young daughter Sarah would take a part. The script was nearing completion. A key role was the character of "General Boy," who would announce that it was time for the "truth about de-evolution." A lawyer friend agreed to play him.

Devo decided to wear their blue work suits, hard hats, and clear masks for the live performance scenes. They gathered together their collection of masks, strange glasses, and costumes to distribute among the "actors." They went shopping at an Army-Navy surplus store for the General Boy outfit, returning with a military dress uniform. The Governance Chambers shoot was scheduled for May 17, 1976. To fill out the seats not already claimed by "Devo-tees," the group advertised on campus: "Mon. 12 noon—Be In A Movie!"

The pieces were coming together. Statler came to town, and they began filming. With such a small budget, everything was being done simply, shot on 16-millimeter film. "Though Chuck was the director, he was mainly there for technical stuff, camera angles and lighting, and to take care of the production end of it," Jerry recalled. "The concepts, the images and ideas were all ours, we always had that together. As a director, Chuck's into the straight-ahead, no-

nonsense industrial approach—no camera moves at all, just static shots and sharp cutting. That certainly influenced me a lot, and I think it's a sensible way to work: the images and the montage, the editing, should do the work themselves. You shouldn't have to resort to fancy camera moves to make it work."

The band was ready to shoot the General Boy scene at the McDonald's "president's room." They had made a large portrait of Booji Boy in a uniform to tape over the picture hanging at the end of the room, creating the look of some sort of Devo war room. But at the last minute, the lawyer slated to play General Boy backed out. With everything tightly budgeted and scheduled, they didn't have much time to spare. They had to come up with someone who could look official, and who would fit into the uniform they'd bought. Mark, Jim, and Bob knew of a good candidate—their dad.

The question was put to him, and Robert Mothersbaugh Sr., upstanding businessman and local churchgoer, agreed. "When you have five kids and you love them—you do this," he later said. "I served three years during the Second World War. I'll let you in on a little secret—I didn't become a general until the boys started Devo! I wore the blue-green Army jacket, pith helmet, black trousers, white shirt, and black tie. The De-Evolutionary Army dress code allowed some flexibility." He even chipped in $300 to help with production costs.

They sat him at the end of the conference table, under the Booji Boy picture. With him in the role, the scene took on a different tone. Mark, as Booji Boy, comes into the room to deliver a set of papers. In the script, Booji Boy was supposed to be General Boy's son. Now, wearing a rubber baby mask, the real-life son was interacting with his real-life father.

"I remember there was relief and excitement when Mr. Mothersbaugh became General Boy, and how it was so much better than what was planned," Bobbie Watson said.

* * *

After the editing sessions in Minneapolis, the film was complete. It commences with the title, *In the Beginning was the End: The Truth About De-Evolution*. The opening scene shows the band in their blue suits and masks, working in the World of Rubber set. It's quitting time and they all depart,

Robert Mothersbaugh, Sr. again adopts the uniform, rank, and role of "General Boy" for their second pre-Warner Bros. film production—a follow-up to *The Truth About De-Evolution*. *Courtesy of Bobbie Watson Whitaker*

Booji Boy removing his cap to wipe sweat from his brow. They pile into Mark's beat-up old blue Chevrolet and drive off. They arrive in front of JB's. As they file into the club, no one seems to notice the sign taped to the door, which boasts the familiar numbers—(15-60-75). Then "Secret Agent Man" begins.

It's hard to believe this is the same band that, just six months before, had tortured the WMMS crowd. Devo's version of the song is tight, polished, and catchy. Behind the band (and mostly obscured by them) is a set of cutout letters spelling "D-E-V-O," a larger version of the set General Jackett had spray-painted in California four years before. The performance footage is intercut with little scenes: A pair of ectomorphic band members in gym shorts and monkey masks paddle Karen Freeman, unrecognizable as promised, in a bathrobe and a strange China-doll mask. A few seconds later, the

Behind the scenes during the filming of *De-Evolution: The Men Who Make the Music* (credited as "directed & produced by Marie Yakubik—with script & music by DEVO, 1977"). *Courtesy of Bobbie Watson Whitaker*

Chinaman appears to be genitally stimulating a coat hanger in the shape of a woman's spread-eagled legs. During the guitar solo, General Jackett, wearing jeans, a decorated leather jacket and sunglasses, wails away on two strapped-together guitars, with a space heater for an amplifier.

Then comes one of the film's most captivating moments. Mark, wearing a John F. Kennedy mask, a pink-and-purple Latin bandleader's shirt and a pair of padded pants, dances with Marina, dressed in some sort of tight-fitting nurse or waitress uniform. Their moves are slow, almost hypnotic, and softly twitchy. It is as clear here as anywhere that the band has achieved an impressive visual command. The paddling and dancing continue, the song ends with JFK waving goodbye, then the scene cuts to the "Shine on America" mural.

Booji Boy, dressed in an orange jumpsuit, enters and runs pell-mell past the mural and up the building's outside staircase. He enters General Boy's inner sanctum.

"Come in, Booji Boy. You're late," the General says. He pronounces the first name "Boogie." Jerry later explained that the spelling change (and inevitable mispronunciation) came as he was putting together the credits for a Devo film (probably not this one), and he ran out of "g's." So he used a "j" instead and liked the way it looked without the "e" at the end.

Booji Boy approaches his father.

"Have you got the papers the Chinaman gave you?" General Boy asks. Booji hands them over, the General gives them a quick glance, then turns to face the camera.

"In the past, this information has been suppressed," he intones seriously, in his nasal accent. "But now it can be told. Every man, woman, and mutant on this planet shall know the truth about de-evolution."

"Oh, Dad," Booji Boy responds enthusiastically. "We're all Devo!" A series of quirky, staccato, synthesized blips follows, keeping time with a series of still images of neon letters, spelling out "D-E-V-O." Then the scene changes to the Governance Chambers. Mark, dressed in a white suit, bow tie, orange rubber gloves, and swimming goggles, is standing between a set of Devo-tees in matching blue surgical caps, dust masks, and sunglasses. Susan Massaro is to his right; Bobbie Watson is to his left, watching dispassionately. Mark begins a loose-limbed, jumpy dance to the intro of "Jocko Homo," then leans over the table as if preparing to deliver a lecture. He gestures animatedly as he begins lip synching. When he asks, "Are we not men?" the scene cuts to the other three band members, in sunglasses, with colored stockings over their heads, giving the response, "We are Devo." When his audience is finally shown, the Governance Chambers is filled with people in the same surgical caps and masks, bobbing in rhythm to the music. The other three band members lie writhing on a large table, their stockinged heads poking out of yellow latex body bags.

"We're on a giant conference table, wearing these rubber costumes from the neck down, and goggles and colored stockings on our heads," Jim recalled.

"So [people from the college] see us in there doing this and they're like 'What the hell?'"

As the song picks up steam, some of the audience members pump their fists in time with "We are Devo," as if they have enthusiastically accepted their fate. "O.K., let's go," Mark says, and the song ends.

This is followed by tuneless synthesizer noises and a collage of grainy, disconnected images as the backdrop to a list of "laws." Also known as the "Devo precepts," these were appropriated directly from B. H. Shadduck's *Jocko-Homo Heavenbound*:

1. Wear gaudy colors or avoid display.
2. Lay a million eggs or give birth to one.
3. The fittest shall survive & the unfit may live.
4. Be like your ancestors or be different.
5. We must repeat.

The music changes then, to an oddly soothing tune—the Beatles song "Because" (from *Abbey Road*), wholly unrecognizable after Mark ran it through a frequency analyzer. This is the poignant soundtrack for the film's most gripping scene. A shirtless Booji Boy is duct-taped to a chair. A man (Ed Barger) enters, pulls off the rubber baby mask to reveal Mark's face, and stabs him. The credits roll.

In the Beginning Was the End: The Truth About De-Evolution was complete. But now what? With his knowledge of the independent film circuit, Statler entered the work in juried festivals, including the highly regarded Ann Arbor Film Festival in neighboring Michigan. For his part, Mark recognized that his band had just completed a wholly new kind of musical project, one that might have far greater value than becoming a decent bar band with record deal potential.

"We thought back in 1975 that by 1976 everybody was going to own a laser disc player," Mark said later. "At least that's what it said in *Popular Science* magazine, and I believed it. So we said, 'There's going to be a new medium—sound and vision.' We were positive that we were going to start something that was going to erase rock and roll, but rock and roll kind of co-opted it, which erased the idea of it being artistic."

Original "Be in a Movie!" flyer with "beautiful mutant" for the filming of the "Jocko Homo" segment of *The Truth About De-Evolution. Courtesy of Bobbie Watson Whitaker*

Susan Massaro, Bob Lewis, and Bobbie Watson at DEVO HQ following the filming of "Jocko Homo" at the KSU Governance Chambers. *Courtesy of Bobbie Watson Whitaker*

Alan in a beret on set during the interview scenes for *The Men Who Make the Music*. *Courtesy of Bobbie Watson Whitaker*

Jerry demands that "if the spud fits—wear it!" *Courtesy of Bobbie Watson Whitaker*Whitaker

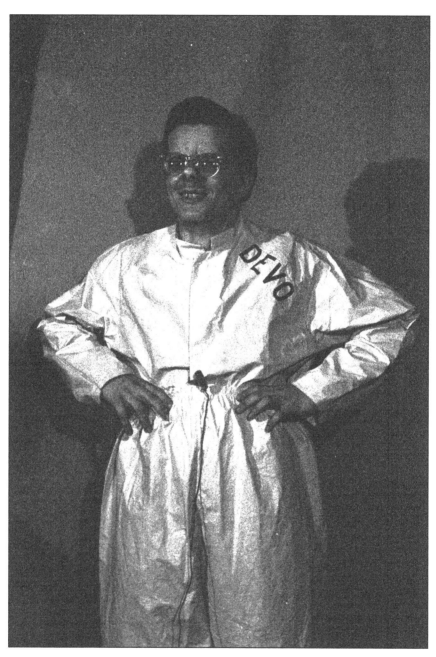

Mark with cellophane-taped facial modifications. *Courtesy of Bobbie Watson Whitaker*

Bob1 blowing bubbles between scenes. *Courtesy of Bobbie Watson Whitaker*

Chapter 14

Bob Mothersbaugh didn't want to quit playing with his brother Jim. But after the film was in the can, Jim's stint in Devo was over. Bob and Jim put together another band called the Jitters, playing much more traditional, Bo Diddley- and Rolling Stones-influenced rock. But Bob was smart enough to know this wasn't his future. The Jitters were a bar band. They played for beers. Devo, even for all its problems, held much more promise. So he took Jim's departure pretty hard. One night, he went out to an Akron bar called the Bucket Shop to drown his sorrows.

The Bucket Shop was a rowdy place. Girls danced on the bar; the floor was always sticky with spilled beer. It was in Akron's Highland Square neighborhood, which cross-pollinated blue-collar homeowners and the city's bohemian crowd. Harlan Hall wasn't far away, and a lot of the Akron-Kent musicians had found apartments nearby. Chris Butler, who had played with the Numbers Band and would soon be playing with Tin Huey, eventually wrote a song about the Bucket Shop girls who liked to flirt with all the boys. The song became the hit that propelled his later band, the Waitresses, out of Akron—"I Know What Boys Like."

But on this night, Bob wasn't interested in having fun. He was sitting at the bar, nursing a beer, when his friend Alan Myers walked in. Alan lived a couple of blocks away, on Dodge Avenue. He had lived there since he was fifteen, when his liberal-minded parents had allowed him to move out of their house and take up the lifestyle of a free spirit. The Dodge Avenue house was kind of a commune for musicians, and although Alan was only in his early twenties, he had been jamming on a wide variety of instruments with a wide variety of players in a wide variety of styles for an unusually long time. He and Bob had played together in yet another of Bob's straight-ahead, blues-based rock bands. That gig had been pretty much a matter of chance.

"One day, I was sitting out on the front porch of my house at 117 Dodge Avenue, and this guy I knew named Crazy Dave was walking down the street," Alan recalled. "In typical small-town fashion, he informed me that the cover band he fronted had just split over artistic differences! Although he stuttered a lot, Crazy Dave was a very nice, warm person, and as it turned out, he was trying to put together another group. He still had a steady gig at a local bar, and it was hard to get a gig in those days, much less anything steady.

"He said, 'Hey Alan. Do you want to join a group and play at this club?'

"I said, 'Sure.'

"So he got a bass player, and enlisted his acquaintance Bob Mothersbaugh. It was the first time I met Bob, although we didn't talk much or anything. I don't remember the name of our band, but we did Chuck Berry and the Rolling Stones for $50 a week."

But by mid-1976, Alan was on a self-imposed musical hiatus. He was working as a cook, going out to see the Numbers Band occasionally, but pretty much keeping to himself. The music scene seemed dead to him; there were no interesting original acts to see, and no one he was interested in playing with. Rock and roll had lost much of its appeal, and he was listening only to jazz. Although he'd only been in the Bucket Shop a handful of times, Alan was feeling bored and lonely that night, and walked up to the bar. That's when he saw Bob sitting on a stool.

"I recall Bob was visibly distraught—maybe even to the point of being in tears," Alan said. "We talked about it, and he said his brother Jim was quitting. He didn't know what to do about the band and was bummed out because things weren't happening."

Alan sat there consoling his friend over beers, and as the conversation progressed, Bob asked if he might be interested in joining Devo. Alan hadn't even heard of Devo, but he said, yeah, he might give it a try. He didn't have anything else going on, after all.

"It seems fateful in retrospect," Alan said. "I suppose I provided something of a catalyst when they asked me to join the band. At that particular moment, we had just the right mixture."

Devo changed almost immediately. Not only were the odd, temperamental electronic drums replaced with a more solid foundation, but Alan Myers was special. Jerry was succinct in his praise: "Alan was one of the most amazing drummers I've ever heard." Much of that stemmed from his unusual musical education. The five years Alan had spent in the Dodge Avenue house had exposed him to a great depth of influences. And, like the rest of his Devo bandmates, he was extremely intelligent, able to process the information he'd fallen into.

"The house on Dodge Avenue became like this enclave," he recalled. "Instead of a living room, we had this collection of musical instruments. It was whatever anybody could get their hands on or borrow. There might have been an electric guitar, but I don't remember it ever being plugged in. We had all this stuff, and there was almost never a song played. We always just used to make sounds. We might get a rhythm or a key going, and everybody would trade instruments. That was what happened at the house basically."

At Litchfield Junior High and Firestone High School, Alan had a classmate named Ralph Carney. In eighth grade, while Ralph Carney was tinkering with percussion, Alan Myers was getting more formal training in the school band They shared a similar taste in beatnik jazz and experimental rock, and Carney was happy to join his pal in playing music outside the marching band environment. So he began hanging out on Dodge Avenue.

"I [played] with Alan starting about 1970, when I first started to jam with people on harmonica, fiddle, and banjo," Carney said. "He and I, plus some older musicians would play and listen to tons of records. They would smoke tons of pot. (I didn't back then.) We didn't really have a 'band,' but we would play at parties sometimes.

"Alan gave me my first saxophone lesson, sort of. He somehow was borrowing a cheap alto around 1972 and would walk around his house playing badly. There was a dog at Dodge Avenue that would howl when he played! I rented a saxophone from the local music store, and he would say, 'Just push the buttons and make patterns.' I mean, it was pretty excruciating to hear him play, but I think some hallucinogens were making their way to his bloodstream on a regular basis back then. I seem to remember a set of vibes in the huge bathroom. I think they were in the john because of the good acoustics!"

Alan continued the story: "I had just picked up a saxophone for like $125, and it was right at the beginning of us knowing each other. If you don't play sax, you really can't last for more than about five or ten minutes because your lips just give out. You haven't developed an embouchure. So, me and Ralph spent five or six hours handing the saxophone back and forth trying to make noises with it. I was giving him some jazz and classical recordings, and he already kind of knew some of this stuff. He had an interest in outside, zany stuff. I hesitate to use a word like that. Then the next day, he went out and rented his own alto sax."

Alan learned to play many instruments, but focused on drums, alto sax, upright bass, and keyboards. His sophistication grew to the point where mainstream music didn't interest him anymore. His tastes gravitated toward early twentieth-century classical, European folk music, and experimental jazz. Along the way, he picked up Frank Zappa's *Freak Out*. The record didn't do much for him, but Zappa's liner notes did. The record sleeve included a list of influences, preceded by the disclaimer, "These people have contributed materially in many ways to make our music what it is. Please do not hold it against them."

"So, in the summer before tenth grade," Alan said, "I went out and picked up some music from this list, and that was the end of my Led Zeppelin collection. I went totally off the deep end...for John Coltrane, Edgar Varese, Arnold Schoenberg, and the rest."

Around 1975, Carney and Alan hooked up with a quintet called Jazz Death, with Carney on sax and Alan on drums. The group—three horns, bass, and drums—played a mix of originals and tunes by Ornette Coleman, Charles Mingus, and Art Ensemble of Chicago.

"We used to play four or five gigs a year," Alan said, "but always like somebody's party. I remember playing the benediction at a Unitarian Church. Somebody would have a club. They would have an open night, and we would go in there—kind of set up and get going. The reaction would always be fifty percent out the door immediately, and twenty-five percent of them were kind of interested. The other twenty-five percent would stick around for some other reason altogether."

Carney continued: "Alan and I would drive up to Cleveland to rehearse, and we mostly gigged up there at coffeehouse-type places. [It was] kinda cold, intellectual jazz. I did most of the scream solos, and I was just nineteen years old!"

By the time Alan joined Devo, Carney had begun playing with Tin Huey, along with Harvey Gold, Mark Price, Michael Aylward, and Stuart Austin. The band was perfect for Carney, a left-of-the-dial mix of jazz, experimental, Captain Beefheart-style rock, and quirky pop. The band had recorded an EP called *Breakfast with the Hueys* and had become about the best band an egghead rock fan could hope for, with Carney squawking and squealing on his sax, Gold and Price singing wry songs about human politics, and the whole band of eccentric savants purposely pushing the sound toward the surreal. Chris Butler would join in 1978, bringing a new element of stability and professionalism. After receiving fawning praise from one of the country's most influential rock critics, Robert Christgau of the *Village Voice*, Tin Huey was signed to Warner Bros. Records in 1978. But the band soon imploded, plagued by a label that had no idea what to do with it. Butler would go on to form the Waitresses, and Carney would sit in with the likes of the B-52s before becoming one of Tom Waits' main sidemen.

Although they had both joined promising rock bands playing in a similar vein, Alan and Carney drifted apart. "Devo was like a cult," Carney said. "Alan cut his hair and it wasn't the same."

Alan's entry into Devo propelled them forward exponentially. Over the following few months, with Bob Casale back on guitar, the band became tight and polished, almost completely removed from their former sound. There would be no more messing around in the studio with windshield wipers and washing machine sounds as rhythm tracks. Alan was technically solid—they nicknamed him "the human metronome." He didn't overplay, but he was capable of complicated parts, like the jerky rhythm of the band's "Satisfaction" cover. He was also on the same intellectual plane as his new bandmates. Not just anyone could fit into the Devo picture, but he did. He even had the same geeky demeanor and skinny physique.

* * *

With Alan's new bounce behind them, Devo began rehearsing more earnestly and writing new material. Although Jerry had been handling most of the lead vocals through the early years, Mark's vocal turn on "Jocko Homo"—and the corresponding performance in *The Truth About De-Evolution*—had proved to be a turning point. Jerry had been the perfect front man for the band Devo was before. Mark was the perfect front man for the band it was becoming. Jerry was durable. As a front man, he could take a punch, and considering the audience reaction of those earlier gigs, Devo needed his sharp tongue and glare at the front of the stage. Mark, on the other hand, was the guy who had performed red-faced under the monkey mask back at the first Creative Arts Festival show, and who had been hiding, nearly voiceless, behind Booji Boy for the past couple of years.

In the early days, Bob Lewis said, "Mark always liked being the scientist in the laboratory. He wasn't uncomfortable about playing music in front of people, but I think he had to kind of force himself to be the front man."

There had been tension about the lead vocalist position from the very start, when Bob Lewis had pushed for his roommate, Fred Weber, to be the Sextet Devo singer. "In the end, Fred wasn't right for Devo," Bob said, "but nobody had any idea Mark would become such a compelling stage presence. Jerry thought he should be the lead singer for our Sextet, but I was convinced it never would have worked. He was clearly offended by my insistence that we ask Fred Weber to sing at the Creative Arts Festival. In retrospect, that decision probably spawned some of the ill will and ongoing conflict that has plagued my relationship with Jerry."

Mark's hiccuppy tenor was carrying the new songs. He could croon like a sentient robot and, while his voice didn't have the range of, say, a Fred Weber, it had personality. It sounded like Devo. He had his masks to hide his shyness, but he was becoming a better performer, with a quirky way of shaking his shoulders and a growing confidence in dealing with hecklers and spuds.

Devo had finally settled on the members who would carry the band through the next decade. Internally, they had solidified, but externally, they were still a band that had yet to make much of an impact, even locally. A trip to an Akron janitorial supply shop would help change that.

Unit Services had folded halfway through 1976. Mark sold off many of his rubber stamps, and Jerry went looking for another job. Through a friend, he found work doing catalog graphics for an industrial supply company called Portage Broom & Brush. Flipping through the company's catalog one day, Jerry spotted a two-piece yellow Tyvek industrial suit. His discriminating eyes popped out. That suit was so Devo!

Jerry found out where the outfits came from—M. F. Murdock Company, a few blocks from Quaker Square. The band went shopping.

"We grew up as spuds in Akron, Ohio, surrounded by janitorial supply houses, rubber factories, catalogs of industrial gear, rubber gloves," Jerry said later. "Instead of being ashamed of it or trying to deny it, we used it. The band went into a janitorial supply house in Akron, saw the yellow suits, tried 'em on and said: 'We'll take 'em; they're hideous!'"

Mark, too, saw the potential. "We were looking for something that made us look glamorous. We kind of looked like giant cheeseburgers in those yellow outfits."

The suits were bright and riveting, vaguely futuristic working-class uniforms. The faceless, lockstep animation the band had been grooming could be achieved with each of the members in these suits. And though they were not made of rubber (they're actually more like paper), they seemed to reflect the rubber factory atmosphere that had so influenced the group. Plus, they were cheap—about $4 apiece.

The printed receipt from an early order of yellow industrial suits from The M. F. Murdock Company. *Courtesy of Bobbie Watson Whitaker*

Those suits were Akron, in a way that only a Rubber City spud could truly appreciate. The band used black electrical tape to spell its name across the front. Devo had found its new skin.

Chapter 15

The summer of 1976 had proved to be a boom time for Devo. But the rest of Akron was in a deep hurt. The United Rubber Workers, a powerful union with international headquarters in downtown Akron, had called a historic strike in late April. Eleven thousand local workers were walking picket lines, with another thirteen thousand, not eligible to strike, watching nervously. The entire city was in a chokehold. As April dragged into May and June into July, President Gerald Ford sent his labor secretary to town to try to break the stalemate, and tire builders were scraping at the bottom of their savings accounts. Proud workers were applying for food stamps and government aid. Grocery stores, gas stations, and restaurants began to suffer, because, aside from maybe those yellow suits at M. F. Murdock, nobody was buying anything.

Akron, since the turn of the twentieth century, had been an industrial center, proudly boasting the title "Rubber Capital of the World." The executive headquarters of the world's largest tire companies were there, along with a great bulk of manufacturing and research, plus the international union. Everywhere, the town carried signs of this legacy, from the Firestone Bank to Goodyear Metropolitan Park, from Goodrich Middle School to General

Street. Through the World War II boom and the gravy years that followed, all of these connected forces had coexisted, and all had profited. The union had grown unusually strong; as the automobile had become a staple of American life, there had been plenty of money to go around. But by the 1970s, foreign competition from the likes of Michelin and Bridgestone had begun to cut into the market share. The Akron companies were bloated and, after strikes in 1967, 1970, and 1973 had become known as the "triennial passion plays," everyone expected the 1976 contract negotiations to be an epic standoff. They were.

By then, Devo was practicing in the basement of "Devo house," a rented home on Greenwood Avenue, a pleasant tree-lined street not far from Highland Square. The owner was a lawyer named Chris Barron, a friend of the band. Susan Massaro and Jerry were living there, as were Bobbie Watson and Bob Mothersbaugh. Bobbie and Bob Lewis had broken up after ten years. The band was peaking creatively, with new songs coming out of the basement, one after another. Susan was upstairs in the kitchen one night, listening to a song she had first heard the band tinker with at Harlan Hall.

"Mark would originally sing 'Blue Balls.' One time, I think it was the night I was baking chocolate chip cookies, and took the bowl of dough downstairs to practice, I teased him about writing a song for me, and he started calling it 'Soo Bawlz.'"

The song would become a fixture in the growing set list. The band had also written a song called "Penetration in the Centerfold," inspired by the new level of graphic erotica in *Hustler* magazine, and "Clockout," with a title straight from the factory. This last entry had an ironic ring that summer. Striking rubber workers roamed around aimlessly, wearing orange T-shirts with the slogan, "URW—Catch up in '76." The pickets decorated Christmas trees at their posts, meant to deliver the message that they were prepared to stay out until winter, if that's what it took. There were fixtures of the strike everywhere. A Black man in a cowboy hat sat every day outside the gate of his Goodyear plant, playing a saxophone. The working-class watering holes, where shots and beers used to be set up along the bar to await three shift changes a day, became places both to grumble and rally around the cause.

One of those bars was a place called the Crypt, a block away from the sprawling Goodyear complex on East Market Street. It was co-owned by a Goodyear production worker named Bill Carpenter, who had taken the place on as kind of a hobby, a rec room away from home. Beer was cheap; it was a place for him and his buddies to hang out. By mid-summer, with everyone hurting, he had slashed the price of beer to twenty-five cents a glass—just enough to pay for the kegs.

Amid all this turmoil among Akron's established culture, an underground music scene was beginning to find some sort of order. Tin Huey was playing when it could get gigs, mostly at JB's in Kent. A young Akron songwriter named Nick Nicholis had put together a band called the Bizarros after hearing New York rock poets like Patti Smith and Tom Verlaine. A heavy metal cover band called King Cobra, led by Harlan Hall resident Ward Welch, had discovered *Creem* magazine and was starting to write songs in the vein of the "street rock" that was taking hold in New York's Bowery district, where the Ramones, Television, and Blondie were beginning to follow the path forged by the Patti Smith Group and Suicide. There was no good reason why Akron, Ohio, was becoming an outpost of a revolution whose first volleys had only just then been fired. But it was.

In Cleveland, a rock critic named David Thomas—pen name Crocus Behemoth—had formed Rocket from the Tombs and played some gigs in 1974 and '75 at the Viking Saloon. The band had spit out some members, who formed Frankenstein and had, by summer 1976, regrouped and changed their name to the Dead Boys, taken from a Rocket from the Tombs lyric. Behemoth, his musical partner (and fellow writer at Cleveland's *Scene* magazine, a weekly music paper) Peter Laughner, and a few others had evolved into Pere Ubu and by late 1975 were gigging around Cleveland with like-minded, hard-art bands the Mirrors and the Electric Eels. Laughner, who approached music as a poet, had an intrinsic, black-sunglasses sense of cool. He soon emerged as one of the scene's most talented songwriters, but also as one of its worst chemical abusers. He did a lot of drugs, and he drank even more.

Devo, it seemed, was finally finished trying to open for the Numbers Band or getting hired as a party joke. The new version of the band played a show in

1976 with King Cobra at the Bombay Bicycle Club, better known as the BBC, in the Portage Lakes area. It was a rough bar that attracted bikers and ex-cons. King Cobra was the de facto house band, and Mark had run sound and done a remote recording for them, wearing a monkey mask, of course.

King Cobra was getting a message, indirectly, from the New York bands. The group was starting to focus more on raw originals, with sometimes playful, sometimes violent lyrics, taking their hard-rock approach in a different direction. And, either consciously or not, they picked up a vital lesson from New York's CBGB's scene: find your own place to play. This had already happened in Cleveland. Pere Ubu had begun to inhabit the Pirate's Cove, in Cleveland's then-bleak, industrial Flats district. Welch wanted to do the same thing. But there was no way the BBC would put up with much of Mark Mothersbaugh in a monkey mask, nor would the biker crowds have much patience for songs they'd never heard played by a bunch of musicians who considered themselves "artists." So Welch and his buddies started casting about for a bar that might allow them to book local, original bands.

By then, the rubber workers' strike had ended, without a clear winner. In late August, the union had negotiated a good contract for its workers, but many of them felt it had not been worth the price of admission. And the skies were darkening over Akron. French tiremaker Michelin had opened its first American production facility while the domestic industry was hamstrung by the strike, and the cornerstone was laid for a quickly growing foreign domination of the tire market. Plants in Akron would soon start closing in harrowing succession, and Asian and European companies would begin snapping up Akron's venerable tire companies. In the immediate sense, Akron felt whipped by a summer of discontent. One young rubber worker's orange T-shirt summed it up. He wore it on the late summer day when the new contract was ratified, modified to read: "URW—Beat Up in '76."

So the pieces were in haphazard place when Ward Welch and his lead guitarist, Buzz Clic, walked into the Crypt that fall. The place had a stage, and the pair asked Carpenter if they might be able to bring in some bands to play. Carpenter, who had spent the summer on strike and had lost interest in keeping his little playhouse, did them one better. If they would run the bar themselves and make the lease payment, they could do whatever the hell they wanted in there. He was finished. The Crypt was theirs. He handed over the keys.

King Cobra was in the midst of a reinvention. Welch started going by "Rod Bent" and the now-mostly original band would soon change its name to the Rubber City Rebels. Welch and Clic earnestly took on their new roles as barkeeps, but they quickly discovered the reality of running an old rubber worker's bar. They had to serve all three Goodyear shifts, which meant they started serving shots and cheap draft at six a.m. But they didn't care. Their reason for doing this was to carve out a stage in Akron. Word was out that Akron had a counterpart to Cleveland's Pirate's Cove, and by winter of 1976, the Crypt was booking a formidable lineup—Devo, Pere Ubu, the Dead Boys, the Bizarros, and, of course, the Rubber City Rebels. But it was hardly as glamorous as it might seem. Welch and Clic spent all day jawing with drunken rubber workers before the bands came in.

"It was, like, old guys named Leftie and Blackie and Louie," Welch said. "And on Friday nights, they'd still be hanging out, and we'd be bringing in the bands—Devo and Pere Ubu—and here's Lefty and Blackie and Louie, and they would hear Devo warm up and—'What the hell is this?' You had to clear out one world and bring in another one."

On December 10, 1976, Devo, now with Mark and Jerry, the two brothers Bob, and Alan Myers, played at the Crypt. Then they played again the next night. That week's issue of *Scene* magazine reported the news that the Crypt was in business: "Akron's King Cobra has found the ultimate solution to the problem of having to play what the bar-owner wants—they bought a bar. The Crypt (in Akron) now belongs to the Cobra boys, and they are reserving the stage of their new acquisition for 'bands with original music.' The Crypt will feature area 'underground' bands such as Pere Ubu, Tin Huey, and The Dead Boys, and hopes to bring in an occasional national act as well. The club's offering December 10 and 11 will be Akron's Devo, and on weeknights King Cobra (not surprisingly) will provide the music."

The following weekend, Devo played the Crypt on two consecutive nights, with Pere Ubu opening. Although Devo was considerably shinier, the two bands shared a similar aesthetic and a similar collection of egghead rockers.

Both groups augmented the traditional guitars-drums lineup with a synthesizer. As front men, Thomas/Behemoth and Mark had a lot in common; although they expressed it in different ways, each drew heavily from the darkness of the industrial landscape around them. Both singers had an idiosyncratic presence—Mark in his eyeglasses and factory costumes and throaty yodel, Thomas in his emotive yelping and understated but studious theatrics. Thomas, somewhere in the three-hundred-pound range, with impossibly thick, frizzy hair, would often perform in a trench coat, eyes fluttering as he beat his breast with a pudgy fist. He used found objects as rhythm instruments, striking a steel window weight with a hammer, for example, with at least as much visual as musical effect. Both Devo and Pere Ubu had a strong, early sense of performance art and would sometimes suffer for this, viewed as joke bands by fans and critics who expected convention in their rock. Nevertheless, both expanded the palette, each in their own way.

Thomas, in retrospect, said Pere Ubu and Devo spoke two different languages, downplaying any artistic connection the two bands may have shared.

"I remember a couple songs they did then that had emotion." he said. "They soon dropped those from the set. I find their 'philosophy,' i.e., what lies underneath the surface devolution material, to be vacuous, populist, and cynical to a repulsive and unnecessary degree. Devo wanted a career more than anything else. We wanted anything else more than a career. They had a strategy. We found the idea of having a strategy to be really small town and hick. They were a pop band. We were a folk band."

Scott Krauss, Pere Ubu's drummer, recalled the night he first encountered the spud boys: "This one friend of mine was telling me that there's this really weird band down in Akron. He said, 'You're not going to believe this, but they all wear these uniforms and sing about the de-evolution of the human race.' So we go down to check this out and it was at a little club called the Crypt. It was definitely one of the weirdest bands I've ever seen. I kept wondering, 'Aren't these guys afraid of getting beat up?' I don't know how it all got worked out, but sometimes they'd come up to Cleveland, and we'd take turns headlining. They got into a bunch of philosophical discussions, Jerry Casale and Mark Mothersbaugh versus David [Thomas] and Allen [Ravenstine, Pere Ubu's synthesizer player], and it was pretty interesting. I think they got the impression that Pere Ubu was never going to make it because we didn't care whether we made it or not. And we thought they were going to the other extreme."

Very quickly, Devo went from a band that had gigged only sporadically in its first three-and-a-half years of existence to a regular working outfit. Through the winter of 1976, the band was playing two shows a week, going back and forth between the Crypt and the Pirate's Cove, usually sharing bills with Pere Ubu or the Rubber City Rebels. Jerry described one of those shows in the liner notes to *Devo Live: The Mongoloid Years*.

"Swept up in the energy of England's punk scene, we are learning to deliver live on stage," he wrote. "Jim Mothersbaugh and his homemade electronic drums are gone. Instead, Alan Myers, the human metronome, pounds out primal beats on a 'real' drum kit. Bob Casale (Bob #2) has joined the Devolutionary Army, adding precise staccato guitar rhythms plus occasional keyboard duties so we can let Mark loose for the rapidly increasing bouts of crowd confrontation. With Bob #1 and myself, this new five-member version of DEVO has only played twice before this night. But the line-up works and will remain this way for the next ten years. Wearing black wrestling shorts and nylons over our heads, we still look like a 'weird art band.' As our tempos have gone nuclear, so have the crowd tempers. Our new precision-machine rock sound polarizes the audience into Pros & Cons. The crowd at The Crypt proves no exception."

Mark's commanding stage presence had come as something of a surprise. But it was working. He was jumping around, walking into the audience, tossing sharp-witted word bombs back at hecklers. And his songwriting had developed to the point that Jerry was no longer the focal point. The band had stopped playing some of his early, twisted sex-and-love songs, written from the perspective of Lt. Casanova.

"Jerry made a big mistake when he threw out all his 'old' Devo songs," Ed Barger observed. "It would have been more Lennon/McCartney had he not given up the early stuff that provided contrast to Mark's talents. Just like his song 'The Death of Lt. Casanova'—Lt. Casanova died one night at the Crypt! I saw it with my own two eyes.

"Devo did 'Jocko Homo,' and Jerry knew it was better than anything he or Bob Lewis were capable of doing. Jerry realized Mark was going to be the star. So he quit writing the type of songs that added a different dimension and another side to Devo and began to concentrate on propaganda. Up until this time Jerry was the so-called 'star' of Devo."

That December, amid the flurry of club shows, Devo went into a Cleveland studio and recorded the song "Mongoloid" on a Revox four-track, touching it up afterward at Krieger-Field. The band turned out a version that showed Devo's growing technical and artistic assurance. The song and its sound would change very little in the hands of Brian Eno when recorded later for Devo's debut album.

The 1976 "Mongoloid" is a thumping, fairly straightforward rock song, with nasal, robotic vocals and droning, fuzzed-out guitars. Written by Jerry, it's a classic of this era, capturing both the new sound and the trademark double-entendre. Although the use of "mongoloid" to describe a person with Down syndrome is now considered offensive, the song conveys a sense of empathy, which, in a span of three-and-a-half minutes, grows to a message of anti-elitism. The song's protagonist functions just fine in a supposedly advanced culture. He wears a hat, has a job, brings home the bacon—just like the fellow drones with college degrees. In fact, he's "happier than you and me."

With a good version of "Jocko Homo" already in the can, the band started to talk about pressing the two songs as a single.

Chapter 16

On New Year's Eve, 1976, Devo was booked to open for King Cobra and headliners the Dead Boys at the Crypt. The ads for the show, decorated with a crude drawing of the Grim Reaper, proclaimed: "Start the New Year with a New Attitude." By then, the Dead Boys had begun driving to New York City to play CBGB's and had endeared themselves to Hilly Kristal, the club's owner. Kristal had become their manager and had made plans to release a Dead Boys record on the house label he was forming. That project never bore fruit—emerging, punk-oriented major label Sire Records intervened—but the buzz was enough to for the ad to bill them as "CBGB-OMFUG Recording Artists."

The Dead Boys were, as the title of their debut album would announce, "young, loud and snotty." They decorated themselves with Nazi paraphernalia and sang songs about being juvenile delinquents and delivering "flame-thrower love." A good chunk of their set was dredged from old Rocket from the Tombs material, including their signature song, "Sonic Reducer" and the dark Peter Laughner ballad, "Ain't it Fun." Laughner wrote the song when he was just twenty-one, bringing an eerie mix of innocence and cynicism to the lyric, "Ain't it fun when you know that you're gonna die young."

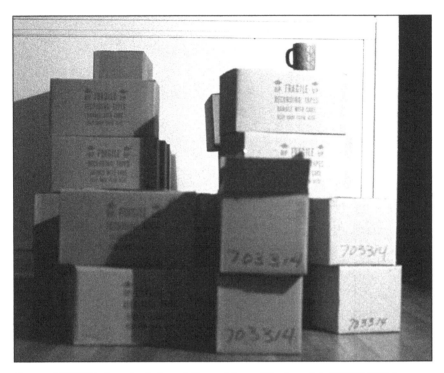

Boxes of DEVO's first single just delivered from Cincinnati to DEVO HQ in Akron. *Courtesy of Bobbie Watson Whitaker*

Dead Boys' singer Stiv Bators was a short, scrawny, tangle-haired self-abuser, with a lot of Iggy in his shimmy. The entire band was bent on destruction as they ravaged their way through a new version of garage-rock aggression. Except for Stiv Bators, whose parents had the foresight to provide him with a stage-ready moniker, the band all took on violent *noms de rock*: guitarists Jimmy Zero and Cheetah Chrome, bassist Jeff Magnum, and drummer Johnny Blitz.

As with the Dead Boys, Devo and Pere Ubu had a knack for crowd confrontation, but from a very different perspective. With the latter two, the message was, "This is our art, and we're gonna make you deal with it." With the Dead Boys, it was—to borrow from their second album title—"We have come for your children."

Jerry, writing in the *Mongoloid Years* liner notes, observed, "Like [the Dead Boys and Rubber City Rebels], DEVO is more than paying its dues within the confines of the psychic barbed-wire. Also, like them, DEVO is fueled by anger and frustration over The Captain and Tennille on local radio and bar bands paid to do covers of 3 Dog Night. That is about where the similarities between us stop. The Dead Boys hate DEVO. Still, we agree to open for them at The Crypt…"

It was freezing that night, but the Crypt—and Devo especially—had quickly developed a following, and the club was full. This was probably vital to Mark's emergence as the front man. He got enough positive feedback to encourage him to keep trying more. Maybe the audiences weren't saying, "There goes a respectable man," as he had hoped in *My Struggle*, but they seemed to think he was cool. This was no small achievement for a bespectacled nerd in satin gym shorts.

But it also led to a clash of egos. Devo's crowd had grown to the point that the band thought they should play last, in the headlining slot. But the Dead Boys had a crowd of their own, many of whom had driven the thirty-five miles from Cleveland. There was a minor argument, but Devo agreed to go on before the Dead Boys. After King Cobra played, Devo took the stage and dove into the new set of material. They had a driving sound, fully rounded with Mark's keyboards, two biting guitarists, and Alan's powerful drumming. Chanted choruses and a harsh tunefulness made this version of the band seem vital—evolved. The weirdness of all those preceding years was fully evident, but so was a new punk force, as Devo made its way through "Clockout," "Soo Bawls," "Space Junk," and "Blockhead."

The Dead Boys were watching the set, celebrating New Year's Eve with Thunderbird wine, which the Crypt sold by the bottle. A drunken Cheetah Chrome and the Dead Boys' roadie, Fuji, made their way to the middle of the crowd to check out the band. Devo had stripped out of their yellow suits and, by late in the set, were wearing black wrestling shorts and T-shirts.

"The little clique from Kent were all hopping around like bunnies while we stood there getting knocked into," Chrome recalled, "and we pushed back when pushed, all in what we assumed to be good fun."

But the action was perceived differently from the stage. Devo, no stranger to confrontation, but also unaccustomed to having a roomful of fans to defend, focused on Chrome as the aggressor. During "Jocko Homo" (or "Mongoloid," depending on who's telling the story), Mark began taunting Chrome.

"Cheetah is a mongoloid!" he chanted, pointing at the red-haired Dead Boy with the dog collar around his neck.

Fuji nudged his buddy. "Why don't you pull down his shorts?" Chrome grinned devilishly, sneaked up to the stage, and gave the boxers a good yank. Down they went, just like in the high school locker room. Marty Reymann happened to be standing right behind Fuji and Chrome when this happened, with Ed Barger a few feet beyond. So when Chrome returned to Fuji's side, Reymann gave him a hard shove. Fuji took a swing at Reymann. Barger lunged forward and took a swing at Fuji. The bodies went down in a pile, with others joining in. The Crypt was having its first real brawl.

In the confusion, Chrome and Fuji dropped to their hands and knees and crawled back to the bar, without anyone realizing they were gone. They picked up their unfinished bottles of Thunderbird and resumed drinking, sharing a good laugh as they watched the Devo fans fight each other.

"After it was over," Reymann said, "Ed told me he had thrown some punches, but didn't even know who he hit. Well, the next week, I had a guy come up to me all pissed off, claiming somebody hit his girlfriend two times! In all the stir, Ed had unknowingly punched out this girl! I was just laughing."

With the Dead Boys already gaining national notoriety for this sort of bad-boy hijinks, the story of the fight was immediately tacked onto into their legend.

"Exaggerated reports of the incident spread fast, causing DEVO to be linked to the U.S. punk music scene," Jerry wrote. "Commercially, it would turn out to be another case of the right thing for the wrong reasons."

The participants, especially the Dead Boys, later downplayed the scuffle. As fisticuffs were a regular part of their repertoire, they probably didn't see this as any big deal—a friendly punch in the arm. In fact, the band would soon use its influence to help Devo crack CBGB's.

Live at CBGB's and confronting The Dead Boys' Cheetah Chrome with Mark "de-pantsed." *Courtesy of Bobbie Watson Whitaker*

"We beat 'em up, but we understood each other," Stiv Bators explained a year later.

Adds Chrome: "I'm kinda surprised to find out that this incident has gained such infamy; I always thought it was kind of a minor thing. I'm also surprised to read what the Devos have to say about it, as I have run into them several times since then and we've always been friendly."

Even so, Chrome would repeat his pants-pulling trick at CBGB's a few months later, proving a Dead Boy could never get too much of a good thing.

"Oh yeah, if memory serves me correctly, I got him both times," Chrome said. "You'd think a smart guy like that would learn to watch his back."

* * *

The shows continued through January. Devo had found its oasis in the Crypt, but there was still only a small group of people who got it. Bob Lewis, Ed Barger, Marty Reymann, and Gary Jackett had remained loyal members at the core of a slowly widening circle. Two friends, Sue Schmidt and Debbie Smith, went to check Devo out one night that winter, and immediately struck up a conversation after being wowed by the first set. The girls, who had played with Peter Laughner in a pre-Pere Ubu band, had been trying to form a group of their own, and it was Alan Myers who introduced them to a drummer friend, Rich Roberts. The trio would soon begin playing as Chi Pig—the name copped from a chicken-and-ribs barbecue joint.

But even as this Akron-Kent-Cleveland musical movement was gaining momentum, there was tension whenever the outside world peeked in. Gary Jackett recalled one of those early Crypt shows, on a January night with the temperature near zero.

"A couple of bikers came in and sat at the bar," he said. "The Chosen Few, I think, was their club. Ten minutes later, and Devo starts playing to the small crowd. In ten more minutes, three more bikers come in. About three-quarters of the way into Devo's set, you look around and there are like twenty Chosen Few in this downstairs bar with all these nerdy, geek Devotees. Rod [Bent] just flipped. They were getting drunk, looking at the band and going, 'What the fuck is this?' You could just feel the room going cold. We quickly realized that everyone was going to get their asses kicked big time. So Rod sneaked out and called the Akron police.

"Suddenly, two cops walked in and said, 'All you guys in the Chosen Few—Out!' Of course, the police walked in about two minutes after the biker guys were drunk enough to be going, 'This is pretty funny! You know, I kind of like these guys.' When the cops came in, it was like, 'We're going to burn this place down. You're all going to die!' They ran them out just when we had won them over."

When the trouble wasn't coming from the outside, Devo's wry sense of humor sometimes invited it in. As the band walked onstage for one of its first Cleveland shows with Pere Ubu, Jerry had his coveralls stuffed full of newspaper, imitating Thomas' portly physique. He ripped out the newspaper and began throwing it around. Thomas was so upset, his bandmates had to plead with him not to cancel the show.

* * *

By March 1977, punk was breaking. Akron and Cleveland were remarkably locked into what was happening in the cultural centers of New York and London, but also remained isolated. Devo, Pere Ubu, and the others had to make extra noise to be noticed. Devo, after struggling through all those years of gestation, accomplished this with perfect timing. That month, both their debut single and their self-produced film were released.

The band put out the 45 of "Jocko Homo"/"Mongoloid" on its own Booji Boy label. The $2,000 borrowed from Kate Myers and Sandy Cohen, which Bob Lewis said he arranged, helped offset the cost. But even with financial backing, the single was still very much do-it-yourself. The band made all the arrangements with the pressing plant and made the record sleeves themselves.

"It was amazing how they sold," Bob Lewis said. "All of a sudden, music stores from France were calling for a hundred copies. Every one of those covers was hand-folded, and we put the little dots on too! It was like the *Little Rascals* for a while."

Mark's recollection was somewhat different, at least as far as local sales were concerned: "I was driving around Ohio, going to record stores going, 'Hey, you guys need another Devo record here?' and the guy would go down to the last bin where it said 'Miscellaneous' and finger through and go, 'Nope, still got the one you brought in last week!' And I'd drive thirty miles back to Akron—'O.K., well, didn't sell any today. But there's always tomorrow!'"

But by midsummer, with influential punk/garage label Bomp handling distribution, the band had sold three thousand copies. More importantly, the single was doing especially well in New York City.

Virtually simultaneous with the arrival of the records from the pressing plant, *In the Beginning Was the End: The Truth About De-Evolution* made

Mark at the Akron Art Institute afternoon concert and premiere screening of *The Truth About De-Evolution* film on March 12, 1977. *Courtesy of Bobbie Watson Whitaker*

its premiere, on March 12, with a screening at the Akron Art Institute, followed by a free Devo concert. The art museum was a center of activity for Akron's small but enlightened cultural elite. The Myers family, with their formidable private collection, were leaders of this faction, and in fact Kate Myers and her husband Sandy hosted a private screening and premiere party at their home before the public opening. It seems logical that Akron's arts community would embrace this event. Mark and Jerry had already endeared themselves to professors in Kent and Akron and had shown themselves to be worthy artists before—and beyond—their current incarnation as a working rock band. The emergence of the film at the same time as Devo's emergence as a live act solidified that impression.

But the three p.m. concert after the art institute screening did not go without incident. Jennifer Licitri recalled the moment that made everyone cringe: "When Devo played in the basement of the Akron Art Museum, the 'Mongoloid' song came up, and in the audience there was a child that was a mongoloid or badly retarded [sic]. It ended up being a huge problem. They just were offending everybody."

Mark got into a conversation with Robert Bertholf that afternoon. He had been working on *My Struggle* for years, and he was looking for advice on getting it published. He had brought along the lengthy manuscript, the nearly three-hundred pages of his photocopied manifesto laid out with his artwork of monkeys, mutated babies, potatoes, and medical diagrams. The book, written by Booji Boy and "compiled by noted contemporary social scientist Mark Mothersbaugh," had an introduction by Jerry in his Chinaman guise. The illustrations included the smiling Chi Chi Rodriguez image that would become the cover of Devo's first album, and the text contained ideas that would define the band's past and future as it careened wildly through surrealistic reveries, prose poetry, sick but hilarious humor, and doctored-up autobiography.

"Everything's in there," Jerry said in a 1995 interview with *Puncture* magazine. "The philosophy is pretty well articulated in my introduction. The kind of irreverence and attack visually, the collage thing we were both doing, Mark kind of really locked into [it] in *My Struggle*, and he produced so much of it. We saw each other every day while he was doing that book and it all came from the art projects we were doing. *My Struggle* today just about covers every offensive and politically incorrect subject you can imagine. I think the pictures kind of tell the story. All the scatology and the conscious satirization of racist and sexist stereotypes and stupid low puns and pop cultural twists and political attacks. It's all there."

This project Mark had been working on for years was mocked up and ready for the world. Bertholf gave him some guidance, and Mark showed his book to the editors at *Scene* magazine. A month later, in the April 14 issue, the music paper previewed the book: "Not to leave any medium untouched, Devo have also put together a book, *My Struggle*, to be on sale soon. Devo keyboardist Mark Mothersbaugh explained that the book's author is 'Booji Boy' (one of Mothersbaugh's onstage characters) and that it's 'about life in Akron and life in general.' "

Mark soon made contact with a mysterious character named rjs, (a.k.a. Robert J. Sigmund or Robert John Sigmond), a friend of the late Cleveland beat-era poet d. a. levy, now a legendary figure, at least in Ohio literary circles. Bob Lewis recalled driving up to Cleveland with Mark to meet with this potential publisher, "R. J. was part of that pre-post-industrial arts climate in Cleveland that self-congratulatorily worshipped levy, Peter (Rocket from the Tombs) Laughner, etc.," he said.

On the back of a postcard, "rjs," after explaining a certain amount of paranoia at having been contacted by a stranger twenty-five years after the fact, described his involvement. "Mark and I were once of a similar spirit," he wrote. "We agreed that I would produce his book when he promised to bring 77 bouncy booby virgin bimbos to help with the manual labor. But when he sold his soul to the devil + moved to lost angeles, I became discouraged + disconnected from him. When he sent me $200, I turned over the unfinished materials to his father, at their estate west of Akron (as per his directions). That was the last inneraction [*sic*]I had with him."

A few copies of *My Struggle* were produced by rjs, and Mark later released it himself. In both cases, the book was credited to the vanity imprint Neo Rubber Band Publications. It was a small, 5½-by-4-inch handbook, bound in red vinyl, although some copies exist with yellow covers. Mark's later editions would have the title embossed in gold. Its appearance was reminiscent of Mao Tse-tung's "little red book." In this sense, Mark was on the same page as Andy Warhol, who, after President Richard Nixon went behind the Communist veil to visit China in 1972, created a series of paintings from the frontispiece of *The Quotations of Chairman Mao*. Mao's status as a revolutionary icon had sexy overtones for pop artists.

Everything seemed to be happening at once for Devo. After the film's premiere at the art institute, a teenager named Michael Hurray interviewed the band for *Heavy Metal*, a local fanzine. The group announced that its first single had arrived and was available for sale. Hurray started asking questions about the band's history.

"Who started the original idea of Devo?" he asked.

Mark quickly pointed at the fellow seated beside him and without hesitation replied, "Him. Bob Lewis."

He continued, "Then Jerry..."

Another member of the band interjected, "And then Mark—[Mark] was the next person." That seemingly innocuous exchange would later come back to haunt them.

* * *

Three days after *The Truth about De-Evolution* premiered in Akron, it was screened at the Ann Arbor Film Festival. The ten-minute Chuck Statler-directed movie won the prize (reportedly $25) for Best Short Film. A buzz was beginning. But Devo was still a local band with gigs to play. The film added a new wrinkle to their club shows. Less than a week after the art institute screening, Devo was back at the Crypt, this time with a film projector in addition to their usual gear. They played the movie at midnight, then followed with their set. They showed the movie again the next night, in what would become a staple of their live performances.

"We would play (our film, *The Truth About De-Evolution*) onstage before we would come out," Mark recalled. "There was no such thing as MTV in the mid-'70s. There was no way to show the stuff, so we would just string a sheet up and then show the film in front of us. Then we'd pull it down and play a set. It seemed to work every time. It seemed to program people perfectly to enjoy an evening of celebrating the downward spiral."

Chapter 17

Less than two weeks after the movie premiere and the release of the "Jocko Homo" single, Iggy Pop's *The Idiot* tour was scheduled to hit Cleveland on March 21 and 22, 1977. This was expected to be an especially hot show, because David Bowie was playing keyboards in Iggy's band, and some cool group from New York called Blondie was opening.

Susan Massaro was especially excited about this. Working as a waitress at Quaker Square's Tavern in the Square restaurant, she'd scored tickets from one of the busboys. She'd never seen Iggy before, and she watched the calendar, eagerly awaiting the show. As the concert approached, she decided she was sure she could get a Devo demo tape into the hands of Bowie and Iggy. She and Jerry had broken up six months before, and she was then dating Bob Mothersbaugh. So she asked Bob if he wanted to go along to try to deliver a cassette. He was game. They could give it a shot.

The following account of what happened next is Susan's. It is flatly rejected by Jerry, and in fact is one of the most disputed of all Devo's stories.

Susan said she asked Mark if he wanted to accompany them to Cleveland, but he and Marina had other plans. She asked Jerry to go, but he thought it was a stupid idea. So she and Bob put together a package with a demo, a photo, and promo materials. She left her daughter in Bobbie's care, and she and Bob headed off to Cleveland. The Agora was a midsize venue downtown, by far the best place to catch up-and-coming acts. An impressive procession of rock royalty passed through there in the 1970s; the Agora was the site of some of Bruce Springsteen's seminal shows, with Kid Leo acting as cheerleader and emcee. The main room had a stage and a wide expanse of wooden floor, with tables and stools around the perimeter.

Bob and Susan arrived a little late and had to push their way through the crowd to get to the front of the stage. Blondie came on, and they both liked them. Susan thought the bass player, Gary Valentine, was cute. After the opening set, Susan and Bob went to the bar for beers, still toting the promo kit, then returned to the front of the stage, positioning themselves so they might be able to make the handoff if the opportunity presented itself.

Iggy and his band came out, Bowie dressed in a flannel shirt, and began playing. Susan was loving the show, but she was also scheming. She got a scrap of paper and scribbled a note indicating she had a package for them and reached over the monitors with it. The hyperkinetic Iggy snatched it up, immediately shredded it, and threw it into the audience.

The show ended. Susan and Bob went to the backstage entrance and tried repeatedly to get through the door, only to be turned away by the club's security. There was growing disappointment. The plan was not going well, but she had another idea. Everyone knew that rock bands, when they played Cleveland, stayed at a place called Swingos Keg & Quarter Hotel, a short hop from the Agora. She asked Bob if he was up for hanging out there, and he said, "Sure."

Debbie Harry and Chris Stein described the hotel in the 1982 biography *Making Tracks: The Rise of Blondie*: "Swingos is famous. It may be the most music-oriented hotel in North America. The rooms are decorated in a tacky bachelor-pad chrome, with black and red rugs, subdued lights, and peeling paint. We heard screams in the night, howls in the halls, and saw festivity, coke dealers in Cadillacs, life in the middle of decay. Perhaps every soul band and half the rock bands in the world have stayed here. Here Cheetah Chrome pushed a soda machine through a wall onto a screwing couple.... Alice's snakes got lost in the lobby. Swingos has seen them all."

(Chrome disputes this story. He says it was Johnny Blitz. He was busy disabling the elevator with a fire hose at the time.)

Bob and Susan entered the lobby of this decadent rock haven. A big crowd of beautiful people were milling about. This might make things difficult. How would they be able to get these two rock stars' attentions? They waited around for a while, then, finally, Bowie and Iggy entered with their entourage. They passed through the lobby quickly and slipped into the bar.

"In retrospect," Susan said, "it's incredible that the fans did not follow. Maybe it was some Swingos protocol, unknown to us at the time. Anyway, Bob and I looked at each other, and just walked into the bar. No one tried to stop us. The room was only moderately busy, so we had full access. It only took a second to find Bowie's booth. I just walked up and started talking. It's hard for me to remember exactly what we said. Iggy wanted to know why I was helping my boyfriend. Bowie asked what kind of music it was, and I don't remember what we said. I think Bob handled that one. The meeting lasted only a minute or two, but I remember Bowie being quite polite and thanking us for the tape, and Iggy, of course, was hyper and cruder. When we left their table, we kind of floated into another booth."

They had done it. Devo's demo was in the hands of two of the most influential musicians imaginable. Bob and Susan tried to be cool as they celebrated their good fortune. Three members of Blondie—Gary Valentine, Clem Burke, and Jimmy Destri—were sitting in the next booth. Valentine leaned over and asked how they knew David Bowie. Bob and Susan slid into their booth and explained what had happened, and the Blondie guys teased them for not bringing an extra tape for them. So Susan, with typical Akron politeness, said she'd be happy to bring one to the next night's show. Blondie invited them to their hotel the following night, and said they'd put them on the guest list for the concert. (Being the opening band, they were staying at a Howard Johnson's.) They all sat and talked about music for a while. Bob and Gary gabbed about guitars; Blondie told them about Seymour Stein, the president of Sire Records who had signed Talking Heads and was a key proponent of the emerging crop of CBGB's bands.

And then Bob Mothersbaugh and Susan Massaro—former nobodies—floated back to Akron on the cloud of one of those nights that can only happen to the young, when the theory that everything is possible seems like a proven fact.

Susan crept in to tuck her daughter Sarah into bed, then recounted the exciting events of this remarkable evening to her best friend Bobbie. "Next day we called Jerry," Susan said, "and of course, he decided he had to go up with us, so he could say and do the right things to impress Bowie and Iggy. We hung out with Blondie at Howard Johnson's for a short while, I think we may have eaten somewhere, and went to the Agora. The show was great, although it could not match the thrill of the night before. I think we got backstage that night, but I don't remember much about it. Gary (Valentine) tried to get us an audience with Bowie, but, unfortunately, he and Iggy had to go into the studio above the Agora and mix the show, as it was to be aired on radio on Sunday. We waited for a very long time, late into the night, and finally decided to go home. Jerry berated us for wasting his time, and that was that."

Jerry's account is considerably different.

"It was me, nobody else in the band," he said. "It was me and I think one of the girls that ended up being in a band called Chi Pig. We wanted to see Blondie.... Iggy's *Idiot* tour, and Bowie was faithfully playing the keyboards. And Blondie (was the opening act). I don't know if Bob1 was along. All I know is I got in backstage with Blondie. Then we got to Iggy, and we gave him a tape, an early demo tape."

Alan Myers' version of the story mirrors Susan Massaro's: "I remember Bob Mothersbaugh took the tape and went up to Cleveland. Susan might have been with him because I think they were an item at the time. They found out what hotel Bowie and Iggy were staying at and hung around the lobby. I think it was Swingos Keg & Quarter. As I recall from his story, they were just about ready to give up and go home then in walked Bowie. I believe Bob approached him with the tape, but it might have been Susan."

In Mark's version, "We had a pretty girl take him a demo tape backstage and hand it to him."

There is general agreement on what happened next. Iggy and Bowie threw the cassette into a box with countless other cassettes they'd been handed on the tour, climbed into Bowie's blue stretch Lincoln Town Car, and departed for the next town, where they'd be given yet more cassettes.

* * *

Part of the spoils of winning the Ann Arbor Film Festival prize was that *The Truth About De-Evolution* went on a tour of colleges and art houses. It was being seen, and audiences were taken with this quirky band that seemed to have something to say and an intriguing way of saying it. One of the people who caught the film was Kip Cohen, an A&M Records rep. Immediately after seeing Devo, he was smitten. "I want this de-evolution band! We've gotta find them."

In April, Jerry's phone rang. It was Cohen. He wanted to fly Devo out to Los Angeles right away for some showcases. Jerry stalled. There was no way they were ready for something like this. They'd only been playing regularly for four months. There was still a lot of screwing around with the set. But Jerry was smooth. He told Cohen no, they couldn't possibly break away from their busy schedule right then. Devo was booked until June, a hot item on the club circuit there in Northeast Ohio—you know how it is. He managed to buy time until July. Cohen said he'd be waiting anxiously. Jerry hung up the phone.

This was some information. A guy in Los Angeles? The same place that less than two years before had found him and Mark scheming to get on a local access charity show to beg for a record contract? He wants us to showcase for a major label?

There would be a lot of work ahead. The band had to get ready. There were weak spots in the material; there was lots of tightening to do. The band that had screwed around for years needed to get polished, and quick. They did have some shows scheduled, a couple of gigs a week through the end of the month. But Jerry realized that maybe—and quicker than anyone thought— the band had outgrown bopping between the Crypt and the Pirate's Cove. So he hatched a plan.

DEVO at Pirate's Cove in Cleveland, 1977, with homemade/clip-on "lighting tree" by Gary Jackett. *Courtesy of Bobbie Watson Whitaker*

Jerry packed a suitcase with some Devo tapes and promo kits, a pair of corduroys and a snazzy sweater, got in a car, and drove to New York. While Devo had always, for reasons of parochial logic, focused on Los Angeles as its musical mecca, New York City was becoming an equally obvious, and far more accessible destination. When Jerry reached the city after a seven-hour drive, he put on his "business" clothes and walked into CBGB's and Max's Kansas City, the other club that was focused on the burgeoning punk scene. With his hair combed, he looked nothing like the guys in baggy yellow suits and 3D glasses in the band pictures. Jerry, no stranger to performance, reached out his hand to Hilly Kristal and introduced himself as Devo's manager.

He went to the office of *New York Rocker*, one of the premier publications of the new rock scene and showed around some pictures and played the single. He talked to Alan Betrock—influential journalist of the underground,

DEVO at Pirate's Cove in Cleveland, 1977. *Courtesy of Bobbie Watson Whitaker*

founder and editor of *New York Rocker*—about doing a story on Devo. Then he sat back and waited. Jerry was pretty smart. He already understood how the business worked, even though he'd operated outside it for his entire career. Based on the promise of a *New York Rocker* feature, CBGB's and Max's Kansas City agreed to book Devo. And based on the promise of bookings at CB's and Max's, *New York Rocker* agreed to do a feature.

Now it was time to get busy. Devo had a series of Cleveland gigs booked at the Pirate's Cove and a new place, the Eagle Street Saloon. These would be the warm-ups for three New York shows in late May, two at CBGB's, and one at Max's Kansas City. Buoyed by the sudden attention, they returned almost immediately to the reality of life in Ohio.

The Eagle Street Saloon had been taken over by a guy named Clockwork Eddie, who had previously run a club called Clockwork Orange until it was shut down by the city.

"I don't know how they got into Eagle Street," Gary Jackett said. "It was like Berlin 1929 in the middle of the German depression. It was a hellhole. It was great, in a horrible way."

Eagle Street was populated by rowdy, hard-rock loving, Bud-drinking bikers. It made the Bombay Bicycle Club look like an ice cream social. Devo got up to play, all focused on grooming itself for the important gigs ahead in New York and Los Angeles. They were honing the set, working on the bits they knew went over well—Booji Boy, the "Satisfaction" cover, the whole "Jocko Homo" opus. But there was one problem. Several problems, actually, but one in particular.

This one guy just kept screaming, "Aerosmith! Play some Aerosmith!" They ignored him. Taunting Cheetah Chrome was one thing; messing with these guys in leather vests would be another.

"Aerosmith!"

"Aerosmith!"

The Booji Boy segment of the night arrived. Mark pulled on the mask and started his sweet, squeaky-voiced routine. Pretty much the antithesis of Aerosmith. Finally, the guy rushed the stage and grabbed the mask with both hands, clenching his teeth.

"I SAID AEROSMITH, GODDAMN IT!!!!!"

And he ripped the mask from Mark's face. Fortunately, Mark had two spares.

Chapter 18

One of the highlights in Devo's set was the cover of the Rolling Stones' classic, "Satisfaction (I Can't Get No)." It had begun with band rehearsing in Man Ray Studios, kicking around the idea of giving a Stones song the same kind of devolved treatment they had already given "Secret Agent Man." Part of this stemmed from a growing ambition. Devo had heard that a Rolling Stones tribute album was in the works and thought that if they could come up with something, maybe they could be included. They started messing around with the song at Man Ray. Bob Casale came up with a lick—a choppy, repetitive guitar pattern—and the rest of the band followed his lead. Mark caught onto the groove and started singing the words to "Paint it Black." But it wasn't working. As the band continued playing, Mark changed tack.

"I can't get no…"

The rhythm was starting to fit.

"…Satisfaction…I can't get me no…satisfaction."

The words began to mesh with the jerky rhythm the band was cranking out. They kept at it. Alan worked out a deceptively simple drum pattern. Bouncing from snare to toms to a sharp little ring-a-ding on the bell of the ride cymbal, his foot working the high hat at an odd interval in the time signature, it almost

DEVO perform with wiggling "worms" in full-body latex sleeves. *Courtesy of Bobbie Watson Whitaker*

seemed as though he was playing backwards on the beat. The guitars were clipped and restrained; Jerry's bass pushed forward and pulled back, pushed forward and pulled back. Even as Mark's monotone vocals climaxed with that impossibly breathless stream of *babybabybabybabybabybabybabybaby*, there was no break at the end as he went into the next line, "Better come back later next week, cuz you see I'm on a losin' streak."

In Devo's hands, the song was all tension and no release, and added an entirely different layer of meaning to the title. When Mick Jagger claimed he couldn't get no satisfaction, there was an unspoken understanding that eventually he would, probably with a couple of hookers in New Orleans. But when Mark Mothersbaugh made the same claim, wearing glasses and a protective yellow suit, you believed him. There was no way that guy would get any satisfaction.

Without hitting the listener over the head, this delivery of "Satisfaction" applied the theory of "Polymer Love," that in an increasingly devolved world, human sex was anachronistic, and human love was irrelevant. Plus, it had a beat, and you could dance to it. The "Satisfaction" cover captured, as well as anything the band had ever done, the spirit of Devo. The soul of the Stones' original was replaced with the funny robotics of Devo. The song was catchy, and it made you want to move, but it wasn't funky, at least not in the traditional sense. It seemed at once familiar and completely new.

"People didn't understand Devo, and we thought it would be easier to show them how to devolve a standard, a classic," Jerry said. "It was kind of like a musical faction of the deconstructivist movement in architecture."

De-evolution in action. Given Mark's seminal moment seeing the Beatles on *Ed Sullivan*, it's a little surprising he didn't tackle a Beatles cover. On the other hand, another new entry in the set, the frantic, driving "Uncontrollable Urge," took one of the Fab Four's early conventions to the Devo extreme. Where "She Loves You" had used the "yeah, yeah, yeah" harmony as a primal hook, Mark advanced the notion during the anxious build-up to "Uncontrollable Urge"—"Yeah, yeah, yeah, yeah, *yeah-yeah-yeah-yeah-yeah-yeah-yeah-yeah*!" He trumped the Beatles by a full nine "yeahs."

Devo had found its sound. Now it was time to see how it would play in the big city. After a final warm-up show with Pere Ubu at the Pirate's Cove on May 19, the band and their friends set off for New York. They wouldn't all fit in the van, so Bobbie and Susan, who had matching Datsun 510s, drove. Ed Barger was along to run sound and act as "the designated heavy...the rest of the spuds were small and skinny and not much help in battle." Bob Lewis accompanied them with his girlfriend Mary King, and Bob Casale's wife, Sherry, came too. As they drove all night through Ohio and Pennsylvania, they talked about the possibilities. In those two little tin-cup Datsuns, the friends who had been together for years recognized that those days above the pizza shop and those nights picking brains with Bob Bertholf and his poetic cronies might be reaching the unlikeliest conclusion. Devo was going somewhere. Nobody knew exactly where yet, but they were definitely going to New York, to the suddenly legendary CBGB's. They had all listened to that first, groundbreaking Ramones album back in Akron, and they knew they were approaching the headwaters.

In retrospect, it seems like everyone who played CBGB's in the mid-1970s became a rock star. Talking Heads, Blondie, the Ramones, Patti Smith, and Television would all be written into rock and roll history after rocking and rolling on the club's ratty, duct-taped stage. Even lesser lights like Mink DeVille and the Dictators benefited, receiving some heightened level of royalty for having been on that particular scene. None of this was completely clear in 1977, but enough of it was.

The band had shows booked on May 23 and 24 at CBGB's, and another on the 25th at Max's Kansas City—a Monday, Tuesday, and Wednesday. They arrived bright and early for their sound check; Ohio kids are raised to be punctual, after all—. Devo was no stranger to raunchy bars, so Hilly Kristal's claustrophobic, 167- by 25-foot club with the stage at the far end of the tunnel didn't raise any particular eyebrows, even as it was tucked in among the Bowery district's soup kitchens and flophouses. The bathrooms were about the worst they'd ever seen, but it didn't matter. The Crypt wasn't much better. And the Crypt was in Akron.

As they checked out the city, Devo and its entourage went shopping in Greenwich Village, hitting Fiorucci and the Capezio store and a bunch of vintage clothing stores. Mark and Jerry, naturally, were mask hunting. At a shop called Unique Boutique, they discovered Gurkha pants, the baggy white shorts worn by British soldiers in tropical climates. The band members each bought a pair to wear onstage. By then, no member of Devo could choose stage clothes without the others, upon approval, buying identical items. The uniforms were part of the ideal—Devo was a collective. There was an echo of the Ramones in this, albeit with a sophisticated edge. The Ramones all wore ripped blue jeans and leather jackets and took "Ramone" as a surname; Devo, even if they changed outfits, had a cohesive front. Kraftwerk, by then, was doing the same thing, and Devo seemed like a cross between the two. Despite the strong personalities, the band intended to present itself as unified, faceless workers, with guitars and synthesizers in their toolbox.

Bob Lewis and Jerry also went scrounging around Manhattan's bookstores. They happened into Samuel Weiser's Books on Broadway. It had been a couple of years since they'd read about Oscar Kiss Maerth's book *The Beginning Was the End*, and they'd never been able to find a copy. Maybe this would be the place. Jerry asked the clerk if they had it.

"And they acted like, 'Why do you want this book?'" he recalled. "The guys that ran the store were all Jewish, and they thought that Oscar Kiss Maerth was definitely a Nazi. They hated anything that had to do with genetics, eugenics, perfection, or any kind of social anthropology. They were so pissed, but they went in the back and got it. Of course they'd sell it to me, but it was like, 'Get out of here.'"

* * *

The band found places to crash. Bob Mothersbaugh and his girlfriend Susan stayed at a loft near CBGB's with Bob and Sherry Casale. Bobbie slept in her car in front of the Ramones' apartment building. Mark and Jerry stayed with an old friend from Kent. One night, to soak in the romance of New York City, some of the group stayed in the Chelsea Hotel, which had given lodging to everyone from Mark Twain to Bob Dylan to Jimi Hendrix. In the darkest moment of the Chelsea's lore, Sid Vicious' girlfriend Nancy Spungeon would die there the following year.

The shows went even better than expected. Back in Ohio, it had been hard to comprehend exactly what a "buzz" meant. The band was sure something was happening, but it had only been a matter of days since Mark's mask had been torn from his face by a clueless, leather-clad spud. Even when Devo won a crowd over, it was mostly with friends in attendance. But now, for three nights, the band was discovering what it meant to be pursued. People had heard the record. They had seen the film. There were music industry talent scouts in the audiences. At one of the shows, a group of high school kids from New Jersey showed up with a black Ford LTD that they had christened the "DEVOmobile." The car had a huge Booji Boy painted on the hood, along with D-E-V-O. Even when the petulant Cheetah Chrome repeated his de-pantsing of Mark at CBGB's, there was a sense of importance in the air. It was hard to figure out how to deal with this.

DEVO's New York debut at CBGB's on May 23 & 24, 1977. *Courtesy of Bobbie Watson Whitaker*

When the band played at Max's, opening for a straight, Rod Stewart-ish band called Allen Turner and Rocks, they hung a big Booji Boy poster behind the stage. They left it up after they were finished, and Turner performed under Booji's watchful eye. After the show, he asked if he could keep the poster. There was something vaguely troubling to this. Even as Devo was being accepted, there was a gnawing suspicion that people weren't really "getting" it. They were becoming musically accessible even as they maintained their deeply groomed philosophy. The more they rocked, the more people listened. But the less, it seemed, they thought about what the band was saying.

Some of this was their own fault. Devo's mix of the high and the low invited fans of the low into the party. Take, for instance, the song "Sloppy (I Saw My Baby Gettin')." The song, co-written with Gary Jackett, comes across in a bar as a frantic porn-fest. The chorus, after all, goes, "She said sloppy, she said sloppy, she said sloppy, I think I missed the hole." But it was intended as a commentary on sexual frustration; Jackett said he wrote it because he was "just crazy for some girl." Sometimes Dadaist theater merely comes across as silly. That's part of the intention. But it's not the final hope.

Still, Devo was in command of the New York audience. These were strangers and, even as Bob Lewis watched, understanding how far Devo had come from the Creative Arts Festival days, and even as his old girlfriend Bobbie Watson took snapshots, and even as Sherry Casale wondered if her husband's radiology career was ending, and even as reliable Ed Barger ran the soundboard, a whole new world was opening up. At Max's, during the song "Praying Hands," Mark went into the audience with his microphone after singing about the occupations of the left and right hands—"while the left hand's diddlin', well, the right hand goes to work." He began to confront bar patrons about their own hands as the band played the hyperactive instrumental interlude.

"Let's find out what people at Max's Kansas City do with their hands," he said, approaching a member of the audience.

"You, sir—what is your left hand doin'?"

"Smoking a cigarette," came the reply.

He approached a woman.

"You—what is your left hand doin,' baby?"

She chirped something in response. Apparently it rubbed Mark the wrong way, prompting him into action.

"Hey—hey! O.K., don't be a spud. Don't be a spud," he said in rhythm with the band. And immediately, he began chanting: "Spud, spud, spud, spud," with one of the band members following suit.

Devo had become precise in handling adverse reactions. They—and now, significantly, Mark—were confident in what they were doing and aware of their role as the Dr. Moreaus of the stage. This was their show. And when they threw that in New York's face, New York seemed to eat it up. This was Devo's field research in the quest to understand humanity.

"We were not really pop musicians; we were scientists, we were musical reporters," Mark said years later. "We were influenced probably more so by multimedia pop artists and conceptualists of the time than influenced by the music that was on the radio. Visual artists—people like Andy Warhol, artists of the '60s that were dealing with concepts and ideas—that's what we wanted to be a part of, as opposed to sitting down with one guitar for the rest of our lives writing songs. We saw the whole world and technology and all things natural and unnatural as potential material for getting our message across."

So the message was getting across, whether fully understood or not. Jerry, writing fifteen years later in the *Mongoloid Years* liner notes, recalled his reaction to the New York shows. Even he, perhaps the most ambitious of the Devo members, realized that this commercial acceptance was a double-edged sword. In the intervening years, that realization became even stronger.

"Though the lights are brighter it's the beginning of the end," he wrote. "Suddenly DEVO's proto-cyberpunk multimedia sensory attack is embraced as Entertainment. An audience of Big Apple spuds, peppered with record biz 'earmen' (tipped off by a snappy column in Alan Betrock's *New York Rocker* magazine), swallow huge doses of de-evolution in an instinctive effort to develop cultural anti-bodies, much like rats learning to live with DDT. Sexy nerds with a sonic plan, DEVO's shows at Max's introduce us to the benefits of artistic license in the pre-AIDS/ PC era. On stage, girls rip the yellow Tyvek (TM) suits from our bodies. Backstage, they complete the ritual with post-performance orgasmic gratuities in the dressing room. The urgency is necessary. Having been paid a total of $500.00, we are forced to dense-pak into our 1970 Ford van, along with our equipment, and lumber back to Akron during the night. The next day, our Rubber City phone starts ringing early. 'I'm sorry. What's that?' 'Who!?' 'Oh from Sire?' 'Elektra/Asylum?' 'Columbia?' 'Really!?' Record company 'hitmen' have decided that DEVO is the new girl in town. The fight begins to see which of them gets her."

The New York stand had been a success. As if to put an exclamation point on this, the band members went out after one of their shows and hung fliers for the already completed gig. Sonny Vincent, from a New York band called the Testors, saw them do this and wondered why. There was something de-evolutionary about this, but it also sent the message that Devo wanted to be remembered.

Everybody was exhausted as they loaded up in the van and the Datsuns and headed back to Ohio. They all fell asleep, including Ed Barger. Unfortunately, he was at the wheel of his van at the time. He ran through a New York red light, his head lolling back on the seat. He snapped back into consciousness just in time, cursing himself for coming so close to killing everybody.

Then it was back to Ohio, back to reality. The following night Devo had a show at the Pirate's Cove, with some local band called the Nerves.

Chapter 19

In mid-June, Devo played an in-store appearance at the Drome in Cleveland. The record store was owned by a guy named John Thompson, known around the music scene as Johnny Dromette. His shop had become a gathering point for the new Northeast Ohio rockers; David Thomas and Peter Laughner worked there, as did the founders of *CLE* magazine, an important chronicle of that unlikely wrinkle in musical time. The scene had remained collegial and, pretty much by necessity, somewhat insulated. There weren't that many of them, and most remained anonymous. Laughner had come close, auditioning for Television (he named his follow-up band Friction after one of the group's songs), but Devo's quickly growing national attention was the exception.

Back in Akron, the singer for the Bizarros, Nick Nicholis—an earnest and organized fellow—had taught himself how to start a record label and was making plans to release an album called *From Akron*, with the Bizarros on one side and Rubber City Rebels on the other. Tin Huey, by then, had whipped a crowd of outsiders into shape as a loyal audience, and the bands were all watching one another and learning. Like Devo, Chi Pig was pairing silly costumes and dances with off-kilter pop. The Rebels had benefited from the Dead Boys' comradeship—Rod Bent (soon to become Rod Firestone in a bratty nod to Akron's rubber royalty) had spiked his hair—and the band was playing originals like "Brain Job" and "Child Eaters" under cheeky stage names, with Clic and Bent joined by Pete Sake and Stix Pelton. Tin Huey's Mark Price was helping produce some of the bands in Akron's Bush Flow Studios. Everyone seemed to be working together and having a good time.

Devo's Drome appearance on the afternoon of June 19 was aired live on the radio, and would become a well-known bootleg, *Workforce to the World*. The band debuted its song "Come Back Jonee" that day. They returned to Akron and began preparing for a second round of New York gigs in early July. Then it would be off to the Los Angeles showcases. But amid all this excitement, tragic news spread through the grapevine. Peter Laughner, the world-weary singer-guitarist with restless potential, was dead.

Late in the evening of June 21, 1977—the first night of summer—alone in a bedroom at his parents' house in Bay Village, he set up a cassette recorder, picked up his acoustic guitar, and pressed "record."

"Well, it's real late at night," he said to the tape machine, his nasal twang sounding ragged. "Everybody's gone to sleep. And I got a six-pack of Genesee and some Lucky Strikes. So I'm gonna do some songs…"

He died the next day. He was twenty-four. The cause was acute pancreatitis related to his alcoholism.

* * *

Devo set out for their second trip to New York, stopping on the way for a July 6 show at the Hot Club in Philadelphia. Hilly Kristal had helped groom a small, like-minded East Coast club circuit between New York, Boston, and Philly. Bob Lewis, always the automotive connoisseur, drove his 1964 tan Oldsmobile Holiday 8 two-door coupe with a 355 Rocket V-8 engine (but alas, no power steering), parking it in front of the club on South Street. In the accompanying van, he had packed five thousand copies of the "Jocko Homo" single for delivery to Stiff Records in New York. The emerging London-based label had agreed to take on distribution, since Devo had

DEVO's New York debut at CBGB's on May 23 & 24, 1977. *Courtesy of Bobbie Watson Whitaker*

quickly outgrown its Booji Boy label. So maybe there was a silver lining when the thief who decided to break into a vehicle that night chose Bob's car, and not the van. (Although it's unlikely that a petty crook would've recognized any value in those stacks of silly-looking records.) Bob and Jerry's luggage got ripped off, and Jerry wasn't about to let it slide. With perhaps a misdirected sense of revenge, he stole a rare bottle of Napoleon brandy from the Hot Club's manager.

Devo returned to New York the following day for a three-night stand at Max's Kansas City, sharing the bills with Suicide and the Cramps. The Cramps had their roots in Northeast Ohio (and Ghoulardi). Singer Lux Interior was from Stow, which neighbors Akron, and had formed the band there with his girlfriend, Poison Ivy Rorschach. And Suicide, although bleaker and more dissonant, shared Devo's desire to smash rock tradition over the head, using synthesizers as part of their weaponry. New York City was all about compression and instancy; nothing was building slowly in the Village by then. Things were exploding. A month after its debut, Devo returned as conquering heroes.

Bob delivered the cases of 45s to Stiff's New York office and he and the band had a long conversation that culminated in a deal with Stiff to release a second single. The shows went even better than the first go-round. Word had gotten out, and suddenly the Max's audiences were studded with stars—aging rockers who wanted to dig the new breed. Keith Richards showed up, crowing, "I wrote that song!" when Devo played "Satisfaction." Robert Fripp, Brian Eno, and Frank Zappa checked them out. A drunken John Lennon came up to Mark's booth after the band had finished and started singing "Uncontrollable Urge" in his face.

Mark couldn't believe what he was hearing. *John Lennon! Singing our song?*

After one of the shows, Fripp invited Eno and the band back to his place and offered his help. He liked them. And he and Eno were in a position to make things happen. The Devo guys thanked him politely. They were trying to keep their cool, but with the LA shows ahead, it was hard to know which cards to play, and when.

The band returned to Ohio and caught a night's sleep before departing for Los Angeles. This trip was going to be a little different. The entourage would be pared down because of the cross-country flight. Bob Lewis would not be included. By then, Bob had already sensed that he was being pushed aside by Jerry. Primarily through his handling of the single, and more generally through his long association with the band, he was emerging as a manager. But there was tension in this.

"I had already told Eddie Barger and General Jackett, sitting in a van across from CBGB's, that if Jerry tried to screw me over there would be a reckoning—and had had a talk with Mark out at 'the ranch' about the fact that there might be consequences to Jerry's behavior—this was a pretty vague conversation, but germane."

The tension was not just between Bob and Jerry, though. Mark didn't like what was emerging as an ugly dissension. He was caught in the middle. He had come into the fold long after Jerry and Bob's early pairing, and he didn't know exactly what their history entailed. Friends in the small Devo circle were, consciously or not, choosing sides, and some informal diplomacy was necessary. Before departing for Los Angeles, Bob Mothersbaugh talked to Bobbie Watson about Lewis' exclusion from the California trip.

"Bob Mothersbaugh was expecting me to be upset," Bobbie said. "But he said I shouldn't be, that it didn't mean Bob was excluded, that this was just an audition. There wasn't anything concrete for Bob to be doing during the short period of time that they anticipated being there. And they only had a certain amount of money to get there and get back on. They wanted a tight budget. He anticipated that we would think it was all Jerry's idea. He wanted it clear that that was not the case, that they all agreed.

"Mark was the one assigned to tell [Bob Lewis]," she continued. "Mark and I had a discussion about his task. He said there was a lot of antagonism between Jerry and Bob and that it was understandable. At this critical time Jerry wouldn't want to deal with that, and Mark was going along with that because he didn't want to blow the chance. If negotiations started and something concrete came up, [Mark promised] he would fly Bob there out on his own money. He valued his input and [Bob] was obviously part of it. [Mark] did respect him as a friend.

"[Bob] was hurt. He was confused. He didn't know how to handle it. He didn't know whether to confront Jerry. He decided against that in the interest of the band because he wanted to see it happen. He believed more, he trusted that this would happen. He believed what Mark said, that he could have joined them out there but there were a lot of things to do here that kept him occupied with the marketing of the 45s."

So the five members of Devo, with Ed Barger along to run sound, left for Los Angeles. And Bob Lewis did not.

* * *

Devo played their first A&M Records showcase on July 25 at the Starwood in Hollywood. *Slash Magazine*, L.A.'s counterpart to *New York Rocker*, threw a big party for the band, inviting lots of film and music industry people. Kip Cohen, the A&M rep who had arranged the shows, was waiting eagerly to see how this "de-evolution band" would come across live. Mark and Jerry sensed, based on the response in New York, that these shows were going to go well. "Outside of New York, L.A. is probably the most devolved city goin'," Jerry told a *New York Rocker* reporter on the eve of the Starwood gigs, "and we just haven't shown them explicit views of the gut, so we're goin' to take the surface off of Los Angeles."

These guys were going to explain Los Angeles to the locals? This seemed like a pretty heady claim, but Devo, at that moment, believed they could do no wrong. They took the Starwood stage, opened the show with *The Truth About De-Evolution*, pulled down the screen, and launched into their set, confident and more controlled than ever in their stage presence. The jerky movements had become sublime; the interaction with the audience, the ability to put on a real show, and the belief that this was what people wanted to hear had reached an apex.

Backstage at the Starwood, a short-haired, skinny, kind of hyper guy in glasses walked into the dressing room. Jerry didn't recognize him at first. The man introduced himself:

"I'm Iggy Pop."

Jerry apologized—this really didn't look like the guy he'd seen four months earlier at the Agora.

Iggy started singing "Praying Hands."

Mark looked at him, surprised.

"How do you know the words?"

"Cuz I've been listening to that tape you gave David," Iggy said.

That tape—the one he'd gotten in Cleveland. Apparently Bowie had thrown it into a bin with a bunch of other tapes, and while he and Iggy were in Germany mixing the *Lust for Life* album, Iggy had gotten bored with the crappy German radio stations and asked Bowie if he had anything to listen to.

"He filled a trash can, a metal wastebasket about this high, with cassettes," Pop recalled. "And he said to me, 'Here, I want you to go through these and see if there's anything good.' I took 'em to my little apartment and—what do you expect? [laughs]—and suddenly, I felt like Columbus. I felt like I'd discovered America. There it was. It was Devo."

Iggy had been learning the songs and had, in fact, been talking about recording the material himself. The label with the contact information had gotten separated from the cassette; all they had was the name—Devo. "They didn't think the band even existed," Mark said. "They just thought we were some art project or something. Which is kinda half-true."

So Iggy, who was back from Germany and had just gotten his first driver's license, was driving down Santa Monica Boulevard in his GTO. He passed the Starwood and saw the name on the marquee: Devo. He'd found them.

Accompanying Iggy backstage were dancer/burgeoning singer Toni Basil, actor Dean Stockwell, and singer Ronnie Blakely. Basil, who would later score an MTV hit with the dance-oriented "Hey Mickey," asked the band who did their choreography.

"Everybody laughed and they pointed at me," Jerry said. "It was like, I never thought it was choreography, but she related to it...and wanted to know, 'How do you get them to do that step?' That was so funny. She totally got off on it. Then she wanted to choreograph us, but we didn't have any money to pay her."

Jerry and Toni hit it off almost immediately. The band was on another high—until they sat down with Kip Cohen. According to Mary B. King in *New York Rocker*, he told them, "On a scale from 1 to 10, you get a 10 for 'star potential,' 10 for stage presence, and 1 for songs." As Mark Mothersbaugh would later recall, "A&M came and saw us and their A&R guy called us to their office after and said, 'Well guys, it's really interesting but the music, I don't get it at all. I don't know how to describe it to you, but say there are five 14-year-old girls standing in front of you: one of them doesn't wear deodorant, one of them needs to change her diet because she has all these pimples, and one of them needs to shave her arms and legs. How do I tell them this? You can't tell them exactly what it is that's wrong.' So, I said, 'We're not your type of girls?' And he said, 'Exactly.' I remember we walked out of there onto La Brea. And Jerry was like 'What an asshole!' And Alan Myers said, 'I kind of feel like if we would have deserved a record contract, he would have given us one.' And we were like, 'What? Shut up! Who asked you? Just play the drums. You're stupid.'"

This was an odd situation to be in. A&M had been providing Devo with apartments at the Oakland Garden Estates in Burbank. But they were cutting off the lifeline, even as Iggy Pop—*Iggy Pop!*—was going ga-ga over them, and this super-cute dancer was flirting with Jerry and they were sure they were on the verge of conquering L.A. the same way they believed they had conquered New York. What were they supposed to do?

With no support, the band was ready to return to Akron. But Jerry smelled blood in the West Coast waters.

"There's no way we're going back," he told them. "This is it. We got to make this happen. We've got to be professional. We're just starting to sound good. We're just starting to play good. Nothing else matters."

So they fished around for places to crash. Jerry hooked up with Toni, who made some calls to friends and found places for most of the other guys to stay. Iggy invited Mark and Bob Casale to stay at his place in Malibu.

All of this was a risk. But they were beginning to realize it was the risk of a lifetime. Jerry had just celebrated his twenty-ninth birthday, and Mark was twenty-seven. Neither of them had particularly promising careers waiting for them back in Ohio, and suddenly, before they'd had a chance to absorb the opportunities that were bombarding them, their pop biological clocks were ticking.

Jerry started working the phones. Toni Basil helped hook him up with management people and used her influence to get club owners to return his calls.

"She helped me because she understood business very well," Jerry said. "She understood this town and how it worked. I was, obviously, theoretically understanding it and trying to be the manager. I didn't have the connections. So she would help get me the people, the numbers, and the callbacks. I just started getting us more gigs so that we were making money. The Starwood wanted us back even though Kip Cohen said, 'Fuck you guys.' Then, she got me to see Marshall Burrows, and we got into the Whisky and Myron's Ballroom. We had a little circuit going."

For about three weeks, Mark and Bob Casale crashed in Iggy Pop's living room. This was kind of like living in a dream and an opium dream at the same time. They were jamming with him at his house, the godfather of punk shaking his thing with the spud boys.

"[Iggy] wanted to record our first album before we did," Mark recalled. "I was like, 'No, we want to do it first,' and he was like, 'Shut up, this would be so good for you.' He was crazy during that time. I have tapes of Devo rehearsing in his living room in Malibu, and him grabbing the microphone... to sing wild shit over the top of our songs."

After the first rehearsal in Iggy's living room, he asked the Devo guys if they wanted to go for a swim. It was a terrible day—stormy, with huge, treacherous waves. They walked to the beach and looked out at the ocean, which bore no resemblance to the flat inland lakes of Ohio. The spuds wanted nothing to do with it. Iggy stripped off his shirt and dove right in, swimming about 150 yards out into the wild Pacific and back.

"Like it was a baby's bath," Ed Barger said.

Barger recalled Iggy as a savior who stepped in when the band needed support. But he was a wild one, nonetheless.

"I'll never forget, he had a '65 GTO in the driveway," Barger said, "and he made us call him 'Jim.' [After his Christian name, Jim Osterberg.] There were sheets of paper about 12 inches wide that hung from walls about 20 feet high. He had a tall step ladder and was doing paintings on these papers. He had these gay guys that would light his cigarettes and care for his every whim. He would pour a pile of cocaine on the table and do it all. And not that anybody wanted any, but none was offered to us.

"Iggy wanted to learn some Devo songs for his upcoming tour. He invited us to his Malibu house to teach him these Devo songs. He wanted to do 'Praying Hands' and asked me to write the lyrics out. So, of course, I wrote them out and handed them to him. Iggy then crumbled the paper into a ball, shook his fist at me and yelled, 'Where are the lyrics?'

"He also had this beautiful girlfriend. The next day when we got there, he had wrecked the GTO, and this beautiful girl had this big bandage on her face. Another time, we were practicing, and Iggy came by with this Black woman. Devo went into 'I need a chick' and Iggy took over on vocals. He sang, 'Iggy's got eight inches!'... 'Iggy's got nine inches!'

… 'Iggy's got ten inches!' This poor woman understood he was making a fool of himself, and tried to drag him away as he pleaded, 'It really is!'"

But the weirdness apparently cut both ways.

"We went to lunch," Pop recalled. "And I remember thinking what an insufferable smartass Mark was, always having to do something stagey and odd. Which at lunch was, when we received our serviettes after ordering, he took his serviette and covered his head with it and continued the conversation with this serviette on his head. You know, it takes one to know one, 'cuz I was that way too!"

* * *

Devo was on the cusp of something. They were five ostensibly square guys from Ohio, suddenly slogging around with rock stars and Beautiful People. They were by no means naïve, but this was a new world for them. One did not sleep on Iggy Pop's couch in Akron. And so they woke up every morning, rubbing their eyes, wondering what was happening to them.

Chapter 20

The Kip Cohen affair had proved to be only a minor speed bump. Devo got a booking right away at Mabuhay Gardens in San Francisco, then another a week later at Myron's Ballroom in L.A., then another, and another, and another. The first time at Mabuhay, the band drew less than a hundred people. The second time, four hundred new fans filled the club. Devo's effect was immediate.

As Sleepers' guitarist Michael Belfer told James Stark in the book *PUNK '77*, "I think Devo were one of the best live bands of that time. Me and a friend came up from Palo Alto to see what was going on and ended up at the Mab. Devo was playing that night. We got in and started milling around and noticed there was a movie screen hanging in back of the stage, which I had never seen in a club before. We weren't sure what was going to happen. All of a sudden their film, the one about devolution came on, and it had the audience transfixed. I remember my friend asking me, 'What the fuck is this?' It had a very intense feel about it. After it ended, it instantaneously dawned on everybody in the club that what we had just seen was the band that was about to come onstage and play. There was this incredible surge that happens where everything goes forward. It felt like gravity had been

David Bowie announces "the band of the future" before DEVO plays at Max's Kansas City. *Courtesy of Bobbie Watson Whitaker*

taken out of the room. They came out playing; it was sort of like being on acid, in the good sense of the word."

After less than a month in Los Angeles, Devo was becoming a regular on the club circuit. The band got booked three nights in a row—August 22, 23, and 24—at the Starwood, the same venue where they'd played the failed A&M showcase. Then, on August 25, back in Ohio, something happened, very quietly, and without the band's knowledge. Bob Lewis filed an application to trademark "Devo."

He had promised a "reckoning." The keystone was set.

* * *

Dean Stockwell, Toni Basil's actor friend, was into the band. In the grand Hollywood tradition, he knew people who knew people. He had a casual friendship with Neil Young and decided one day to play him a tape of Devo. He played "Mongoloid" and "Satisfaction" on a cheap cassette player, and Young liked it. So Stockwell took him to see the band at the Starwood. It's hard to know how well they recognized their connection then, especially as Young was a denim-and-flannel, post-hippie rock-and-roller who sometimes wore fur-lined boots, and Devo was none of those things.

But there was a connection. Young, in a famously spontaneous fit of anger and sadness, had written the song "Ohio" after the 1970 Kent State shootings. He and Jerry had been equally affected by the event and had channeled their emotion into music. Young had been succinct in his musical response, Jerry less direct but more complete. But their reactions were the same. That Devo was here at all, playing the Starwood seven years later, had a lot to do with the "four dead in O-hi-o."

With the band's star rising, the fence-straddling between Ohio and California began to fade. Devo played steadily through September, with a four-night stand at the Starwood followed by another at the legendary Whisky-a-Go-Go. The Whisky had been the launching pad for the Doors and had continued as a showcase for provocative up-and-comers. Its history was written into the menu, with a Joan Jett Take-Off drink ("a Runaway best seller"), the Cheap Trick Bun E. Burger (after drummer Bun E. Carlos) and, paying homage to KROQ's most influential disc jockey, the Rodney Bingenheimer Special (Tab cola). Soon, a Devo item would be added to the menu—a bowl of nuts and chips (potato, no doubt.)

Devo was sharing the bill with Blondie and a new, primitive but strangely endearing punk band called the Germs. Bingenheimer was a fan of the latter group, whose whiny young singer, Darby Crash, a.k.a. Bobby Pyn, was taking rock-and-roll destruction seriously. The three bands were scheduled to play an afternoon matinee before their regular evening sets. The Germs went on first, with Crash strutting onto the stage in a leopard-skin jockstrap. During a sloppy cover of Chuck Berry's "Round and Round," he began breaking bottles over his head, then hurled himself off the stage and into the glass shards below. He was taken to the hospital, stitched up, and returned in time to catch Blondie's set.

Despite Kip Cohen's flat-out rejection of Devo, the buzz had continued. Record label scouts were coming out to the shows. After one of the Whisky performances, Gary Jackett found a scrap of paper on the floor. He picked it up and read it: "Devo—these guys are going to be huge."

* * *

With the band staying longer and longer in L.A., Bob Lewis was feeling more and more like he'd been cut off for good. Mark had promised that if things started to heat up, he'd see to it personally that Bob was brought back in. But now things were heating up, and Bob was still sitting at home in Akron. He wrote Mark a letter, outlining his quickly growing concerns. Mark was still not certain how much the band owed Bob. According to several members of the Devo circle, Jerry had been deceptive, or at least vague about what role Bob had had in developing Devo. So at first Mark was sympathetic, in part because he knew a blow-up between Bob and Jerry would be disruptive to the band's progress. But when news reached Los Angeles about Bob's trademark filing, Mark was as angry as the rest. He felt like Bob had gone behind their backs. Bob was in danger of painting himself into a corner, and he was going to have to be certain he knew what he was doing.

Ed Barger, meanwhile, was feeling secure in his position. He had extensive experience doing crew work for Belkin Productions, the Cleveland region's dominant concert promoter. He was very good behind the soundboard, knew how to run lights and handle the roadie chores. He'd built a sound tower for Pink Floyd, so he could certainly handle the setup at the Whisky. And Mark must have felt an allegiance to him, considering how supportive Barger and Marty Reymann had been early on. "Like so many others, I was thinking if these guys were successful—I would get out of spudland myself," Barger said. "I knew Jerry was evil, but I was also convinced of Mark's talent. I still believe that Mark was a good person and would have shared with Bob Lewis and everybody had it not been for Jerry."

* * *

DEVO in latex "pinhead" caps and yellow suits at Max's. *Courtesy of Bobbie Watson Whitaker*

Devo still made a good Halloween band, and the Starwood booked them for its "Super Halloween Punk-In" with the Mumps and, according to the event flier, "more surprises." As the band played that night to yet another full house, there must have been a grinning sense of satisfaction. It was two years to the day since they had been pelted with beer cans before clearing Cleveland's WHK Auditorium. One year before, they weren't even playing, still teaching Alan the set, and working up this alchemy from their base metals.

Devo took a break from the almost nonstop schedule to fly back to New York for a pair of shows at Max's Kansas City in mid-November. By then, they were the toast of New York. The Akron contingent made the trip to meet their old friends in Manhattan. Susan Massaro and Bob Lewis were there to greet them. Things seemed different. Jerry was sleeping with a minor celebrity. Their old friends were telling stories about being Iggy Pop's roommate and hanging out with Blondie. To Bob Lewis, California had once been the backdrop for writing *The Staff* essays with Jerry. Now it seemed like an entirely different world.

Although things were tense, Bob was still willing to help out. His driving prowess was put into use when the band was running late for an uptown meeting with David Bowie. "It was amazing, like being in the Batmobile," Susan recalled. Bowie, back from Germany, had heard from Iggy that this band they'd been trying to track down not only existed, but was the best thing he had heard in a long time. Devo appealed to just about every aesthetic Bowie held dear. Their songs were artful; their performance was provocative. They were intellectuals who could also rock with intensity. They were thoughtful adventurers, just like him. He told them he was interested in producing an album. And, just to cement an already clear mythology, he asked to introduce them at Max's.

The band waited backstage with Bowie. Max's was packed; the smoky air filled with anticipation. Robert Fripp and Brian Eno were there. Susan, who just eight months before had scratched her way into a few seconds of face time with Bowie, was now standing in the Max's dressing room, chatting with the Thin White Duke as if he were one of the Rubber City Rebels. Devo stood there in their yellow suits, accustomed by now to the attention, but still electrified by the excitement of it all. They waited as David Bowie walked onto the club's stage, dressed in jeans and a black leather bomber jacket.

"This is the band of the future," he announced. "And I'm going to produce them in Tokyo this winter."

"And we thought that was a great idea," Mark said years later, "because we were going to be sleeping in the van that night."

This wasn't exactly true. The band was staying at the Chelsea Hotel. But still, this was something. It was a little hard to share the good fortune with the rest of the Akron crowd, the former "Devo-tees." Although not all of them could have expected to be included in the success, they had maintained their loyal friendship. Susan and Bobbie had moved from the Greenwood house to an apartment on South Portage Path in Highland Square. That had become Devo's Akron mailing address, and the former girlfriends had helped keep things together on the home front. Bob was still willing to lend a hand, and his help was being accepted. Before one of the shows, during the afternoon sound check, Bob Mothersbaugh had played guitar for Susan. But Bob was also, by then, seeing a Los Angeles girl named Maria, and she was there with him.

Mark greets the New York crowd. *Courtesy of Bobbie Watson Whitaker*

"It's honestly still very painful to think about this last trip," Susan said twenty-five years later. "Everything was different."

* * *

And so the band returned to Ohio. Devo played a triumphant December 3 show at the WHK Auditorium, the scene of the WMMS crime. The show, arranged by Johnny Dromette, was opened by Destroy All Monsters from Ann Arbor and the Styrene Money Band from Cleveland. The auditorium was still in dreadful shape, but the atmosphere had changed. Almost everything had changed. Bob Mothersbaugh's girlfriend, twenty-year-old Maria Linda Borisoff, was pregnant. They were going to be married in four days by a Cuyahoga Falls minister. Jerry was not happy about this. According to Gary Jackett, the prospect "flipped Jerry out." Bob Casale had left his wife shortly before the trip to California, and "part of the whole Devo thing was that we're going to get all these chicks. We're going to be a big rock band,

Bob 1 solo at Max's. *Courtesy of Bobbie Watson Whitaker*

and have all this fun," Jackett said, recalling Jerry's attitude. "Suddenly, Bob put a wrench into the plan. He was going to have to be a family man."

And Devo, though only a few months removed from the local scene, were now, for all intents and purposes, rock stars. "Devo was stunning that night," said Tim Story, who was sitting behind the soundboard with Johnny Dromette. The show was polished. The band was tight. Every aspect of Devo's performance had benefited from the incessant gigging in California.

They returned to Akron, finally, that night. Mark, reunited with Marina, crashed in Bobbie's darkroom. Perhaps it was the photo processing chemicals or the total absence of light, but Mark slept better than he had in months.

★ ★ ★

Booji Boy encore. *Courtesy of Bobbie Watson Whitaker*

Less than a week later, Devo was zigzagging across the country again, first for a show at Mabuhay Gardens in San Francisco, then back to Max's. Brian Eno came to the New York shows. He wanted to talk to the band.

After leaving Roxy Music in 1973, Eno, former foppish glam rocker, had become famous, not only for producing Bowie, John Cale. and Robert Fripp, but also for the way he produced. He was all right-brain, a Zen master who used the studio as an instrument. He didn't just record bands, he sculpted them. He quizzed them. He told them to make it sound like water, and then when it sounded like water, he told them to turn it upside down. The English musician had, by the time of this meeting, been courting Talking Heads, the artiest of the CBGB's bands and, in many ways, the group that had the most in common with Devo—the weirdest of the accessible bands, or the most accessible of the weird bands. Either way you turned it, Eno was not going to pursue the Dead Boys. But he was going to pursue Devo.

He asked to meet with them for lunch the following day in a hotel room overlooking Central Park. The five band members were there, along with

Ed Barger. Barger already had a long-distance relationship with Eno. The only phone number Eno had for Devo was at Man Ray Studios, and when he called there, it was usually Barger on the other end. So, there in the New York hotel room, they ordered room service and they talked.

"Brian Eno was a quiet guy, and the discussion over lunch was more about people feeling each other out," Barger said. "Devo was wondering what this guy wanted from them, and Eno was like a scientist observing the spuds under a microscope. Devo was always suspicious of everybody. Eno was as weird as Devo and enjoyed seeing the spud squirm. Like them, he took pleasure in watching the experiment go wrong."

The band didn't have a record contract yet, but Eno offered to front the money and said he and David Bowie would produce an album. The rest would follow, he promised.

Shortly after this meeting, Eno sat with a British reporter and talked about his next project. Devo, he said, has "the best live show I have ever seen. What I saw in them always happens when you encounter something new in art—you get a feeling of being slightly dislocated, and with that are emotional overtones that are slightly menacing as well as alluring.... I am very interested in knowing why that happens...and I spend as much time in that sort of reflection as I do in the work. You see, in this work, you arrive at attractive positions for which sometimes you have no defenses.... When you make a piece of work, you are postulating a little world of your own, with a set of rules, and you try to see how they work. Then, how do they apply to real life? That's where the 'Oblique Strategies' come in—employing accidents as a part of the work to make the connection. In both Devo, Talking Heads, and myself, I see an interest in working out the terms of what that perception is."

The "Oblique Strategies" were tarot cards Eno employed in the studio. He would set them out before a musician he was working with and gesture toward them—pick a card, any card. The card would contain an instruction: "Honor thy error as a hidden intention," for example. The "oblique" part consumed the strategy part. This would be a far cry from General Boy's "nose-to-the-grindstone" ethic, a far cry from Mrs. Fox's organ lessons, a far cry from the nuns at St. Patrick's. But Devo was already a far, far cry from Ohio.

DEVO at The Crypt, Akron, Ohio in the photograph that was cropped, altered, and colorized for the cover art for their Booji Boy Records debut single. *Courtesy of Bobbie Watson Whitaker*

Alan Myers keeping the beat in the second image that was mutated and merged to make the "Jocko Homo/Mongoloid" cover. *Courtesy of Bobbie Watson Whitaker*

General Jackett airbrushed "Booji Boy" record sleeve inscribed with "Sloppy" lyrics. *Courtesy of Gary Jackett*

DEVO sound check at Max's Kansas City, New York, in July 1977. *Courtesy of Bobbie Watson Whitaker*

Alan Myers and family in NYC. *Courtesy of Bobbie Watson Whitaker*

Susan Massaro and Bob Mothersbaugh at the historic Hotel Chelsea. *Courtesy of Bobbie Watson Whitaker*

Alan Myers, Bob Lewis, and Mary King on the NYC subway. *Courtesy of Bobbie Watson Whitaker*

Chapter 21

The blizzard began during the midnight shift, after an evening of rain, when school kids and snowplow drivers were sleeping. The bottom fell out of the barometer, the wind took people's breath away, and before they could draw another, Akron and the rest of Ohio were paralyzed by the storm of the century. A small plane tumbled like a child's toy across a field at Akron Municipal Airport. Giant trees snapped like matchsticks. Store windows shattered, power lines fell, water pipes burst, and snowdrifts buried cars. It seemed to happen all at once, and it would not go away. By dawn on Thursday, January 26, 1978, the entire region was frozen. Streets were indistinguishable in the white landscape. The wind, gusting to seventy-five miles per hour, drove snow against every surface, and had pushed the temperature from thirty-four degrees at five a.m. to thirteen at six a.m. Nothing looked right; nothing sounded right; nothing felt right.

The members of Devo woke up that morning in their temporary lodgings at Susan and Bobbie's Portage Path apartment house, which had become Devo's informal headquarters. They looked out the window to find the biggest snowflakes they had ever seen, the size of silver dollars. It just kept falling. Schools were closed—many businesses, too. The tire companies kept the

Christmas time at 103 S. Portage Path with Mark, Bob2, Susan Massaro, and Bob Lewis, 1976. *Courtesy of Bobbie Watson Whitaker*

factories open, though. Workers who could make it in would be able to stay as long as they pleased—plenty of coffee and free heat. Hard times had begun after the 1976 strike, and everyone in Akron knew this work was becoming more and more precious. Just two weeks before this snowstorm, Goodyear production workers had been stunned by the news that Akron's largest tire company was closing its main plant, ending car tire production in Akron, and putting 1,380 people out of work.

"Akron is a dead town," one worker had told the *Akron Beacon Journal* after the announcement. And this blizzard seemed to prove it. The storm was going to cause problems for Devo. The band was supposed to play its "farewell" show that night at the Pirate's Cove, but getting to Cleveland seemed impossible. And in the growing frenzy to sign Devo, Dave Robinson of Stiff Records was supposed to be flying in to Ohio the next day with Island Records' Chris Blackwell. Would the airports even be open? Meanwhile,

DEVO chart with record company offers from Warner, Bewlay, Island, and Virgin. *Courtesy of Bobbie Watson Whitaker*

Devo had a lot of work to do. In Susan and Bobbie's cozy brick apartment, the band had set up a chart in a highly organized attempt to sort out the record deals that were being tossed at them. Coming from record executives' mouths, everything sounded like milk and honey. On paper, none of it looked particularly appealing.

Warner Bros. and Island had made serious offers. There was a lot of money involved. And Devo, still without an experienced manager, was left to its own devices. In the Voyager laserdisc *DEVO: The Complete Truth About De-Evolution*, Jerry explained the agonizing process in an essay called "Drooling for Dollars."

"[T]hose six-figure deal numbers were mind-boggling to Rubber City bottomfeeders used to living hand-to-mouth.... We read a book by Arista Records chief, Clive Davis, entitled *Inside the Record Business*. The irony of one of the record business' most notorious 'hitmen' dispensing tips on success was lost on DEVO. So, as fledgling Punk-scientists, we did as he suggested. We made a chart to analyze and compare the offers."

This was an awful lot of math for a bunch of art majors and former bar band members. The snow piling up outside seemed to reflect the overwhelming numbers the band was trying to sort out. Devo and its close circle of friends talked it through. Mark and Jerry went to the library. They studied law books. There was no way they were going to let themselves get screwed. Or at the very least, they wanted to understand how badly they were getting screwed. Devo's distrust of the music industry seemed written in their DNA; it began early and stayed with them throughout their career.

Bob Lewis, despite his growing suspicion that Jerry was trying to push him aside, remained willing to help. He had worked as a roadie the day after Christmas, when the band played a Cleveland Agora show with the Dead Boys. And he was handling the marketing of singles to Stiff Records. Stiff was set to release "Jocko Homo"/"Mongoloid" in the United Kingdom in a few weeks and was preparing to put out a second single, "Satisfaction" b/w "Sloppy," right on its heels. The "Satisfaction" single would be released on the Booji Boy label but distributed by Stiff. The English label, growing in reputation as a New Wave powerhouse, also had a special interest in yet a third 45—with "Be Stiff" on the A-side and "Social Fools" on the B-side. "Be Stiff"—wouldn't that be a perfect corporate anthem?

The band decided that afternoon to try to make it up to Cleveland for the Pirate's Cove show. As they loaded up their gear in a snowy driveway, they packed a copy of their latest film, for the song "Mongoloid," which was to make its premiere that night. This "new de-evolution film," as *Scene* called it, was directed by Bruce Conner, a respected experimental filmmaker. The band had met him through Toni Basil in Santa Monica. She played him "Mongoloid," and he flipped for it, offering his services without ever having seen the band. The film was a series of vintage black-and-white movie stills set to the music. It carried echoes of Mark's artwork, using old images, cut-and-paste style, but in a new context, with evocative effect. The four-minute film would be marketed through unusual means. It was sold by San Francisco distributor Canyon Cinema, Inc. as an educational documentary, "exploring the manner in which a determined young man overcame a basic mental defect and became a useful member of society." The marketing materials described the film's "insightful editing techniques [that] reveal the dreams, ideals and problems that face a large segment of the American male population… [with] background music written and performed by the DEVO orchestra."

Devo made its slow, careful way up to Cleveland. The snow continued to fall through the night. Plows were unable to keep ahead of it. Everyone got there and back, but the next day, they would have to drive to Cleveland again. The bigwigs were coming to town.

* * *

Friday wasn't any better. Gov. James Rhodes, announcing that President Jimmy Carter had signed a declaration of emergency, said, "Ohio is in trouble." Countless people were without heat or power. Three people had died; snowplows were stranded; and a trucker on a roadside near Akron was buried under a twenty-foot snowdrift, surviving on melted snow with a tube stuck through the window for air.

When Chris Blackwell, the Caribbean-born president of Island Records flew in from the Bahamas, he was still wearing beach clothes as he touched down in icy Ohio. Devo picked up him and Dave Robinson at the airport. As they headed back south, Blackwell sat shivering in the back seat, wide-eyed, no doubt wondering what manner of place had spawned this Devo band. As soon as they got to Akron, the locals drove him to a department store to buy some proper clothing. Hey, this is winter in Spudland, the Devo boys tried to explain.

They finally made it back to the Portage Path apartment, rubbed the cold out of their hands, and sat down to talk. Jerry and Mark liked Chris Blackwell. Although, on this day, they seemed literally to come from different worlds, Chris, to Jerry's recollection, was "charming, personable and pleasantly low-key."

Chris hung out with the band and their friends, learning about Akron and hearing about the little explosion in the local scene. Debbie Smith and

Sue Schmidt of Chi Pig dropped by and got to talking with the Island president. He asked how they got their name. They explained that it came from the sign in front of a barbecue joint. "Chi," for chicken, and "Pig" for ribs. Chris thought that was pretty cool and wondered if they had ever tried to get their hands on the sign. A light bulb went off. And with that, the little group—two quirky New Wave girls and a famous record company president—set off into the snowy Akron night to try to steal the Chi Pig sign. They failed, but the fact that he was willing to go along suggested that maybe Chris Blackwell was the kind of guy who could understand Devo's appreciation for the absurd.

Devo was impressed with Blackwell. Maybe he wasn't the "baby-faced killer" that an Atlantic Records executive had described. Maybe he was just a regular guy who happened to be in a position to make them all rich and famous. Mark and Jerry and the others weren't jaded yet. Despite the teachings of devolution, the sobering lesson of the Kent State shootings and all the rest, Blackwell seemed to offer hope that maybe there was some sanity to the music business.

Then a very strange thing happened.

Chapter 22

A week or so after Chris Blackwell's Akron visit, the phone rang in the Portage Path apartment. It was Richard Branson, the president of Virgin Records. He said he wanted to fly Devo to Jamaica, that he had a deal to discuss. Mark looked out the window at the still-dismal snowscape. Jamaica? That sounded pretty good. They probably have palm trees or something there. So he got off the phone and asked who wanted to go to Kingston. Jerry was in the midst of an ongoing fight with his girlfriend, Linda Waddington. Bob Mothersbaugh was newly married, and Alan was getting close—they both wanted to spend these waning days in Akron. So Mark and Bob Casale took Branson up on his offer.

In a reversal of Blackwell's wardrobe misjudgment, the two Ohio boys boarded their flight wearing snowsuits and big winter hats. They touched down in balmy Jamaica, peeling off the layers to expose their February-white Midwestern skin to the tropical sun. This was not a bad deal. They were being treated like rock stars, even though they still had no deal. The plane tickets alone had cost something like $300 apiece, money neither Mark nor Bob could have come up with on their own. The two friends had talked on the flight. Virgin's entry into the bidding could only help matters, and they wanted to make a good impression on Branson. They knew he was emerg-

Mark returns to Ohio following the German recording sessions. *Courtesy of Bobbie Watson Whitaker*

ing as a formidable mogul. So they wanted to be cool, to let him know that they already had good offers, and yes, Mr. Branson, we'll certainly consider Virgin as we sort through all these lucrative deals, but we're not some rubes from Ohio who will jump at the first carrot dangled before us. We know what we're doing.

Mark and Bob checked into their hotel, stashed their hats and coats and freshened up. Kingston, Jamaica, was an intimidating place. Mark had never been there before, hadn't ever seen anything like this. He looked out of his hotel room window and saw a Great Dane in rigor mortis on the roadside as people went about their business, sidestepping the dead dog with hardly a notice.

It was with this image that he and Bob went down the hall to the room where they were to meet Branson. They walked in and were greeted by this millionaire and his minions—all these young South American guys who were pushing to make Virgin a major player. As impressive as meeting

Branson was, though, Mark and Bob's eyes widened when they saw the huge pile of marijuana on the table. Despite Kent's liberal, post-hippie milieu, drugs were still a rather precious commodity. Even more rare was good pot, which, Mark suspected, this probably was. They were in Jamaica, after all. Back in Ohio, someone would score a little stash, and everybody would stare at it for a week, discussing its potential quality. "I hear this African stuff's supposed to be really hallucinogenic," someone would comment, even though it had probably been plucked from a roadside in Mexico. Finally Saturday night would come, and a roomful of people would roll a pencil-thin joint and pass it around, trying to catch a buzz.

"I think I'm high," they'd say. "Maybe I'm high. Yeah, I might have felt something. My throat's definitely feeling raw."

But here, as Mark and Bob tried to maintain an air of sophistication, someone was rolling a joint the size of a cigar, lighting it, and handing it to them. Mark took a hit. Definitely not Ohio pot. Bob took a hit. The joint went around, and everyone loosened up a little, even though Mark was still trying to stay focused so he could make some intelligent response when Branson started breaking down his deal.

"What do you guys think of the Sex Pistols?" Branson asked.

"Well, we like them," Mark said. In fact, he explained, Devo and the Pistols had partied together just a few weeks before, when both bands were gigging in San Francisco. While Devo's shows were building toward a climax, the Pistols were in the midst of their implosion. It was, in fact, during the same week the two bands had met that the Sex Pistols played their last show, on January 14 at the Winterland Ballroom. Johnny Rotten finished the concert with his trademark whine, uttering the immortal last words, "Ah-ha-ha! Ever get the feeling you've been cheated? Good night." Three days later, they were finished. Mark told Branson he was really sorry about what had happened, that he thought the Pistols were cool, and really thought highly of them.

Branson smiled.

"Well, I'll tell why you're here," he said. "Johnny Rotten is in the next room, and he wants to join Devo. He wants Devo to be his new band after the Sex Pistols."

Mark squirmed. He looked down at his shoes. Branson continued. "And if you want to make that announcement, we can go out to the beach—we've got all the British press here—*Melody Maker*, *Sounds*, *New Music Express*—and we can go down to the beach and make that announcement right now."

Mark looked at the huge joint in his hand. Was he hearing this right? Maybe it was the pot. Maybe this Jamaican stuff had done a number on his head. He looked up at the smiling Branson, realizing for the first time how very large the man's teeth were. They seemed to glisten. This was a carnivore. And Mark began to blush, embarrassed for everybody in the room and for Johnny Rotten in the next room. And then he began to snicker. And he looked at Bob, who also began to snicker. And quickly the snickers turned into belly laughs. It was like one of those moments in church, where the harder you try not to laugh the more impossible it becomes to stop. They were laughing like a pair of nincompoops. Full, round, holding-the-stomach, tears-running-down-the-cheeks laughter.

Mark tried to stammer out some sort of answer, but the pot and the absurdity just made him laugh more.

"Really, Richard," he said, trying desperately to regain his cool. "I'm not laughing at you."

Finally, Mark and Bob managed to explain that it would never work, that Devo had great respect for Johnny Rotten, but it wasn't what Devo had worked for all those years. They parted, and Mark and Bob went back to their room, staring and not saying a word. They'd blown it. Not only that, but they were now certain that they were surrounded by sharks. It was going to be Devo against the world. And the world was becoming a very strange place indeed.

✷ ✷ ✷

And so it was off to Germany. Ed Barger dropped the band off at the airport, and they waited anxiously for the plane that would carry them into Brian Eno's waiting arms, and into their future. Jerry had gotten sidetracked making one last telephone call to Linda. They talked—and talked and talked right through the boarding call and the boarding and the takeoff. As Mark and the others lifted off for Germany, Jerry found himself booking another flight. He'd be at least half a day behind his bandmates.

Devo wasn't paying for any of this. Despite the increasing industry lust for the band, they remained nearly penniless, having subsisted on club shows for a year. But they looked good on paper. They were getting flown around the world, and everything seemed like just a matter of time. Eno was paying for the studio sessions. Warner Bros. had been kind enough to front the money for the flights. It didn't seem to matter at the time. Money was invisible. All that mattered was that they were headed to Conrad Plank's legendary studio. Housed on an old Victorian farm in Wolperath, not far from Cologne, the studio had become legendary as a landmark of the krautrock movement. Kraftwerk had recorded its first album there, the record that Jerry had loved listening to back in the apartment above Guido's. Plank had worked with GuruGuru, Can, and Neu—bands that had pioneered electronic music and set a tone for Devo to carry forward.

Already, even before arriving in Germany, the band was looking past this first album. On a piece of paper torn from a spiral notebook, they had plotted out the songs for the first two albums. At the top of the page was scrawled, "Intelligent suggestions based on [an] exhaustive pole." While the contents of the albums would change somewhat, it was clear that Devo had a plan and was ready and able to produce at least two records based on their impressive warehouse of material.

Album #1: "Satisfaction," "Too Much Paranoias," "Praying Hands," "Uncontrollable Urge," Mongoloid," "Jocko Homo," "Social Fools," "Be Stiff," "Gut Feeling/Slap Your Mammy," "Sloppy," and "Come Back Jonee."

Album #2: "Anthem," "Clockout," "Timing X-Soo Bawlz," "Pink Pussy," "Blockhead," "Wiggly World," "Gates of Steel," "Secret Agent Man," "Space Junk," and "Smart Patrol-Mr. DNA."

The songs weren't yet listed for the third record, but a potential title was there: *The Golden Energy Album*. Devo's sound was still dominated by guitars, but the plan was to move beyond them. Electronics were advancing quickly, and Devo's futuristic bent—the Jetsons half of *The Jetsons Meet the Flint-*

stones—was lassoed to their engine. "We saw the whole world and technology and all things natural and unnatural as potential material for getting our message across," Mark once said.

The plane touched down, and Devo reunited with Eno. David Bowie had originally wanted to be involved with the production, but he had just begun working on a film in Berlin. He had offered to handle production in his downtime, but that didn't sound like a very efficient way to move forward, especially with so much riding on the finished product. Devo and Eno had decided to put the cart before the horse by recording without a contract, so they would need to get down to business. But that first day, without Jerry, all the band could do was set up equipment and jam.

"Holger Czukay [of Can] was hanging out most of the time," Mark recalled. "So, we have a tape of four-fifths of Devo jamming with Holger and Brian Eno. David Bowie was hanging out, so he picked up a guitar for a little bit. So it was just the seven of us, playing music at Connie Plank's studio."

* * *

Eno was eager to get started. He'd loved Devo's shows in New York, just as he had loved Talking Heads' shows. Now he was in a position to produce both bands. In each, he saw an artistic sensibility he could relate to, bands that were open to new sounds, that were interested in expanding rock music's vocabulary. This fit with his ability to "play" the studio as an instrument, to experiment with the sound by running it through synthesizers, even as the music was being played live. As a producer, he was on firm technical ground, but his greatest interest was in allowing creative accidents to happen.

By the time Jerry arrived at Connie Plank's studio, everyone was beginning to feel comfortable. Bob Mothersbaugh had found an oddball German amplifier and was experimenting with its sounds. When he touched his finger to the metal tip of his unplugged guitar cord, a cool sound came out, sort of a cross between a bleep and a whistle. It was different than a synthesizer sound, and as the band jammed on "Uncontrollable Urge," he added that sound near the end. That was the kind of thing Eno loved. But what he

DEVO return from recording in Germany. *Courtesy of Bobbie Watson Whitaker*

didn't realize was that this band, so full of ideas and creativity, had also become very calculated. There were very few loose threads to unravel and discover what lay underneath. That scrap of paper with the albums mapped out was the very type of planning Eno tried to avoid.

Devo had brought along a box full of previous studio tapes. They had become very good in the studio, and they had a clear idea of where they wanted to go in these sessions. Eno, for his part, had brought the "Oblique Strategies" cards, and, more broadly, an oblique strategy. He wanted to do what he typically did—pull things inside out, turn them upside down, hold them up to a mirror, strip them down, and build them back up. As the sessions began, he started to recognize that there was a fundamental difference of opinion between him and Devo. They knew what they wanted to do, and he knew what he wanted to do. Almost immediately, tension crept into the isolated studio.

"'Anal' is the word," Eno said years later in an interview with *Mojo* magazine. "They were a terrifying group of people to work with because they were so unable to experiment. When they turned up to do this record in Germany, they brought a big chest of recordings they'd already done of these

The band disembarks upon return to Ohio. *Courtesy of Bobbie Watson Whitaker*

same songs. We'd be sitting there working, and suddenly Mark Mothersbaugh would be in the chest to retrieve some three-year-old tape, put it on and say, 'Right, we want the snare drum to sound like that.'

"I hate that kind of work. I just do not see the point of trying to replicate such peculiar circumstances: the snare drum sounds good like that because all the other things around it are like they are, so do you really want to replicate the whole thing? 'No, we want to have that snare drum, but the guitar sound we want like this'—and it was back in the chest again for another tape! This seemed impossible, foolish and stupid. Stupid in that it was a waste of time: here we are in another situation, another time, another place, why not do something for this situation?

"Their picture of recording, for me, was very old-fashioned, like a Platonic Ideal of recording, that somewhere there existed the ideal state of this song, and they thought they could identify several of the ingredients, they were in the chest there somewhere, and my job as a producer was to try to remake these ingredients and fit them back together. A nightmare. I'd be

Welcome Home DEVO. *Courtesy of Bobbie Watson Whitaker*

sitting there at the desk, and there are EQs, echo sends, all those kinds of things, and my hand would sort of sneak up to put a bit of a treatment on something, and I could feel Jerry Casale bristling behind me. It was awful! He would stand behind me all the time, then lean over and say, 'Why are you doing that?' As if you can know why you do something before you do it, always!"

Meanwhile, the studio phone provided constant distraction. The fact that Devo was in Connie Plank's studio, recording its album with Brian Eno, had turned the heat up even higher. Warner Bros. was calling. Virgin was calling. A&M had gotten back into the hunt. They all wanted this album, and their offers were escalating. Someone walked into the studio one day with the new issue of *Melody Maker*. Devo was shocked to find its picture on the cover. Stiff was getting ready to push the singles hard. Things were growing beyond their control, but at least they were growing in the right direction.

Bob Casale and Mark had left Jamaica believing they'd ruined their chances with Virgin, but Branson had only grown more persistent, almost obsessive in his pursuit. And Warner Bros. was right in lockstep. During the Eno sessions, a Warner representative showed up at the studio and asked if the band needed some walking-around money. Sure, they said. So they each got a little wad of cash, maybe a hundred bucks apiece.

Their studying had paid off. Devo was still acting as their own manager, but by now, Stan Diamond, David Bowie's lawyer, was working with them in the negotiations process. The band had a good strategy. They wanted to try to work out two record deals, each with separate territorial rights. That way, if the band didn't do well in one part of the world, the losses wouldn't eat into the profits from the other territories.

There was one major sticking point, however. Bob Lewis, back in Akron, had the trademark to Devo. Stan Diamond, realizing that no record deal could be finalized without the band owning rights to itself, drew up a set of papers—an "Assignment"—allowing rights to transfer back to the band. He contacted Bob about this and sent him the papers. Bob wasn't sure what to do. He had filed for the trademark to protect himself, but if he stuck to his guns, there might be nothing to protect himself from. Devo could get dropped before even being signed. And he didn't want to screw his friends. He had invested seven years in Devo—only Jerry had been around as long—and he wanted to see it come to fruition. He understood how important it all was. So, in what he later described as "a moment of weakness," he put his signature on the document. Devo was free.

Chapter 23

If being in a band meant just playing music, life would be pretty simple. But those days were long gone for Devo. By March 1978, the de-evolution band had plenty of field research to prove its notion that moving forward can also mean moving backward. Devo was being bombarded by offers, the arcanum of negotiation, legal details and, of course, the immediate task of completing their debut album. Amid all this, the phone rang yet again at Connie Plank's studio. This time it was Stiff Records. The "Mongoloid" single was making waves, and the label was about to release "Satisfaction," the second of the three singles it had planned for the spring and summer. Although Devo had rock-solid street credibility in New York and Los Angeles by then, the band remained an enigma in London, Stiff's prime territory. So Stiff wanted to book some shows before Devo left Europe. The month of February had been spent recording, and the album was turning out well. Devo agreed to take the March 9–12 bookings. But there was a problem. They had no stage gear—neither costumes nor equipment. So they made a phone call to Akron.

The loyal old spuds on South Portage Path sprang into action. Bob Lewis submitted applications to the Akron Federation of Musicians to allow the band to play in England. He and Susan and Bobbie and the others boxed up some yellow suits and black gym clothes and shipped those and the stage gear off to Europe.

With temporary visas and the album in the can, Devo arrived in London on March 6. Although Abba's "Take a Chance on Me" was No. 1 on *Melody Maker*'s U.K. charts that week, the country was primed for the raw energy and studied weirdness of this band from a place everybody seemed intent on pronouncing "Ak-rawn." The first show was scheduled for a club called Eric's in Liverpool, with concerts to follow at Leeds University, the Free Trade Hall in Manchester and the Roundhouse in London. Mark, having had his musical epiphany years before, watching the Beatles on *Ed Sullivan*, felt as though he'd reached some hallowed—if not particularly romantic—place. Liverpool was a dingy, gray, industrial port town. As he took all this in, a music journalist asked him what Akron was like.

"Actually, it's a lot like Liverpool," Mark responded. He was referring to the landscape. But the reporter went away with the impression that Akron might be a Liverpool-esque hotbed like that which had spawned the Beatles and the *Mersey Beat* movement. A seed had been planted that would soon begin to show strange flower back in Ohio.

Devo played their first show, not certain what to expect. The U.K. punk scene, inflamed by the likes of the dearly departed Sex Pistols and the emergent Clash and Buzzcocks, was becoming increasingly violent. Devo's yellow janitorial suits may have seemed cheeky back in America, but here they seemed downright sensible, what with all the saliva flying about. American bands wondered about the British punk custom of spitting on a band to show its appreciation; Devo was about to do the same. Eric's, having seen its share of hooliganism, had installed a cage around the stage as a security measure. When Devo took the stage that night, playing live for the first time in well over a month and the first time off American soil, they found themselves surrounded by the wildest scene they'd ever experienced. Punk rockers were hanging off the sides of the cage, screaming and spitting. It was intimidating and exhilarating, all at once. The band never even saw what Eric's looked like, as they were surrounded by a wall of bodies for the entire set. It could have been an *Island of Lost Souls* outtake.

The following few nights erased any doubt—Devo was on fire. Word spread quickly through the compressed English scene that this band David Bowie had gone bonkers over was the real deal. They were intensely controlled on stage, but the music was primal and frantic. Devo had a sonic assault and sense of humor equal to the Sex Pistols. Devo, like many of the British punk bands, also had a message. It wasn't as directly political as the Pistols' middle-finger-waving, anti-government rants, and it's likely that the subtlety and intellectualism of the Idea was lost amid the hysterics.

But at this moment, none of that mattered. In less than a week of concerts, Devo had managed to drive its reputation right through the bars of that steel cage and directly to the ears of Richard Branson and all the others. Somebody had to get this record. It was time to finalize the deal. Devo returned to Akron at the beginning of May. Branson was ready to go, and he engaged the band in a series of secret meetings. Devo had favored one particular aspect of his offer. He was willing to include a film production deal as part of the package, which would help Devo fulfill one of its original intents to pursue the project as a full manifestation of artistic expression.

"Devo was about art," Mark said years later. "We were multimedia from the beginning. That's what interested me about Andy Warhol. He wasn't limited to just being a printmaker. He was also a photographer, produced the Velvet Underground, made feature films—he was even a fashion designer. He was more interested in concepts and ideas. That's how we saw ourselves."

In fact, that's why the band had been so excited about being aligned with Bowie. He seemed to be the next incarnation of Warhol, and Devo wanted to take it from there. So when Branson was ready with his offer, Devo was ready, too. The Virgin Records contract had everything the band wanted. After the U.K. shows, Branson upped his financial offer. He included the film production package. He was willing to split up the world's territories into two separate contracts. Mark and Jerry and the others had done their homework. They knew this was an incredibly good deal. So they signed with Virgin.

* * *

Almost immediately, Warner Bros. went ballistic. Wait a minute, they said. Jerry made a verbal agreement with us. We have already put money into Devo. Remember the plane tickets? Remember the spending money? That was all in good faith. Apparently, the band had gone so far as to O.K. a press release announcing Devo's intent to sign with Warner. In late May, Warner Bros. sued Virgin and Devo.

This was a sobering moment. Everything had built up so incredibly well. The band had a nearly perfect contract with Virgin. They turned to Richard Branson. "Don't worry," he told them. "I can handle this." He flew Jerry and Mark back to England for the proceedings and put them up on his houseboat while he went to court with his lawyer, Ken Barry. What he found at the other table was a regiment of grim, dark-suited English barristers hired by Warner Bros. The American company was going to play hardball.

After a tense courtroom duel, the two companies reached an agreement. There would be two contracts. Branson's Virgin would have the rights to Europe and Warner Bros. would have the US and the rest of the world. To Mark, this represented "two shitty record deals." To Jerry, "after hip capitalist Branson and corporate Bros. Warner finalized carving up DEVO's collectively owned carcass, we got what we wanted—a worldwide record deal with two first-class corporations."

The ultimate outcome was that Devo's debut album would finally be put into production. They had settled on a title, *Q. Are We Not Men? A. We Are Devo!*, borrowing the key phrase from the band's anthem, "Jocko Homo." The epithet that had once been little more than an inside joke was becoming a catch phrase.

It was already clear that Devo no longer belonged to Akron. Now the band was becoming certain they didn't belong in Akron. In mid-May, Devo met with a local attorney named William Whitaker to discuss incorporation in Ohio and California, confirming their intention to relocate soon to Los Angeles. Whitaker had been a Kent State student at the same time as the band members, although he was not a Devo insider. But he, like some of the others, had been interviewed by James Michener for his book on the May 4 shootings, quoted under the pseudonym Paul Probius. So he helped the band tie up some of its final loose ends in Ohio.

Devo, having seen a bit of the world, recognized the importance of this decision. Record companies, Mark once said, "didn't really understand us and they didn't like the music. We were afraid that if we stayed in our hometown we really would be a one-off thing—we'd do one album and be buried quickly." The spuds' survival instinct pointed west.

Devo's calculated defection from the local scene both reflected and influenced a series of significant changes in Akron. By spring 1978, the Crypt had folded after the rubber worker who owned it was offered $14,000 for his liquor license. But by then, the scene had found an unlikely foothold in a larger national venue. Akron was becoming known as a hotbed of New Wave, helped in great part by the discovery of Devo and Mark's misunderstood "Liverpool" analogy. A phrase started appearing in the music press: "the Akron Sound."

The previous December, the Rubber City Rebels had decided to escape the hellish winter and drove out to Los Angeles. Thanks in part to their friendship with Mark Mothersbaugh, the Rebels got booked into the Starwood. Their manager then came up with a brilliantly mischievous plan to draw some attention. On Christmas Eve, he donned a pair of coveralls and climbed up onto a billboard catwalk above the Sunset Strip. On the whitewashed background, he painted, "Rubber City Rebels, Akron, Ohio."

The billboard stayed that way for days, long enough to draw the desired attention. A Sire rep, perhaps recognizing Akron as sudden mark of credibility, attended the Starwood show. Seymour Stein soon came to see them, and before long he drew up a contract. But the Rebels pushed their luck a little too far, making demands on Sire that didn't sit well with Stein. He dropped them, but the attention was enough to score an eventual deal with Capitol.

Meanwhile, the Dead Boys had become a fixture in New York's Bowery, and the bands that had remained in Northeast Ohio were plying their trade in what suddenly seemed like a musical boom town. Pere Ubu were signed by Blank, a New Wave imprint of Mercury, and the Bizarros were about to do the same. Chris Butler had been kicked out of the Numbers Band for spending too much time on his burgeoning Waitresses side project, and had joined Tin Huey, which was also being courted by the major labels.

Just about every original band in Akron was being eyeballed. The groups were riding on Devo's yellow synthetic coattails. When Tin Huey entered negotiations with Warner Bros., Mark shared the details of Devo's deal, and the Hueys, scaling down the numbers to suit their own realistic expectations, used the contract as a template.

And so Robert Christgau came to Akron. The influential *Village Voice* writer had been hearing snippets of what was happening in a place never considered a hotbed of original music. Butler had written him a letter; Nick Nicholis had mailed him the *From Akron* two-band album on his Clone label. Christgau made a few phone calls, arranged to crash at Nicholis' house, and ventured into the industrial Midwest in March. When his long feature appeared in the April 17 *Voice*, it captured the Akron-Cleveland-Kent scene at perhaps its highest point. Christgau explored why Northeast Ohio, of all places, had become such a fertile breeding ground of avant-garde rock and roll.

He gave some credit to WMMS, which in its freeform days had played the likes of the Velvet Underground, Captain Beefheart, and Soft Machine. (Although scenesters undoubtedly would have argued this point; WMMS virtually ignored the local bands inspired by those groups.) In conversations with Nicholis, he also observed that Ohio, unlike New York, offered unlimited garage and basement space, allowing bands to practice and evolve and experiment more thoroughly. He gave props to Johnny Dromette's record store—"a more impressive New Wave outlet than any in New York"—and to Jim Ellis' *CLE* magazine.

More than anything, though, he captured a moment in time. Stiff Records, aided by a local musician and man about town named Liam Sternberg, was working on an Akron compilation, which would also include a teenage singer named Rachel Sweet, whom Sternberg was mentoring. Everyone was at the tantalizing cusp of possibility, and the harsh realities of disappointing record sales, infighting, and the splintering of the club infrastructure were not yet a factor. What Christgau found was the charming sincerity of Nicholis and the sweetness of the Chi Pig girls, all in their finest state.

Christgau's Akron visit coincided with Devo's first London gigs, so in their stead he interviewed Bob Lewis, "their quasi-manager and longtime conceptual collaborator," and Susan Massaro and Bobbie Watson, who introduced themselves as Susan Devo and Bobbie Devo. The writer described the girls' Portage Path apartment as a Devo "commune," and wrote about the band almost in the past tense, as if their stardom was a foregone conclusion.

"When a Warners exec told [Devo] that he liked to sign one 'art band' for every act he knew was going to sell three million," Christgau wrote, "he was politely asked what art band would balance off Devo."

Chapter 24

There's a phrase from the *Little Rascals* that Devo has always been fond of applying to themselves: "Hey, kids—let's put on a show!" From Jerry's tampon coat to the white sheet tacked up to the wall for film projection to the thrift-store Booji Boy mask, their do-it-yourself bent had always run toward the homespun. So maybe it's not surprising that when the time came to make another film—even with a record company budget—the old ways prevailed.

They decided to make the "Satisfaction" film in Akron, where they knew how to operate. Chuck Statler was brought in from Minneapolis to direct, and the band arranged to use the stage of the Old Strand Theatre downtown for the performance footage. The old movie house, like much of Akron, had fallen into neglect. It wasn't as bad as Cleveland's WHK Auditorium, but like the nearby landmark Akron Civic Theatre, it was limping along on a small budget. There was a lot of crossover between the local crowd that supported the Old Strand and the 1920s Moorish Civic and the local crowd that supported Devo. They seemed to understand the importance of what the mainstream ignored.

Devo took some of their budget money and went shopping for wardrobes. They chose the local Gold Circle, part of a regional chain of discount stores,

Eddie Barger and Mark on the set of "Satisfaction". *Courtesy of Bobbie Watson Whitaker*

sort of a B-version of Kmart. They had an idea of what they wanted as they started sorting through the racks, using their highly trained sense of kitsch to spot just the right combination of double-knits, bad slacks, white plastic loafers, and leisure shirts. They dragged these treasures back to the dressing rooms and began trying out the combinations, looking in the mirrors as they affected their dance moves. With the whole entourage making a big commotion, the manager finally came back and told them to get out of the store.

"Hey, we're spending lotsa money here, making a purchase," they argued. So he sent a couple of salesmen over to keep an eye on them as they continued sorting through the merchandise.

"We outfitted the band in a total double-knit, religious evangelist, middle-class salesmen's uniform... some damn cheap clothes!" the band recalled later that year. "All for $186.00 for 5 people."

Preparations for the filming of "Satisfaction" with Mark and Jerry. *Courtesy of Bobbie Watson Whitaker*

Chuck Statler filming a scene for "Satisfaction." *Courtesy of Bobbie Watson Whitaker*

Mark and Jenny Licitri caught petting in the backseat by General Boy. *Courtesy of Bobbie Watson Whitaker*

"Satisfaction" scene as filmed by Chuck Statler. *Courtesy of Bobbie Watson Whitaker*

Once again, the "Devo-tees" were recruited for supporting roles. Selma B. Smith, the mother of Debbie Smith from Chi Pig, would play an angry mother in a house dress, with a rolling pin and hair curlers. Her anger would be directed toward Mark, trying to score some late- night couch action with Linda Waddington, Jerry's girlfriend. In the back seat of a car driven by General Boy, Mark would try to cop a feel from Jenny Licitri, another of Jerry's old flames. Licitri, who worked as a go-go dancer, was nicknamed "Boob"—but not for the obvious reason. She had been fond of Yogi Bear's pal Boo Boo as a kid, and the name had stuck.

The performance part of the film showed Devo in the yellow suits, playing with the controlled, mechanical precision that had become their trademark. Mark wanted a guitar that looked like Devo sounded. He borrowed Bob Lewis' prized blonde Telecaster, the one he had bought from the Fender salesman at Dayho Electric. Mark sloppily duct-taped a boxy frequency analyzer to the front, with cables hanging down and extra guitar strings dangling from the headstock, so it looked like something from a mad scientist's home studio.

The most striking footage was of a tall, lanky punk from California known as Spazz Attack. As the song plays, Spazz, dressed in garish red pants and a bondage collar, throws himself into a flip, landing flat on his back. He looks like he's being electrocuted, mirroring a scene with Booji Boy in a playpen, wearing a shiny silver spacesuit. As Mark yelps out "baby baby baby baby baby baby baby baby baby baby baby," Booji sticks a fork into a toaster and shakes spasmodically.

As riveting as the *Truth About De-Evolution* film had been, this new clip was Devo's definitive aesthetic moment. It was funny and entertaining, but it also made an authoritative visual statement. Here was a band that looked like it sounded and sounded like it looked, and it didn't look or sound like anyone else. With General Boy as their leader and the likes of Spazz Attack in their elite forces, Devo was ready to make an assault.

All of this must have been rather confounding to the record executives preparing to sell the band's debut album. Art bands were supposed to eschew all aspects of business, except for the receipt of advances and royalty checks.

Mark Mothersbaugh with cigarettes in "Satisfaction" close-up. *Courtesy of Bobbie Watson Whitaker*

But Devo was the art band that also boldly declared a commercial intent. On June 6, 1978, Mark applied for articles of incorporation with California's secretary of state to create Devo Inc. It was an "if you can't beat'em join 'em" gesture. Devo recognized the insanity of the record business, but rather than run from it, they decided to mimic it internally, with the hope of the greatest financial reward.

* * *

As Devo was filming the "Satisfaction" concert sequence, the band ventured out of the Old Strand and into downtown Akron for a photo session. Bobbie Watson, who had photographed them many times already, was there, along with another local photographer, Janet Macoska. Chris Stein from Blondie was in town visiting, and he also took some shots. The band posed in a nearby bus shelter, a wide concrete structure with a modernistic oval opening. They also ventured down to a local joint called Chili Dog Mac, a few doors north of the Civic, standing in front of the sign in their yellow suits.

It was as though the band wanted to mine this rich landscape one last time before pulling up stakes and relocating permanently to Los Angeles. "Akron's a good place to be from," Jerry once said sardonically, calling it "boot camp to the world." Now they were leaving.

One of the last things they plucked from their surroundings was the cover image for the upcoming album. Mark had included a picture in *My Struggle* of professional golfer Chi Chi Rodriguez, copped from a package of practice golf balls. The smiling Rodriguez, in his trademark porkpie hat, hearkened back to Jerry's "American Dream" installation (performance) for the M-A-T-E-R art class. Graphically, it screamed, "Devo." It seemed, even in its careful representation of a sports icon, to suggest that mutation lay beneath the cheery veneer. When the picture was taken out of its original context, it had a strangely enigmatic presence.

The picture was initially chosen without regard to its source. It had been used on a line of golf products distributed by the Kent Sales & Manufacturing Company. The designer, Richard Blocher, worked for the local Fred Bock Advertising Agency. Blocher, coincidentally, was a close friend and golf partner of Susan Massaro's father. He had drawn the original illustration with colored pencils. Mark had spotted it several years before and tossed it in with his massive collection of found images.

The band had already used the picture as the cover for the "Be Stiff" single on Stiff, but when the artwork was presented to Warner Bros., there were immediate concerns. First was the problem of copyright. And, accord-

Cast and crew consulting the "Satisfaction" storyboards. *Courtesy of Bobbie Watson Whitaker*

ing to Jerry, the company's manager of business affairs was a golf fan and felt Devo was making fun of poor Chi Chi Rodriguez. So the band offered to contact the golfer and ask for his permission. In a weird set of local coincidences, Rodriguez's agent was Eddie Elias, a sports marketing legend who lived in Akron. But with deadlines pressing, the company decided instead to have its art department alter the image sufficiently to avoid legal problems.

"And after some resistance from us," Jerry said, "Mark and I decided okay. So Mark gave the art man a picture that he had pulled out of a newspaper of some artist's conception of a computer-generated mélange of faces from the last four presidents—Nixon, Kennedy, Ford and Johnson...and showed what they'd look like if they were one man. Now this was truly in keeping with the Devo spirit as much as the Chi Chi image. So we said, 'Okay, take the lips from this president, that eye, that hairline and include it in Chi Chi's head.'"

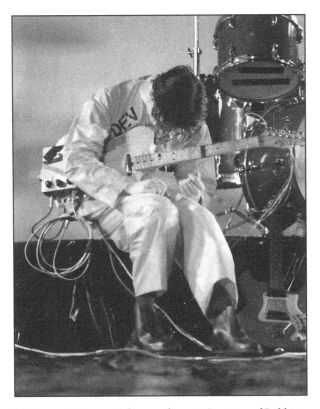

Mark naps between takes on the set. *Courtesy of Bobbie Watson Whitaker*

From there, everything veered into quintessentially Devo absurdity. A Warner Bros. executive, looking at the airbrushed image, decided it still resembled Rodriguez too closely. According to Jerry, he "personally altered our album cover by crossing the eyes off of Chi Chi, taking the scoop marks out of the golf ball, so you couldn't tell it was a golf ball, and changing the hat band, because he maintained that every golfer knew that was Chi Chi's hat. He sent his version back with a message saying, 'Here,' with a messenger waiting—'sign off on this and you guys got the green light—you can have your album cover.'"

Meanwhile, Rodriguez had granted permission to use the original image. But by then it was too late. The plates had been made and the presses were

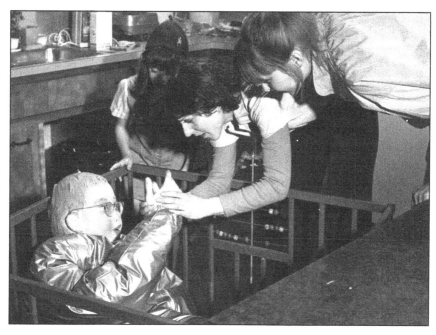

Debbie and Sue from Chi Pig babysit for Booji Boy between scenes. *Courtesy of Bobbie Watson Whitaker*

ready to roll. So Warner Bros. decided to pay Rodriguez $2,500 just to keep everyone honest, and Rodriguez simply asked for a box of records.

"His response from his lawyer was, at the end, when he got his box of records: 'Hey, this doesn't look like me,'" Jerry continued. "He at least, being good natured, didn't press charges for defaming his image. We were able to come out with something that—by the corporate interference and misunderstanding of the business side of Warner Bros. Records—actually unwittingly produced something far more DEVO than the original…image of Chi Chi's much more handsome face over the golf ball."

Rodriguez, years later, recalled the transaction in a newspaper article. "I had never heard of them when my manager told me they called," he said. "They seemed like nice kids with some crazy ideas about music, but I never did meet them. I tried to listen to their music, but I felt sorry for them. I couldn't understand what they were saying."

A passport photo of Mark Mothersbaugh, 1977. *Courtesy of Bobbie Watson Whitaker*

In late June, with the album almost ready for release, Devo flew to Knebworth, England, to play in front of the largest crowd they'd ever seen—an estimated 120,000 people. The "Midsummer Night's Dream" Festival also included Genesis, Jefferson Starship, Tom Petty, the Atlanta Rhythm Section, and Roy Harper. Devo was still a club band, without a proper road crew and without any practical preparation for such an event.

Their attitude was, "Hey, kids—let's put on a show!"

The band members dressed themselves in gray coveralls and hung out with the roadies just offstage, watching the other bands. When Devo's turn came, these five men in workmen's clothes walked out and set up the equipment in front of a vast sea of people, then ran off to the mobile dressing

Mark Mothersbaugh and Bob Lewis at DEVO HQ in Akron. *Courtesy of Bobbie Watson Whitaker*

rooms, changed into their yellow suits, and ran back onto the stage, to the same vast sea of people, with no idea they'd just been watching the same quintet hauling gear.

For all the canniness of preparation, however, the show was a monumental failure. The Knebworth audience had its ears ready for old rock standbys. Devo at first confused, then incited the crowd, which completely trashed the band. Devo retreated from the thunderous booing. They ran back to the dressing rooms, changed back into the coveralls, ran back onto the stage, and broke down the equipment. General Boy would have been proud.

Bob Lewis détourned/pen and ink "Warners and Virgin" (1977) dancewear sales catalog page. *Courtesy of Bob Lewis*

"Intelligent suggestions based on [an] exhaustive pole" for songs on Albums #1, #2 and 3—The Golden Energy Album. *Courtesy of Bobbie Watson Whitaker*

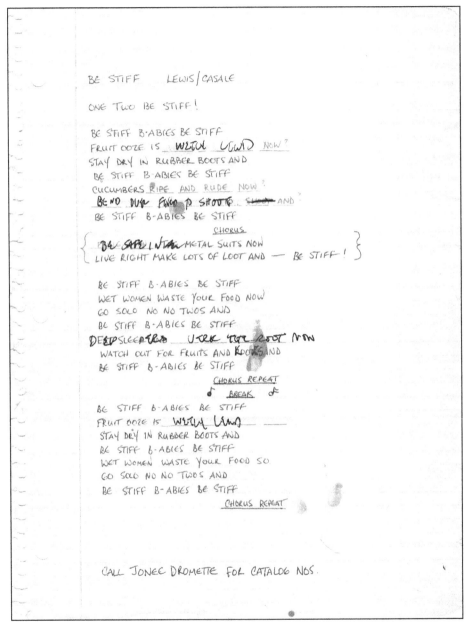

Original handwritten lyrics for "Be Stiff." *Courtesy of Bob Lewis*

Chapter 25

Q. Are We Not Men? A. We are Devo! was released in England in late August 1978 and came out in the United States two months later. With its October release, Devo embarked on their first proper tour, a grueling stretch of American and European dates that would carry into early 1979. By then, the stage show had reached its apex. The floor was covered with a sheet of black plastic, like a giant trash bag. Mark, as Booji Boy, would crawl underneath and emerge by tearing a hole in the plastic and wriggling forth, as if from the womb. The lighting was intention- ally weird, with bright green fills from one side, orange from the other, and 1,000-watt television lights shooting from below, all playing off the yellow suits. Bennett "Bud" Horowitz, the band's lighting designer, found some adjustments in order for this new kind of rock band. "I was used to lighting people to make them look good," he said. "Devo, Jerry specifically, wanted to look as ugly as possible."

Somehow, it worked. Devo had gone forth with the dual intention of sticking to their iconoclastic guns, and of convincing the world that this was the way rock and roll should be. They didn't want to be outsiders in the traditional sense. They wanted to be the outsiders who set the template for the mainstream. They wanted the nerds to overthrow the jocks.

Setup and sound check for *Saturday Night Live*. Courtesy of Bobbie Watson Whitaker

* * *

A few weeks after the release, on September 22, Neil Young & Crazy Horse played the Richfield Coliseum, a basketball arena nestled between Akron and Cleveland. Despite his primary association with rock's hippie-era mainstream, Young was emerging as an adventurous shape-shifter. He'd taken a shine to Devo, casting them in a vanity-project feature film call *Human Highway*. The footage included film of Young and the Devo members in a late-night jam session that reached its climax with Mark, in his Booji Boy guise, singing the words "rust never sleeps," an improvised phrase that may have come from a sign at an Akron auto shop, and that had made its way into his vast mental warehouse of material. The riff they played that night became Young's classic "Hey Hey, My My (Into the Black)."

"Rust Never Sleeps," would be immortalized as the title of Young's next tour and the resultant live album. Young took more than just those three words away from the session with Devo. The incomplete "Hey Hey, My My"

Booji Boy with fork in toaster scene from "Satisfaction". *Courtesy of Bobbie Watson Whitaker*

had taken on a new edge, and when Young took it into the studio to work it out, he brought the film along.

"We went to play 'Hey, Hey,' and we weren't hittin' it that good," Crazy Horse guitarist Frank "Poncho" Sampedro recalled in Jimmy McDonough's book, *SHAKEY: Neil Young's Biography*. "Neil showed us the film of him playin' it with Devo. I didn't think we could ever play it that good, but that inspired us to play harder. From then on, we played the shit outta that song."

Bob Lewis was at the Coliseum show. Bob had learned that the band had enlisted Young's manager, Elliott Roberts, to handle their affairs. He felt he'd been cut out and had been quietly preparing his response. After the concert, he was to meet with Roberts. Bob went to Roberts' hotel room along with along his lawyer, William Whitaker, who had helped Devo with their incorporation papers a few months earlier. Roberts wanted to resolve the tension between Lewis and the band, or at least to reach some kind of settlement that would get rid of this growing distraction.

"I don't think there was any raging hatred against Bob Lewis," Alan Myers said. "Unfortunately, he just wasn't able to reach an agreement on what sort of compensation he might be due. Bands go through that a lot with former members. As I understood it, in the case of Bob Lewis, it was more about his role in the conceptual development of the Devo philosophy. Of course, I wasn't there until later, so I don't have firsthand knowledge of Bob's contribution or expectations."

Bob was expecting some kind of meaningful part in Devo Inc., a creative or managerial position. But Elliot Roberts, of course, already had the manager job. As they discussed Bob's future, Roberts offered a job racking records in Cleveland, a low-level promotional position. Bob flatly refused.

Roberts, according to Bob Lewis, responded, "You'll never work in this town again!" Which was fine with Bob, because he wasn't particularly interested in working in Cleveland in the first place. According to Bob, however, Roberts had misrepresented the Warner Bros. offer, possibly opening up a long stretch of headaches in the process.

"In later discussions with Peter Gregg and then Jerry, this rather interesting tidbit comes to light," Bob said. "When Roberts came to try to settle—he was supposed to make an offer of an in-house job at Warner Bros. in California, acting as a special liaison for the band's interests. This would have been a relatively highly paid position which, if I were able to work with the Warners' people, would have greatly benefited the band and myself. Instead, Roberts offered a job racking records with Warners in Cleveland. Why? Who knows? Jerry isn't a big Roberts fan, that's for sure. Who knows what would have happened if Roberts had done what he was supposed to do? As far as I'm concerned, Elliot's failure to properly transmit the offer was the reason it didn't get worked out more amicably."

* * *

Devo, meanwhile, was focused on more immediate concerns. A few days into the tour, the band was scheduled to play two songs on *Saturday Night Live*, which represented by far the biggest exposure they'd ever received. This would be the second show of the season, coming on the heels of the

DEVO performing on *SNL. Courtesy of Bobbie Watson Whitaker*

Rolling Stones' appearance the week before. It was a strange juxtaposition, considering that Devo's first song would be their cover of "Satisfaction." Or maybe it wasn't so strange. It was because of a series of coincidences and chance meetings, ironies and mutations that Devo was there at all. In a directly chronological sense, this was de-evolution.

The band arrived at the NBC studios, mingling backstage with the Not Ready For Prime Time Players, the group that had made the Lorne Michaels-produced program an unlikely hit. John Belushi, Dan Aykroyd, Laraine Newman, Gilda Radner, Jane Curtin, Garrett Morris and Bill Murray had become stars. Their skits were repeated in classrooms and offices each week; *SNL* was driving popular culture as much as any other entertainment of the late 1970s. Even though there was a certain antiestablishment edge to the program, Devo was a dark horse. With the exception of the "Midsummer Night's Dream" festival, they had never played to more than 1,000 people. And they had never been played on mainstream radio. But on this night, millions would be watching.

DEVO performing on *SNL*. *Courtesy of Bobbie Watson Whitaker*

One of them was General Boy. Robert Mothersbaugh Sr. had gone out that week and bought a VCR, a new bit of technology that would allow him to capture one of his proudest moments as a father.

"That was really important for me as a father to see, because I knew then that Devo had an audience," he said. "I knew that my sons could make a buck and that they'd be all right."

Ed Barger, who had remained as the band's sound man, recalled Jerry making a snide comment about the beloved Rolling Stones backstage, "and everyone on the show was bummed."

This was probably a result of nervous energy. The whole band was excited about this appearance. Jerry and Dan Aykroyd had shared a laugh over the fact that, a year before, when Jerry had sent a tape of the de-evolution film to him, Aykroyd had thrown it in the trash. So this appearance was a victory in many ways. Jerry, to celebrate, had made his first cocaine purchase, saving it for after the show. When he saw Belushi backstage, he thought he'd be a nice guy and offer him some.

DEVO disrobe on *SNL* television debut. *Courtesy of Bobbie Watson Whitaker*

"Don't mind if I do," Belushi said, pulling a glass straw from the pocket of his Blues Brothers jacket. He stuck the straw into the vial and snorted the entire contents. Jerry's face went blank as Belushi handed back the empty vial, laughing.

The host that night was Fred Willard, star of the TV show *Fernwood 2-Nite*. He and Aykroyd performed the first skit, a parody of a low-budget law firm called "Two Guys Who Are Lawyers." That was followed by a segment in which Belushi played an aging Hollywood stuntman. As it wound down, Devo took their places on the stage, waiting nervously in their yellow suits through the commercial break. Lorne Michaels came over to the edge of the stage. They were on in thirty seconds, he said. Millions of people were watching. "Don't fucking blow it," he advised. "Ten, nine, eight, seven…"

The commercial break ended. Fred Willard, standing on the set, looked into the camera. "Ladies and gentlemen," he said, "Devo!"

"Then the lights hit us," Jerry said, "we can see the audience and they can see us, and we have to go. It was the most adrenaline I've ever felt in my life."

DEVO performing on *SNL*. *Courtesy of Bobbie Watson Whitaker*

And despite the rush, and despite the butterflies and the pressure and everything else, Devo delivered. The performance that night was as perfect as anything they had ever done. Every movement was controlled, giving the illusion of frantic action, when actually they were hardly moving. Jerry, especially, appeared to be a robot, executing precise half-turns, twitching as though he was drawn in stop-action animation. Although their specific personalities were obscured by the yellow suits and 3D glasses, the collective personality was mesmerizing. These were not rockers who closed their eyes and bobbed their heads and poured out the feeling. These were funky bone machines. They were electric and electrocuting. The song stopped on a dime, and everyone froze, Jerry waiting a long beat before jerking the neck of his bass upward, then snapping his left hand up in a wave, as if to announce, "Take me to your leader." Then he dropped into a bow and popped back up, in subtle, twisted homage to the Beatles' *Ed Sullivan* gentility.

And then the show went on. Devo returned later in the night, this time in a clip from *The Beginning Was the End*. Booji Boy delivered the documents to General Boy, and then it got weird. This band that had seemed to crack open pop music half an hour before went hallucinogenic with "Jocko Homo." They weren't just goofing. They were saying something. It wasn't clear whether this was a joke or a bold social statement, and that was exactly the point.

This had been the rarest of opportunities. It didn't matter to the masses that some of the world's premier hipsters dug Devo. That would have done them fine in the year-end top-ten lists, but it never could have planted the seed that was planted that night. Without this national appearance, Devo might have passed as a super-cool inside joke. But now the world had seen exactly what a New Wave band looked like and acted like. These weren't the raw English punk rockers dressed in a shredded version of some previous rock fashion. This was something entirely new, vaguely disturbing but wholly entertaining. The aliens from Planet Akron had landed.

V. Vale, publisher of the fanzine *Search & Destroy*, talked about this in James Stark's book *PUNK '77*. "At first, when punk rock started, when we walked down the street wearing our black leather jackets, people would yell out 'Fag!' at us. They thought we were gay or something, me and my friends. They knew something was going on that they didn't like, but they didn't know what to call it. Then in 1978 there was like a 'consciousness' shift because people would yell out, 'DEVO!' I guess Devo were the first band to get some national recognition; they were heard by these kids from the suburbs who would drive into San Francisco Friday and Saturday nights just cruising around yelling at people."

That "Devo" had become a new kind of insult was a sublime compliment. An announcement had been made. The shrink-wrapped yellow albums appeared, with Chi Chi Rodriguez bravely smiling. Devo took the *SNL* moment on the road. Every seed of a densely structured past was in flower. Devo would, in some ways, get better, but they would never be more perfect. This was the beginning, and the beginning was the end.

Chapter 26

On December 26, Devo filed a lawsuit in California against Bob Lewis. The move was strategic. The band and their lawyers figured if this was going to go to court, better to make the first move so the proceedings would take place in California. That way, Bob would have to front the money to bring witnesses, most of whom lived in Ohio, out to the West Coast. The relationship with Bob had deteriorated significantly. His meeting with Elliot Roberts had been a punctuation mark in a years-long dialogue. Now with a set of corporate lawyers in the picture, there was no more messing around. Bob's insistence on a piece of the pie had been a drag and posed a threat to the band's relationship with Warner Bros., and the band and the record company were ready to be rid of him once and for all.

Meanwhile, the reviews for *Q. Are We Not Men?* began to appear, and the band was finding itself as confused as the critics and some fans seemed to be. In *Creem* magazine Readers' Poll, Devo's debut was listed as Best New Wave Album of 1978, ahead of releases by the Ramones, Elvis Costello, Patti Smith, and Blondie. But readers also put Devo at No. 3 on the "Worst Group" list—even as they gave them the No. 3 spot on the "Best New Group" list. Lester Bangs (perhaps not surprisingly, given his straight-punk sensibilities) called Devo "tinker-toy music," while *Rolling Stone* praised the album's sense

Band members pose in both directions. *Courtesy of Bobbie Watson Whitaker*

of authority. "Devo," reviewer Tom Carson wrote, "presents their dissociated, chillingly cerebral music as a definitive restatement of rock & roll's aims and boundaries in the Seventies."

Amidst all this, the band returned to the States, and to Akron. A January 4, 1979, show at the Akron Civic Theatre was billed as Devo's Homecoming Concert. The event was written up in the hometown paper, the *Akron Beacon Journal*, but it was clear that the mainstream still didn't quite get it. Devo was—and maybe always would be—trapped between wanting to be accepted by a mass audience and wanting to change the way that audience thought about music, about performance, about the condition of their lives. But it was hard for audiences to get past the band's sound and presentation. They were the group that had done that weird Rolling Stones cover, the ones in the yellow suits with the baby mask. Not a lot more was getting through. The title of *My Struggle* was proving to be an ironic truth.

The band's families eagerly awaited this show at the downtown landmark. General Boy, still aglow with the *Saturday Night Live* appearance, was going to see living proof of his boys' success. Akron teenagers bought tickets to

Mark and the band tour downtown Akron with photographers (including Blondie's Chris Stein) in tow. *Courtesy of Bobbie Watson Whitaker*

the concert and rode their bicycles downtown. "We had kickass seats," recalled Mark and Bob 1's cousin Alan Mothersbaugh, who was twelve at the time. "And a whole row—my uncle, all my dad's family was at this thing."

Devo, meanwhile, was somewhat ambivalent about this homecoming. Coming home to what? The place that, with precious few exceptions, had shunned and antagonized them? It was ironic that the show was promoted jointly by WMMS, the radio giant at whose Halloween party three years before the band hand been pelted with beer cans, and by Belkin Productions, the regional goliath of concert promoters that probably would just as soon have been shilling a Springsteen show. Devo's prior Akron gigs had been at the Crypt, which was an outsider joint by necessity. Even though "Akron" had become part of the band's calling card, part of its quirkiness, it was also a place they recognized they'd had to escape. But now they were back.

In the familiar surroundings, they loaded in their gear, Ed Barger running the soundcheck, just as he'd done at the Crypt. They hung out with family members and old friends backstage. They were interviewed by a Kent State

DEVO recharges in downtown Akron. *Courtesy of Bobbie Watson Whitaker*

graduate student named Scott Lee Powers for a thesis he was writing. As they basked in this triumph and all its ironies, a stranger approached.

A US marshal. He thrust an envelope at the band. Before they knew what was happening, they'd been served with a lawsuit. Bob Lewis was asking for $1.5 million in compensatory damages and $1.5 million in punitive damages. He was suing them for theft of intellectual property.

"I talked to Mark about [Warner Bros. assigning Elliot Roberts as Devo's new management], and he said that Jerry was the boss," Bob recalled. "It wasn't a high-pressure thing; it was just a quiet resignation on the rest of the band's part. Mark said, 'He's got to do what he has to do, and so do you.' Right away, I asked them to change the name of the band, to relinquish all of the intellectual property related to Devo. The General, the bios, manifestos, graphic design, philosophies, characters, even the Poot. Jerry wasn't interested. So...I filed the lawsuit Lewis v. Casale, Mothersbaugh, Mothersbaugh, Casale, Myers, Devo Inc."

The band kept the lawsuit quiet that evening. It may have been unsettling, but they weren't going to let it destroy this moment. "It did not seem to affect their performance," Ed Barger said. "At their worst, Devo was always great live." This was true. Devo was as polished and urgent that night as they had been on the TV a few months before, putting a charge into a depressed downtown that had fallen silent.

Bob Mothersbaugh, who played with a wireless guitar transmitter, ran down the aisle of the theater during a guitar solo. "We were like, 'Bobby! Bobby!'" Alan Mothersbaugh said. "He put his pick in his mouth and shook our hands real hard, all in the middle of this song. We were so excited. He had that guitar that had been customized, cut down so it was like a thin plank of wood. My dad—he's like, 'That's a real expensive guitar—and he didn't care, he just shaved the shit out of it!' You know, that depression-era thing."

Twenty or so years before, central Akron had been full of nightlife, enjoying the ripple effect of young tire builders with money in their pockets and a Saturday night to blow. But by 1979, the ugly term "Rust Belt" was emerging, and, although no one wanted to admit it, Akron was right in the middle of it. Tire building—the backbone of the local economy and the local psyche—was fast becoming a local anachronism. The jobs had moved south to "right-to-work" states. The short-term gains of the 1976 strike had lasting effects. There was no way Akron's blue-collar workers could continue to dominate every aspect of life here as they once had. And downtown was a dark and empty place. A bar called the Bank—formerly an actual bank, now a ratty, cavernous nightclub with marble bathrooms and a huge, ornate vault that served as a store- room—had begun to book the Numbers Band and would soon become the local New Wave haven. On any given weekend night, all up and down Main Street, the only noise and the only light came from there.

But on the evening of January 4, the noise and the light emanated from the Civic. Devo came home and conquered.

And then they left. It would be thirty years before the band set foot on an Akron stage again.

Chapter 27

In late 1979, Bob Lewis sent a letter to his old friend and professor, Ed Dorn:

> Briefly—present status.... Got some songs on an album called *Bowling Balls from Hell* coming out on Clone Records [under the stage-name Hurricane Bob—from the tropical storm of the same] and have even been doing some writing.

"In re. Devo," he continued, "the boys have currently exhausted all avenues of delay, harassment and procedural fencing—and trial is scheduled in Federal District Court for late March. In the meantime, hopefully they'll make big bucks and decide to settle for same."

Bob had successfully argued that the significant part of his involvement with Devo had taken place in Ohio, and that the trial should be held there, giving a huge boost to his ability to fight his case.

The *Bowling Balls* album he referred to was part of the ongoing attempt from within the tightly knit local scene to make itself heard. Released on Nick Nicholis' local label, it was a cross section of the unconventional, arty music being concocted in Akron basements and garages. In addition to the contribution from Hurricane Bob (which included Bob Lewis, the members of Chi Pig, and Numbers Band saxophonist Terry Hynde), the record

Freedom of Choice LP promotional photograph by Jules Bates/Artrouble.
Courtesy of Jules Bates/Artrouble

included cuts from Chris Butler's side project the Waitresses and collaborations between Tin Huey horn player Ralph Carney and Pere Ubu vocalist David Thomas. By then, many of the Akron bands had been signed and had released their debut albums, but nobody had gotten a lot of attention, and certainly not at the level of Devo. The Rubber City Rebels were doing well as a Los Angeles club band, and Doug Fieger from the Knack had agreed to produce their Capitol Records debut.

The Stiff Records Akron compilation had been released, with the "Shine on America" mural on a cover that also included a tire-scented scratch-and-sniff panel. Rachel Sweet's New Wave/country hybrid had caught the ears of some music industry people, as had the Waitresses. But the coattail effect was not as strong as many had hoped.

* * *

Meanwhile, the commercial era of Devo began to unfurl.

On New Year's Eve, 1979, the band, fully relocated to Los Angeles, played a concert at California's Long Beach Arena. Their set included what is believed to be the first live performance of a new song called "Whip It."

Before the show, Mark gave his old friend and former roommate Ed Barger an inscribed copy of *My Struggle*. Inside the cover, Mark had written, "Although others remain incredulous, you know, for you were there." Barger, still the group's soundman, had been with Mark since long before the two had ever heard of Devo, and he was one of the few from the Akron contingent who had proven himself valuable enough to remain as part of the inner circle.

After the concert, Jerry came out to the house mixing board and congratulated Barger for a great show, something he had never done before. Shortly thereafter, Barger was fired, an act he claimed was Jerry's attempt to exert control over the operation. The last remaining Ohio tie had been cut.

* * *

Throughout the release and world tour of *Freedom of Choice*, the group's most successful album, the Bob Lewis intellectual property lawsuit continued to loom. Bob had tracked down a tape of the interview conducted by teenager Michael Hurray back at the 1977 Akron premiere of *In the Beginning Was the End: The Truth About De-Evolution*. Bob realized that this obscure bit of evidence could well be the smoking gun, and he and William Whitaker were planning to save it for the courtroom. Meanwhile, the depositions continued, filled with testimony from Bobbie Watson, Susan Massaro, and others, detailing their perceptions of Bob's importance to the development of the band's concept.

Bob's deposition took place in an eighteenth-floor conference room at a Century City law office. Robert Mangels, the attorney for Devo, asked Bob what made him think he was the one who had come up with the Devo concept. Realizing his answer might change the course of the whole thing right then, he dropped the bombshell prematurely. He told Mangels there was a tape on which Mark had professed Bob's importance. Mangels appeared taken aback, Bob said, and demanded that the tape be produced.

A couple of days later, during another deposition that was observed by Jerry and Mark, Whitaker set a tape deck on the table. He pressed play. The old cassette rolled. Hurray asked his question.

"Who started the original idea of Devo?"

"Him," Mark clearly replied. "Bob Lewis."

Bob looked across the room, at his old friends and their attorney. As he recalled it, Mark looked baffled, Jerry was enraged, and Mangels looked deflated.

On February 13, 1981, the record company settled with Bob. Part of the agreement was that the amount never be revealed, but Bob did acknowledge that it was "into the six figures." A few days after the settlement, he wrote a letter to Ed and Jennifer Dorn: "As for the good news of which I spoke, I got a call on Friday the 13th from DEVO HDQ, saying essentially 'Uncle,' and while I think that the major tragedy of the affair still lives on in the bifurcation of vision, and in the breakdown of the 'trust,' the settlement which we effected will at least release me from the grinding stone of abject poverty, and might supply both the room and the capital needed for the projects now simmering on the back burners."

The fallout for Devo was hard to take. The band's relationship with Warner Bros. had been founded on a lawsuit, and now this one came just as the label was pushing the group toward stardom. Bob had hurt Devo. He realized it and said years later that he took "no personal pleasure from the whole episode."

In the Beginning Was the End:

The Truth About De-Evolution.

Both phrases proved to be wickedly prophetic.

Postscript

The settlement with Bob Lewis marks the end of Devo's Ohio story. Their career and its narrative continued, of course, as the group went on to create and perform artistically ambitious, commercially successful music and videos that helped define the American culture of the 1980s. Five more albums and worldwide concert tours followed *Freedom of Choice* before the band went dormant in 1991. By then, Mark had recorded the theme music for the CBS Saturday morning show *Pee-wee's Playhouse*, leading Nickelodeon to enlist him for soundtrack work on its children's series *Rugrats*. He opened a studio called Mutato Muzika in a round, green building on the Sunset Strip and brought Bobs 1 and 2 into the operation, which thrived on soundtracks, commercials, and other musical projects. Jerry went on to direct music videos for Soundgarden, Silverchair, Foo Fighters, and others, while also directing television commercials and writing and performing in solo music projects. He would also open a wine company.

Mark continued making visual art, a daily habit that carried all the way back to the *My Struggle* project. His work was shown in galleries and museums, including a major retrospective, *Mark Mothersbaugh: Myopia*, curated by the Museum of Contemporary Art Denver in 2014. Jerry remained politically

The band departs. *Courtesy of Bobbie Watson Whitaker*

engaged and outspoken, an eloquent voice on the subject of devolution, whose essence continued to find new relevance with each unfolding of human history.

The band's legacy picked up almost immediately after Devo stepped aside. In the early '90s, Nirvana recorded "Turnaround," the B-side to the "Whip It" single. Soundgarden and Superchunk recorded "Girl U Want." Moby did a death metal cover of "Whip It." Growing numbers of rock bands paid homage. Guided by Voices singer Robert Pollard listed Q*: Are We Not Men? A: We Are Devo!* among his favorite albums of all time; punk orator Henry Rollins proclaimed that there are just two kinds of people: those who get Devo, and those who don't.

"Where do I see them?" Iggy Pop asked rhetorically in 2010, pondering their legacy. "Is there another really creative New Wave band? That's pretty much where I'd see them—as the truth of the New Wave. The actual truth is with that group. The others are more—a song here and a song there, recombinant imagery, skinny ties, paranoia. But I don't see the creativity matching them."

Following headlining spots on the 1996 and 1997 Lollapalooza tours that celebrated the band as returning heroes, Devo continued to perform on a casual but regular basis, maintaining a presence in the cultural consciousness. They released another studio album, *Something for Everybody*, in 2010.

While their concert tours had included Cleveland dates throughout the band's career, Devo would not perform again in its Akron hometown until 2008, when they headlined a fundraiser for Barack Obama's presidential campaign. The venue was the Akron Civic Theater, the site of Devo's last Akron performance in 1978. Sharing the bill were the city's other most notable rockers, Chrissie Hynde and the Black Keys.

The homecoming was important for a Rust Belt city that cleaves closely to its native celebrities, and for good reason. The era that spawned Devo was a painful one for Northeast Ohio, as the identity and confidence of its industrial heyday corroded and collapsed. For a generation, the region yearned for relevance. When "Rubber Capital of the World" became an empty slogan, it was important to find other touchstones to fill the void. Devo had become one of those, whether they chose to or not.

Chrissie Hynde had always openly embraced her hometown roots, wearing Akron-themed T-shirts as her standard public uniform. The Black Keys, too, made Akron part of their iconography, releasing an album titled *Rubber Factory*, so named because they had recorded it in a former General Tire building. And LeBron James, the city's most notable public figure, has always identified prominently with his hometown, referring to himself as "just a kid from Akron."

While Devo maintained a less fervent connection to Akron, the city heartily filled in its side of the equation. In 2015, the city's administration and the Civic Theater arranged to hang a mural-size print of Janet Macoska's Chili Dog Mac band portrait next to the marquee on Main Street, a prominent statement of loyalty in the middle of a recovering downtown. An annual series of DEVOtional fan conventions alternated between home bases in Akron and Cleveland. A local Devo 5K race was established in 2017 and became an annual event in downtown Akron, usually with Jerry as an honorary guest. Mark was granted an honorary PhD by Kent State in 2008 and was handed the key to the city by Akron's mayor in 2016 when the *Myopia* exhibit opened to great public fanfare at the Akron Art Museum and the Museum of Contemporary Art Cleveland.

And in 2021, to celebrate Devo's nomination for the Rock and Roll Hall of Fame, the City of Akron issued a proclamation declaring April 1 "Devo Day," launching a monthlong promotion to drum up votes. As part of the effort, the city installed fifty energy dome-inspired sculptures around town, created from discarded tires, painted red, and stacked in upwardly descending sizes to replicate the ziggurat shape. But because of the initiative's launch date, it was widely believed to be an April Fool's hoax. Even the hometown *Akron Beacon Journal* reported it as such.

Under the headline, "Akron's 'Devo Day' proclamation sounds a little foolish, doesn't it?," the article wink-winked its way through the "news," closing with the suggestion that Elvis would be in town to commemorate the event.

In the city where the idea of plastic reality had first taken hold, it seemed only fitting that an attempt to place Devo in an institution with the immortal figures of rock history would be mistaken as a prank.

But it wasn't a joke. It was real.

But if it was real, it was meant to be laughed at. And if it was a joke, it was meant to be taken seriously.

There, then, is the true heart of Devo. Part of the culture of the Ohioan, especially of the Ghoulardi generation, is to expect to be the butt of the joke. The well-practiced defense is to be quicker to the punch line.

Devo did devolve. Its '80s story includes the standard rockumentary elements of drug abuse and strained relationships and commercial compromises and artistic missteps. The reason there seems to be a sort of tragedy in that is because they knew it was coming, and despite all the thought and effort, all the conceptual depth of their long formation, there was no escape.

"Even though we had always said from the beginning, very self-consciously, that the beginning was the end, and that the truth about devolution embodied that idea, the end always comes as a surprise," Jerry Casale once said. "The specific end, you never understand, and you never can foresee, and that is the perverse joke of it all."

For all the confusions of packaging, fame, and perception, Devo was, and will always remain, one of the most well thought-out, most well executed ideas for a rock band ever to find a niche in the mainstream psyche. Despite all the planning, there were lots of accidents along the way, but maybe the biggest accident was that people, briefly, got it. And that they didn't really get it.

Devo was one of the most misunderstood bands in rock history and in a way that made their idea richer. Jerry could laugh, as he had done back at Kent State, and that laugh meant there was something bigger going on. Mark could pull on his Booji Boy mask and squeak out truth in the voice of the innocent. Five skinny guys in yellow Tyvek and flowerpot hats could step onto a stage and make everything more urgent and more funny and more important than anyone could have expected.

There was always a question. (Are we not men?)

And there was always an answer. (We are Devo.)

Acknowledgments

Many thanks to the following individuals who gave generously of their time for interviews, opened their archives and provided photographs or essential information:

David Allen + Artrouble, Brian Applegate, Arno, Kathy Atkinson, Ed Barger, Walt Batansky, Anita Bates (The Jules Bates Foundation), Robert Bertholf, Richard Blocher, Mykel Board, Joep Bruijnjé, Chris Butler, Ralph Carney, Gerald V. Casale, Roger Casale, Buzz Clic, Jim Clinefelter, Cheetah Chrome, Patrick Cullie, Holger Czukay, Rod Firestone, Doug Gillard, Harvey Gold, Vernon L. Gowdy III, James Grauerholz, Peter Gregg, Randy Hansen, Don Harvey, Susan Schmidt Horning, Bruce Hensal, Gary Jackett, Donna Kossy, Sammy Larson, Nicky Latzoni, Robert Lewis, Justin Keiser (Kent State University Special Collections/Library), Jennifer Licitri, Tim Maglione, Susan Massaro Aylward, Alan Mothersbaugh, Jim Mothersbaugh, Mark Mothersbaugh, Robert Mothersbaugh, Sr., Alan Myers, Nick Nicholis, Scott Orsi, Ray Packard, Tony Pemberton, John Petkovic, Michael Pilmer, Robert Pollard, Iggy Pop, Rod Reisman, Martin Reymann, Ebet Roberts, KRK Ryden, Rocky Schenck, Klaus Schleusener, Debbie Smith, Rev. Ivan Stang, Chuck Statler, Allan Tannenbaum, Malcolm Tent, John Thompson (a.k.a.

Johnny Dromette), Michael Watters, Fred Weber, Rev. Toth Wilder, Rutherford Witthus (Curator of Literary Collections/Edward Dorn Papers at the University of Connecticut's Thomas J. Dodd Research Center), Billy Zoom, the members of the MSN (now Facebook) Spudtalk newsgroup, and now long-defunct alt.fan.devo.

The authors would like to thank Director Jon Miller and staff members Amy Freels and Thea Ledendecker of The University of Akron Press for bringing this edition to life. For critical feedback on the early manuscript drafts, we thank our friends and volunteer readers: Nina Antonia, Chuck Klosterman, Eric Nuzum, Mark J. Price, and Jeff Winner.

We are especially grateful to Bobbie Watson Whitaker for documenting so many of the events recounted in this book, and for generously sharing her photo archives.

Finally, Jade would like to acknowledge his wife Cathy Sowell and his parents for their unconditional love, support, and encouragement. David gives everlasting thanks to Gina, Evan, and Lia Giffels for their patience and support while he toiled on the Island of Lost Souls.

Bibliography

Introduction
INTERVIEWS:
Casale, Jerry. "De-evolution for the Modern Squad." Interview by Wil Forbis of *Acid Logic*, 2000.
Casale, Jerry. Interview by *INKnineteen*, May 2000.
Casale, Jerry. Telephone interview by Jade Dellinger, June 11, 2001.
OTHER SOURCES:
Encyclopedia Britannica. https://kids.britannica.com/students/article/Devo/606640.
Shadduck, Dr. B. H. *Jocko-Homo Heavenbound* (Roger, OH: Jocko-Homo Pub. Co., 1924).

Chapter 1
INTERVIEWS:
Akron Beacon Journal. "Forever Ghoul," Oct. 25, 1998.
Casale, Jerry. "Devo: Sixties Idealists or Nazis and Clowns?" Interview by Michael Goldberg. *Rolling Stone*, 1981.
Casale, Jerry. Interview by Australian 3-PBS 106.7 (date unknown).
Casale, Jerry. Interview by David Giffels, July 18, 1997.
Casale, Jerry. Interview by *INKnineteen*, May 2000.
Casale, Jerry. Interview by *New Vinyl Times*, v. 1 #11, 1980.
Casale, Jerry. Interview by Sharisse Zeff of *Upbeat*, August 1980.
Casale, Jerry. Telephone interview by Jade Dellinger, June 11, 2001.
DeFrange, Tim. Email interview by Jade Dellinger, Sept. 10, 2000.
Gregg, Peter. Posted to Spudtalk newsgroup Oct. 2001 through Feb. 2002.

Lewis, Bob. Email interviews by Jade Dellinger, Oct. 2001.
Lewis, Bob. Interview by Jade Dellinger, Jan. 8, 2001.
Reisman, Rod. Telephone interview by Jade Dellinger, Dec. 15, 2000.
Thomas, David. Posted to www.projex.demon.co.uk/archives/heenan.html (date unknown).
Watson, Bobbie. Interview by Jade Dellinger, Oct. 15, 2001.

OTHER SOURCES:

Tom Feran and R. D. Heldenfels, *Ghoulardi: Inside Cleveland TV's Wildest Ride* (Cleveland: Gray & Company, 1997).
Love, Steve and David Giffels, *Wheels of Fortune: The Story of Rubber in Akron*, (Akron: The University of Akron Press, 1998).
Ohio Department of Health birth record for Gerald Casale.
Rough Rider, 1966 (Roosevelt High School yearbook).

Chapter 2

INTERVIEWS:

Mothersbaugh, Mark. Interview by Brad Shank for *Music Alive!*, vol. 21, #1, Oct. 2001.
Mothersbaugh, Mark. Interview by E-Online HotSpot (date unknown).
Mothersbaugh, Mark. Interview by "E. K." for RocknRollreporter.com, 1996.
Mothersbaugh, Mark. Interview by Jettlag, Sept. 1980.
Mothersbaugh, Mark. Interview by Michael Pilmer, April 26, 2001.
Mothersbaugh, Mark. Interview by TalkCity.com, Aug. 26, 1998.
Mothersbaugh, Mark. Interview by Victoria Reynolds Harrow for *Northern Ohio LIVE*, March 2000.
Mothersbaugh, Mark, Live 105 Modern Rock interview, published in *Spud Magazine*, 1988.
Mothersbaugh, Robert, Sr. Telephone interview by Jade Dellinger, July 26, 2000.

OTHER SOURCES:

Billboard, November 22, 1980, Vol. 92, No. 47.
Boy, Booji (a.k.a. Mark Mothersbaugh), *My Struggle*, (Cleveland: NEO Rubber Band, 1978).
Graff, Gary and Daniel Durchholz (eds.), *Music Hound: Rock—The Essential Album Guide*, (Detroit, MI: Visible Ink, 1996).
Mothersbaugh, Jim. Address to DEVOtional Fan Convention, Cleveland, 2001 (transcript).
"Mr. Potato Head," www.yesterdayland.com/popopedia/shows/toys/ty1048.php.
Ohio Department of Health birth record for Mark Mothersbaugh.
Oriflame (Woodridge High School yearbook), 1968.
Mothersbaugh, Robert, Sr. Address to Devo "Day of Atonement" Fan Convention. Cleveland, 2000 (transcript).
Woodarian (Woodridge High School student newspaper), May 28, 1968.

Chapter 3
INTERVIEWS:
Bertholf, Robert. Telephone interview by Jade Dellinger, May 17, 2001.
Butler, Chris. Telephone interview by Jade Dellinger, April 10, 2001.
Casale, Jerry. "Oh Yes, It's Devo: An Interview with Jerry Casale." Interview by Brian L. Knight of *The Vermont Review* (date unknown).
Casale, Jerry. "De-evolution for the Modern Squad." Interview by Wil Forbis of *Acid Logic*, 2000.
Casale, Jerry. "Devo's Primal Pop." Interview by *Newsweek*, Oct. 30, 1978.
Casale, Jerry. "Devo: Sixties Idealists or Nazis and Clowns?" Interview by Michael Goldberg. *Rolling Stone*, Dec. 10, 1981.
Casale, Jerry. Interview by David Giffels, April 2000.
Casale, Jerry. Interview by Jeff Winner, March 11, 1993.
Casale, Jerry. Interview by "On Tour" (KCET-Los Angeles), August 1997.
Casale, Jerry. Interview by Ron Kretsch of *Cleveland Free Times*, June 14, 2000.
Casale, Jerry. Interview by *Search & Destroy* #2, 1977.
Casale, Jerry. Telephone interview by Jade Dellinger, June 11, 2001.
Casale, Roger. Email interview by Jade Dellinger, April 10, 2001.
Jackett, Gary. Telephone interview by Jade Dellinger, Jan. 18, 2001.
Lewis, Bob. Email interviews by Jade Dellinger, Sept. 30, 2001; Oct. 12 & 16, 2001.
Lewis, Bob. Interview by Rob Warmowski, c. 1996, https://warmowski.wordpress.com/2010/03/01/devo-founder-bob-lewis-my-1997-interview/.
Lewis, Bob. Telephone interview by Jade Dellinger, Jan. 8, 2001.
Mothersbaugh, Bob. Email interview by Alex Brunelle and Tom Chiki, Nov. 9, 2004.

OTHER SOURCES:
Akron Beacon Journal archives, "Kent State," 1970.
How-to Newsletter mention in *Akron Beacon Journal*. "Of Loss and Learning." April 30, 2000.
Cento, "Edward Dorn: An 80's Reminiscence," https://writing.upenn.edu/epc/authors/dorn/DORN_CENTO/dorn_wolff.html.
Dorn, Edward. *Way West: Stories, Essays & Verse Accounts: 1963–1993* (Santa Rosa, CA: Black Sparrow Press, 1993).
Gordon, William A. *Four Dead in Ohio: Was There a Conspiracy at Kent State?* (Laguna Hills, CA: North Ridge Books, 1995).
Th President's Commission on Campus Unrest Special Report, 1970; "Shut it Down!" (newsletter), May 1970.

Chapter 4
INTERVIEWS:
Barger, Ed. Email interviews by Jade Dellinger, Dec. 1–18, 2001.
Butler, Chris. Telephone interview by Jade Dellinger, April 19, 2001.
Casale, Jerry. Telephone interview by Jade Dellinger, June 11, 2001.

Gregg, Peter. Posted to Spudtalk newsgroup, Dec. 10 & 11, 2001.
Hensal, Bruce. Telephone interview by Jade Dellinger, June 18, 2001.
Jackett, Gary. Telephone interview by Jade Dellinger, Jan. 18, 2001.
Lewis, Bob. Email interviews by Jade Dellinger, Sept. 26, 2001 through April 10, 2002.
Lewis, Bob. Telephone interview by Jade Dellinger, Jan. 8, 2001.
Licitri, Jennifer. Telephone interview by Jade Dellinger, Oct. 18, 2001.
McGough, Dale. Telephone interview by David Giffels, Oct. 13, 2002.
Mothersbaugh, Mark. Interview by Diana Fischer for icast.com (date unknown).
Mothersbaugh, Mark. Interview by *Search & Destroy* #7 (1978).
Reisman, Rod. Telephone interview by Jade Dellinger, Dec. 15, 2000.
Reymann, Martin. Telephone interview by Jade Dellinger, Nov. 7, 2001.
Storage, Bill. Email interview by Jade Dellinger, Dec. 24, 2003.
Watson, Bobbie. Email interviews by Jade Dellinger, Sept. 25 & 27, 2001.
Weber, Fred. Telephone interview by Jade Dellinger, Jan. 24, 2001.

OTHER SOURCES:

Adventure Comics #416. Reprint of the Golden Age March–April 1948 *Wonder Woman* (issue #28). March 1972.
Akron Beacon Journal. "Akron police hold suspects in N.M. robbery, slaying." March 1, 1978.
Akron Beacon Journal. "Charged With Showing Obscene Film." Sept. 15, 1971.
Akron Beacon Journal. "City Charges Obscenity in Films." May 23, 1971.
Akron Beacon Journal. "Fistfight puts jail inmate in city hospital." March 11, 1978.
Akron Beacon Journal. "'School For Sex' Is Closed." Sept. 8, 1971.
Akron Beacon Journal. "2 businesses hit by halts." Feb. 25, 1976.
District of Ohio Eastern Division case between Robert Lewis, Plaintiff vs. Gerald V. Casale, et al, Defendants.
Mothersbaugh, Mark, *The Sad Story of a Very Dead Man . . . My Struggle, or Life in the Rubber City* (manuscript), ca. 1971.
Payne, J. Gregory, "May 4 Archive." https://www.may4archive.org/.
Watson, Barbara Jo (Bobbie). Deposition taken on June 15, 1979, in the US District Court Northern
Youngstown Vindicator. "Speeding Auto Leaves Bodies Strewn on W. Federal." Nov. 12, 1971.

Chapter 5

INTERVIEWS:

Barger, Ed. Email interview by Jade Dellinger, Dec. 13, 2001.
Casale, Jerry. Interview by Jeff Winner, March 11, 1993.
Casale, Jerry. Telephone interview by Jade Dellinger, June 11, 2001.
Jacket, Gary. Telephone interview by Jade Dellinger via telephone, Jan. 18, 2001.
Lewis, Bob. Email interview by Jade Dellinger, Sept. 26, 2001 & Oct. 17, 2001.
Lewis, Bob. Interview by Rob Warmowski, c. 1996, https://warmowski.wordpress.com/2010/03/01/devo-founder-bob-lewis-my-1997-interview/.

Masarro, Susan (Aylward). Email interview by Jade Dellinger, Sept. 28, 2001 & March 5, 2002.
Watson, Bobbie. Email interview by Jade Dellinger, Sept. 25, 2001.

OTHER SOURCES:
Devo Rap Sheet (ca. 1976 press release).
Eric Mottram, "Left for California: the Slow Awakening," *Sixpack* 5 (London & Lake Toxaway, NC, 1973).
The Staff 2 (Hollywood, CA, July 14, 1972) in the Collection of the Eric Mottram Archives at King's College London, UK.

Chapter 6
INTERVIEWS:
Casale, Jerry. "Oh Yes, It's Devo: An Interview with Jerry Casale." Interview by Brian L. Knight for *The Vermont Review* (date unknown).
Casale, Jerry. Telephone interview by Jade Dellinger, June 11, 2001.
Cullie, Patrick. Email interview by Jade Dellinger, April 8, 2002.
Jacket, Gary. Telephone interview by Jade Dellinger, Jan. 18, 2001 & Feb. 2, 2001.
Maglione, Tim. Email interview by Jade Dellinger, Aug. 15, 2000.
Mothersbaugh, Mark. Interview by Marshall Thomas for *BBC Rock Hour* (date unknown).
Mothersbaugh, Mark. Interview by Victoria Reynolds Harrow for *Northern Ohio LIVE*, March 2000.
Reisman, Rod. Telephone interview by Jade Dellinger, Dec. 15, 2000.

OTHER SOURCES:
Gritter, Headley. *Rock-N-Roll Asylum* (New York: Delilah Books, 1984).
Mothersbaugh, Bob. "Readers Vs. Breeders" and "Polymer Love," *The Staff*, reprinted in *Shelly's* magazine, Kent, Ohio, Spring 1975.
The Numbers 1970–2020: Fifty Years of Original Music. Numbersband.com (band history of 15-60-75).
Shelly's magazine, Kent, Ohio, Spring 1975.

Chapter 7
INTERVIEWS:
Bertholf, Robert. Telephone interview by Jade Dellinger, May 17, 2001.
Casale, Jerry. Telephone interview by Jade Dellinger, June 11, 2001.
Lewis, Bob. Email interviews by Jade Dellinger, Sept. 30, 2001 & 2002.
Lewis, Bob. Telephone interview by Jade Dellinger, Jan. 8, 2001.
Reisman, Rod. Telephone interview by Jade Dellinger, Dec. 15, 2000.
Reymann, Marty. Telephone interview by Jade Dellinger, Nov. 7, 2001.
Weber, Fred. Telephone interview by Jade Dellinger, Jan. 24, 2001.

OTHER SOURCES:
Bertholf, Robert. deposition taken on June 14, 1979, in the US District Court Northern District of Ohio Eastern Division case between Robert Lewis, Plaintiff vs. Gerald V. Casale, et al, Defendants.

Boy, Booji (a.k.a. Mark Mothersbaugh), *My Struggle*, (Cleveland: NEO Rubber Band, 1978).
The Daily Kent Stater, "Devo Clan Returns Triumphant." Page 11. April 23, 1974.
Devo, The Complete Truth About De-evolution (Voyager laserdisc 1993).
Dorn, Edward. *Recollections of Gran Apacheria* (San Francisco, CA: Turtle Island, 1974).
Dorn, Edward. *Way West: Stories, Essays & Verse Accounts: 1963–1993* (Santa Rosa, CA: Black Sparrow Press, 1993).
Lewis, Bob. Letter to Ed & Jennifer Dorn, ca. 1974.
Mashin' Potatoes: Tribute to Devo (compact disc), Beat Happy! Music (1998).
Students for a Democratic Society, Kent State University chapter, communique to members, ca. 1972.
Watson, Barbara Jo (Bobbie). Deposition taken on June 15, 1979, in the US District Court Northern District of Ohio Eastern Division case between Robert Lewis, Plaintiff vs. Gerald V. Casale, et al, Defendants.

Chapter 8
INTERVIEWS:
Casale, Jerry. "De-evolution for the Modern Squad." Interview by Wil Forbis for Acid Logic, 2000.
Casale, Jerry. Interview by Donna Kossy for *Puncture*, 1995.
Casale, Jerry. Telephone interviews by Jade Dellinger, Feb. 19, 2001 & June 11, 2001.
Casale, Jerry, 1978 telex sent to a (unknown) UK music magazine.
Devo (unidentified member). Interview by Warner Brothers CyberTalk, Aug. 19, 1996.
Harvey, Don. Email interview by David Giffels, June 26, 2002.
Lewis, Bob. Email interview by Jade Dellinger, Sept. 30, 2001.
Lewis, Bob. Telephone interview by Jade Dellinger, Jan. 8, 2001.

OTHER SOURCES:
Akron city directory, 1974.
Bertholf, Robert. Letter to Ed & Jennie Dorn, December 7, 1973.
Boy, Booji (a.k.a. Mark Mothersbaugh). *My Struggle* (Cleveland: NEO Rubber Band, 1978).
The Daily Kent Stater, "Devo Clan Returns Triumphant." Page 11. Apr. 23, 1974.
Kossy, Donna. *Strange Creations: Aberrant Ideas of Human Origins from Ancient Astronauts to Aquatic Apes* (Los Angeles: Feral House, 2001).
Lewis, Bob. Letter to Ed & Jenny Dorn. July 13, 1974 (postmark).
Maerth, Oscar Kiss (trans. by Judith Hayward). *The Beginning Was the End: How Man Came into Being through Cannibalism—Intelligence Can Be Eaten* (NY: Praeger Publishers, 1974).
Mothersbaugh, Jim. Address to DEVOtional Fan Convention, Cleveland, 2001 (transcript).
Shadduck, Dr. B. H. , *Jocko-Homo Heavenbound* (ibid.).

Time, "Books: Top Bananas." Review of *In The Beginning Was the End* by Oscar Kiss Maerth. R. Z. Sheppard. June 24, 1974.

Chapter 9
INTERVIEWS:
Barger, Ed. Email interviews by Jade Dellinger, Dec. 1 & 4, 2001.
Casale, Jerry. Interview by David Giffels, July 18, 1997.
Casale, Jerry. Telephone interview by Jade Dellinger, June 11, 2001.
Cullie, Patrick. Email interviews by Jade Dellinger, April 8 & 10, 2002.
Gregg, Peter. Posted on the MSN Spudtalk newsgroup, Oct. 20, 2001.
Hensal, Bruce. Telephone interview by Jade Dellinger, June 18, 2001.
Jacket, Gary. Telephone interview by Jade Dellinger, Jan. 18, 2001.
Lewis, Bob. Email interviews by Jade Dellinger, Sept. 27, 2001, through Oct. 21, 2001.
Lewis, Bob. Telephone interview by Jade Dellinger, Jan. 8, 2001.
Mothersbaugh, Jim. Interview by David Giffels, Sept. 4, 2002.
Mothersbaugh, Mark. Interview by David Giffels, July 18, 1997.
Mothersbaugh, Robert, Sr. Telephone interview by Jade Dellinger, July 26, 2000.
Reymann, Martin. Telephone interview by Jade Dellinger via telephone, Nov. 11, 2001.
OTHER SOURCES:
Bertholf, Robert. Deposition taken on June 14, 1979, in the US District Court Northern District of Ohio.
Boy, Booji (a.k.a. Mark Mothersbaugh), *My Struggle* (Cleveland: NEO Rubber Band, 1978).
Chestnut Burr (Kent State yearbook), "Shelly's Book Bar: Breeding Thought in the Poetic Arena," Ron Kovach, 1975.
Lewis, Bob. Letters, ca.1974 to Ed & Jenny Dorn.
DEVO: The Complete Truth About De-Evolution (Voyager laserdisc 1993).
DEVO RAP SHEET (Devo-issued press release, ca. 1976).
Island of Lost Souls, MCA Home Video, 1993 (original release: Paramount Productions, 1932).
Mothersbaugh, Jim. Address to DEVOtional Fan Convention, Cleveland, 2001 (transcript).
Mothersbaugh, Mark. Email to Jade Dellinger, Nov. 29, 2020.
Mothersbaugh, Robert. Address to DEVOtional Fan Convention, Cleveland, 2001 (transcript).
Watson, Barbara Jo (Bobbie). Deposition taken on June 15, 1979, in the US District Court Northern
Shelly's magazine, (Kent, Ohio, October 1974).

Chapter 10
INTERVIEWS:
Barger, Ed. Email interviews by Jade Dellinger, Dec. 4–18, 2001.

Casale, Jerry. Interview by Jeff Winner, March 11, 1993.
Casale, Jerry. Telephone interview by Jade Dellinger, June 11, 2001.
Jacket, Gary. Telephone interview by Jade Dellinger, Jan. 18, 2001.
Lewis, Bob. Email interviews by Jade Dellinger, Sept. 27–Oct. 17, 2001.
Licitri, Jennifer. Telephone interview by Jade Dellinger, Oct. 18, 2001.
Mothersbaugh, Bob. Interview by Paul Provenza for checkout.com, 2001.
Mothersbaugh, Mark. Interview by *Ampersand*, Oct. 1981.
Mothersbaugh, Mark. Interview by Diana Fischer for icast.com, (date unknown).
Reymann, Martin. Telephone interview by Jade Dellinger, Nov. 7, 2001.
Watson, Bobbie. Email interviews by Jade Dellinger, Sept. 27 & 28, 2001.

OTHER SOURCES:
Akron Beacon Journal. "Artist Making His Stamp By Updating Past's Images, Feb. 2, 1975.
Akron Beacon Journal. "Chris Meets Artist Max: Lesson Was Beyond His Wildest Hopes," Nov. 11, 1971.
Akron Beacon Journal. "Is Art Lost in Akron?" Aug. 27, 1973.
Akron city directory, 1975.
Boy, Booji (a.k.a. Mark Mothersbaugh). *My Struggle* (Cleveland: NEO Rubber Band, 1978).
Lewis, Bob. ca. 1974 letter to Ed Dorn.
Lewis, Bob. Jan. 17, 1975 (postmark) letter to Ed and Jenny Dorn.
Mothersbaugh, Robert. Address to DEVOtional Fan Convention, Cleveland, 2001 (transcript).
Shelly's magazine, (Kent, Ohio, April/May 1975).

Chapter 11
INTERVIEWS:
Barger, Ed. Email interview by Jade Dellinger, Nov. 29, 2001.
Hensal, Bruce. Telephone interview by Jade Dellinger, June 18, 2001.
Jacket, Gary. Telephone interview by Jade Dellinger, Jan. 18, 2001.
Casale, Jerry. Interview by Jeff Winner; March 11, 1993.
Casale, Jerry. Interview by Jim Infirmary. *New York Rocker*, July 1977 (published July/August 1978).
Casale, Jerry. Interview by *New Musical Express*, March 18, 1978.
Casale, Jerry. Telephone interview by Jade Dellinger, June 11, 2001.
Cullie, Patrick. Email interviews by Jade Dellinger, April 8 & 10, 2002.
Gregg, Peter. Posted on the MSN Spudtalk newsgroup, Oct. 29, 2001.
Lewis, Bob. Email interviews by Jade Dellinger, Oct. 11 & 12, 2001, April 1, 2002.
Mothersbaugh, Mark. Interview for IRC/Apple Computer, Inc. Online chat at Sundance Film Festival, Jan. 25, 1996.
Mothersbaugh, Mark. Interview by Michael Pilmer (date unknown).
Mothersbaugh, Mark. Interview by *Search & Destroy* #7, 1978.

OTHER SOURCES:
Lewis, Bob. Letter to Ed and Jennifer Dorn. Jan. 17, 1975.
Lewis, Bob. Letter to Ed Dorn. Undated (c. 1975).
Daily Kent Stater ad for *Pink Flamingos*, Apr. 4, 1975.
Eastern Division case between Robert Lewis, Plaintiff vs. Gerald V. Casale, et al, Defendants.
Bertholf, Robert. Deposition taken on June 14, 1979, in the US District Court Northern District of Ohio. District of Ohio Eastern Division case between Robert Lewis, Plaintiff vs. Gerald V. Casale, et al, Defendants.

Chapter 12
INTERVIEWS:
Barger, Ed. Email interviews by Jade Dellinger, Dec. 1 & 13, 2001.
Bators, Stiv. Interview by Larry Wichman for *Velvet Magazine* (date unknown).
Casale, Jerry. Interview by *Search & Destroy* (#2), 1977.
Casale, Jerry. Interview by *Trouser Press*, Sept. 1979.
Casale, Jerry. Telephone interview by Jade Dellinger; June 11, 2001.
Jacket, Gary. Telephone interviews by Jade Dellinger, Jan. 18 & Feb. 2, 2001.
Lewis, Bob. Email interview by Jade Dellinger, Sept. 26, 2001.
Licitri, Jennifer. Telephone interview by Jade Dellinger, Oct. 18, 2001.
Massaro, Susan (Aylward). Email interview by Jade Dellinger, Sept. 28, 2001.
Mothersbaugh, Jim. Interview by David Giffels, Sept. 4, 2002.
Mothersbaugh, Mark. Interview by Joe Garden for *The Onion*, July 10, 1997.
Mothersbaugh, Mark. Interview by Michael Shore of *OMNI*, 1982.
Mothersbaugh, Mark. Interview by *Seconds Magazine*, 2000.
Mothersbaugh, Mark. Interview by *Trouser Press*, Sept. 1979.
Reymann, Martin. Telephone interview by Jade Dellinger, Nov. 7, 2001.
Massaro, Susan (Aylward). Email interview by Jade Dellinger, Sept. 28, 2001.
OTHER SOURCES:
Akron Beacon Journal. "Akron police hold suspects in N.M. robbery, slaying," March 1, 1978.
Akron Beacon Journal. "Coventry man indicted in Greenlese slaying." April 17, 1976.
Akron Beacon Journal. "Evidence illegal, case halts." May 10, 1976.
Akron Beacon Journal. "Fistfight puts jail inmate in city hospital," March 11, 1978.
Akron Beacon Journal. "2 businesses hit by robbers," Feb. 25, 1976.
Bussy, Pascal. *Kraftwerk: Man, Machine and Music* (Wembley, Middx., England: SAF Publishing, Ltd., 1993)
Casale, Jerry. Liner notes for *DEVO Live: The Mongoloid Years* (compact disc), Rykodisc, 1992.
CLE magazine 3A.
Devo. *DEVO Live: The Mongoloid Years* (compact disc), Rykodisc, 1992.
Heylin, Clinton. *From the Velvets to the Voidoids: A Pre-Punk History for a Post-Punk World* (NY: Penguin Books, 1993)

Massaro, Susan (Aylward). Deposition taken on June 15, 1979, in the US District Court Northern District of Ohio Eastern Division case between Robert Lewis, Plaintiff vs. Gerald V. Casale, et al, Defendants

Mothersbaugh, Jim. Address to DEVOtional Fan Convention, Cleveland, 2001 (transcript).

Pressler, Charlotte. "The De-Evolution Band." *CLE* magazine, No. 1, Winter 1977.

Chapter 13
INTERVIEWS:

Casale, Jerry. Interview by *Rock Video Magazine*, June 1984.

Casale, Jerry. Interview by Sammy Larson, 1993.

Casale, Jerry. Telephone interview by Jade Dellinger, June 11, 2001.

Jacket, Gary. Telephone interview by Jade Dellinger, Jan. 18, 2001.

Lewis, Bob. Interview by Rob Warmowski, c. 1996, https://warmowski.wordpress.com/2010/03/01/devo-founder-bob-lewis-my-1997-interview/.

Licitri, Jennifer. Telephone interview by Jade Dellinger, Oct. 18, 2001Massaro, Susan (Aylward). Email interviews by Jade Dellinger, Sept. 17–24, 2001.

Mothersbaugh, Jim. Interview by Victoria Reynolds Harrow for *Northern Ohio LIVE*, March 2000.

Mothersbaugh, Mark. Interview by Diana Fischer for icast.com.

Mothersbaugh, Mark. Interview by Tim Pedersen for Roland Users Group, 1997.

Mothersbaugh, Robert, Sr. Telephone interview by Jade Dellinger, July 26, 2000.

Smith, Debbie. Telephone interview by Jade Dellinger, April 11, 2001.

Statler, Chuck. Video interview by Jade Dellinger and David Giffels, Sept. 22, 2022.

Watson, Bobbie. Email interview by Jade Dellinger, Sept. 26–27, 2001.

OTHER SOURCES:

DEVO: The Complete Truth About De-Evolution (Voyager laserdisc 1993).

Devo. *Hardcore Volume 1: '74–'77* (compact disc), Rykodisc, 1990.

Lewis, Bob. Postcard to Ed and Jenny Dorn, Apr. 9, 1976 (postmark).

Massaro, Susan (Aylward). Deposition taken on June 15, 1979 in the US District Court Northern District of Ohio Eastern Division case between Robert Lewis, Plaintiff vs. Gerald V. Casale, et al, Defendants.

Mothersbaugh, Mark. Email to Jade Dellinger, Nov. 29, 2020.

Shadduck, Dr. B. H. *Jocko-Homo Heavenbound* (Roger, OH: Jocko-Homo Pub. Co., 1924).

Watson, Barbara Jo (Bobbie). Deposition taken on June 15, 1979, in the US District Court Northern District of Ohio Eastern Division case between Robert Lewis, Plaintiff vs. Gerald V. Casale, et al, Defendants.

Chapter 14
INTERVIEWS:

Barger, Ed. Email interview by Jade Dellinger, Dec. 1, 2001.

Butler, Chris. Telephone interview by Jade Dellinger, April 10, 2001.
Carney, Ralph. Email interview by Jade Dellinger, July 20 & 24, 2000, Jan. 26, 2001.
Casale, Jerry, July 1977 interview by Jim Infirmary for *New York Rocker*, published July/August 1978.
Casale, Jerry & Mothersbaugh, Mark, Australian newspaper article, 1980 (clipping—source unknown)
Casale, Jerry. Telephone interview by Jade Dellinger, June 11, 2001.
Gold, Harvey. Interview by David Giffels, Sept. 3, 2002.
Lewis, Bob. Email interview by Jade Dellinger, Oct. 17, 2001.
Lewis, Bob. Telephone interview by Jade Dellinger, Jan. 8, 2001.
Massaro, Susan (Aylward). Email interview by Jade Dellinger, Sept. 17 & 20, 2001.
Myers, Alan. Telephone interview by Jade Dellinger, Jan. 24, 2001.

OTHER SOURCES:
Frank Zappa & The Mothers of Invention, *Freak Out!* (1966, Verve LP).
Gritter, Headley. *Rock-n-Roll Asylum* (New York: Delilah Books, 1984).

Chapter 15
INTERVIEWS:
Barger, Ed. Email interviews by Jade Dellinger, Dec. 4 & 6, 2001.
Firestone, Rod. Interview by David Giffels, June 2001.
Firestone, Rod (a.k.a. Ward Welch), email interview by Jade Dellinger, Dec. 7, 2000.
Jacket, Gary. Telephone interview by Jade Dellinger, Jan. 18, 2001.
Krauss, Scott. Interview by Colin McFrangos, (date unknown).
Nicholis, Nick. Interview by David Giffels, June 1999.
Massaro, Susan (Aylward). Email interview by Jade Dellinger, Sept. 28, 2001.
Mothersbaugh, Mark. Interview by Michael Pilmer, April 26, 2001.
Nicholis, Nick. Interview by David Giffels, June 1999.
Schmidt Horning, Susan. Email interview by Jade Dellinger, Nov. 9, 2001.
Thomas, David. Email interview by Jade Dellinger, July 4, 2002.
Watson, Bobbie. Email interview by Jade Dellinger, Sept. 27, 2001.

OTHER SOURCES:
Casale, Jerry, liner notes for *DEVO Live: The Mongoloid Years* (compact disc), Rykodisc, 1992.
Devo, *Hardcore Volume 1: '74–'77* (compact disc), Rykodisc, 1990.
Heylin, Clinton. *From the Velvets to the Voidoids: A Pre-Punk History for a Post-Punk World* (NY: Penguin Books, 1993).
Love, Steve and David Giffels. *Wheels of Fortune: The Story of Rubber in Akron* (Akron: The University of Akron Press, 1998).
Scene (Cleveland), Dec. 9, 1976 & Jan. 27, 1977.

Chapter 16
INTERVIEWS:
Bators, Stiv. Interview by *Search & Destroy* #4, 1977.

Casale, Jerry. Interview by Donna Kossy for *Puncture*, 1995.
Casale, Jerry, July 1977 interview by Jim Infirmary for *New York Rocker*, published July/August 1978.
Chrome, Cheetah. Email interview by Jade Dellinger, May 21, 2002.
DEVO (unidentified member) interview in *Search & Destroy* (#3) in 1977.
Horvath, Alan. Email interview by Jade Dellinger, Feb. 19, 2002.
Jacket, Gary. Telephone interview by Jade Dellinger, Feb. 2, 2001.
Lewis, Bob. Email interviews by Jade Dellinger, Sept. 26, 2001 & Feb. 19, 2002.
Licitri, Jennifer. Telephone interview by Jade Dellinger, Oct. 18, 2001.
Massaro, Susan (Aylward). Email interview by Jade Dellinger, Sept. 20, 2001.
Mothersbaugh, Mark. Interview by Joe Garden for *The Onion*, July 10, 1997.
Mothersbaugh, Mark. Interview by Michael Hurray for *Heavy Metal*, March 12, 1977.
Mothersbaugh, Mark. Interview by *Seconds Magazine*, issue 5001, 2000.
Mothersbaugh, Mark. Interview by Tim Pedersen for Roland Users Group, 1997.
Reymann, Marty. Telephone interview by Jade Dellinger, Nov. 7, 2001.
Schmidt Horning, Susan. Email interview by Jade Dellinger, Nov. 9, 2001.
Smith, Debbie. Telephone interview by Jade Dellinger, April 11, 2001.
Watson, Bobbie. Email interview by Jade Dellinger, Sept. 28, 2001.

OTHER SOURCES:
Boy, Booji (a.k.a. Mark Mothersbaugh). *My Struggle* (Cleveland: NEO Rubber Band, 1978).
DEVO Live: The Mongoloid Years (compact disc), Rykodisc, 1992.
Heylin, Clinton. *From the Velvets to the Voidoids: A Pre-Punk History for a Post-Punk World* (NY: Penguin Books, 1993).
"rjs," Postcard. March 2002 & April 25, 2002.
Scene (Cleveland), April 14, 1977.
WKDD-Radio Rap Sheet, Dec. 1976.
Watson, Barbara Jo (Bobbie). Deposition taken on June 15, 1979, in the US District Court Northern District of Ohio Eastern Division case between Robert Lewis, Plaintiff vs. Gerald V. Casale, et al, Defendants.

Chapter 17
INTERVIEWS:
Casale, Jerry. Interview by *INKnineteen*, May 2000.
Casale, Jerry. Telephone interview by Jade Dellinger, June 11, 2001.
Chrome, Cheetah. Email interview by Jade Dellinger, May 21, 2002.
Devo (unidentified member). Interview by *Search & Destroy* #2, 1977.
Jacket, Gary. Telephone interview by Jade Dellinger, Feb. 2, 2001.
Mothersbaugh, Mark. Interview by Jere Chandler for *REWIND*, 1997.
Mothersbaugh, Mark. Interview by *Search & Destroy* #7, 197.
Myers, Alan. Telephone interview by Jade Dellinger, Jan. 24, 2001.
Pop, Iggy. Interview by Jade Dellinger, June 16, 2010.
Mothersbaugh, Mark. Interview by Jere Chandler for *REWIND*, 1997.

Mothersbaugh, Mark. Interview by *Search & Destroy* #7, 197.
Schmidt Horning, Susan. Email interview by Jade Dellinger, Sept. 17, 2001.

OTHER SOURCES:
Harry, Debbie and Chris Stein (ed. Victor Bockris), *Making Tracks: The Rise of Blondie* (London: Elm Tree Books, 1982).
New York Rocker, July/August 1978.

Chapter 18
INTERVIEWS:
Barger, Ed. Email interview by Jade Dellinger, Sept. 26, 2001.
Casale, Jerry. Interview by Paul Freeman for cnn.com, May 23, 2000.
Casale, Jerry. Telephone interview by Jade Dellinger, Feb. 19, 2001.
Jacket, Gary. Telephone interview by Jade Dellinger, Jan. 18, 2001.
Massaro, Susan (Aylward). Email interviews by Jade Dellinger, Oct. 10 & 11, 2001.
Mothersbaugh, Bob. Interview by Paul Provenza for checkout.com, 2001.
Mothersbaugh, Mark. Interview by Jim Infirmary for *New York Rocker*, July 1977, published July/August 1978.
Mothersbaugh, Mark. Interview by Music World On-Line, (date unknown).
Vincent, Sonny. Email interview by Jade Dellinger, Oct. 5, 2002.
Watson, Bobbie. Email interview by Jade Dellinger, Oct. 1, 2001.

OTHER SOURCES:
DEVO Live: The Mongoloid Years (compact disc), Rykodisc, 1992.

Chapter 19
INTERVIEWS:
Barger, Ed. Email interview by Jade Dellinger, Dec. 8–13, 2001.
Casale, Jerry. Interview by *INKnineteen*, May 2000.
Casale, Jerry. Interview by Jim Infirmary for *New York Rocker*, July 1977, published July/August 1978.
Casale, Jerry. Telephone interview by Jade Dellinger, June 11, 2001.
Lewis, Bob. Email interviews by Jade Dellinger, Sept. 26 & 28, 2001.
Massaro, Susan (Aylward). Email interview by Jade Dellinger, Oct. 11, 2001.
Mothersbaugh, Mark. Interview by Diana Fischer for icast.com, (date unknown).
Mothersbaugh, Mark. Interview by Jere Chandler for *REWIND*, 1997.
Mothersbaugh, Mark. Interview by Joe Gardner for *The Onion*, 1997.
Mothersbaugh, Mark. Interview by Tim Pedersen for Roland Users Group, 1997.
Nicholis, Nick. Interview by David Giffels, June 1999.
Iggy Pop. Interview by Jade Dellinger, June 16, 2010.

OTHER SOURCES:
Casale, Robert Edward. Deposition taken on April 3, 1979, in the US District Court Northern District of Ohio Eastern Division case between Robert Lewis, Plaintiff vs. Gerald V. Casale, et al, Defendants and the US District Court Central District of California case between Gerald Casale, Robert Casale, Robert Mothersbaugh,

Mark Mothersbaugh, Alan Myers and Devo, Inc., a corporation, Plaintiffs vs. Robert Lewis, Defendant.

Heylin, Clinton. *From the Velvets to the Voidoids: A Pre-Punk History for a Post-Punk World* (NY: Penguin Books, 1993).

Krystal, Hilly. CBGB's history on cbgb.com.

Laughner, Peter. *Peter Laughner* (Miami Beach: Smog Veil Records, 2019).

New York Rocker, July/August 1978.

Romanowski, Patricia and Holly George-Warren (eds.), *The New Rolling Stone Encyclopedia of Rock & Roll* (NY: Fireside, 1995)

Watson, Barbara Jo (Bobbie). Deposition taken on June 15, 1979, in the US District Court Northern District of Ohio Eastern Division case between Robert Lewis, Plaintiff vs. Gerald V. Casale, et al, Defendants.

Chapter 20

INTERVIEWS:

Barger, Ed. Email interview by Jade Dellinger, Dec. 4–9, 2001 & April 30, 2002.

Casale, Jerry. Telephone interview by Jade Dellinger, June 11, 2001.

Devo, uncredited transcript of ca. 1978 interview by "Puddie and Liz," found in the files of Festival East Concerts, Inc. in Buffalo.

Eno, Brian. Interview by Caroline Coon. "Brian Eno." *RITZ*, October 1977.

Eno, Brian. Interview by Roman Kozak "Math Qualities of Music Interest Eno." *Billboard*, May 13, 1978.

Jackett, Gary. Telephone interview by Jade Dellinger, Feb. 2, 2001.

Lewis, Bob. Email interview by Jade Dellinger, Sept. 28, 2001.

Massaro, Susan (Aylward). Email interviews by Jade Dellinger, Oct. 10–11, 2001.

Mothersbaugh, Mark. Interview by Jere Chandler for *REWIND*, 1997.

Story, Tim. Email interview by Jade Dellinger, Oct. 11, 2001.

Watson, Bobbie. Email interview by Jade Dellinger, Sept. 27, 2001.

OTHER SOURCES:

Bowman, David. *This Must Be the Place: The Adventures of Talking Heads in the 20th Century* (NY: HarperCollins, 2001).

Jimmy McDonough, *Shakey: Neil Young's Biography* (NY: Random House, 2002). Mieses, Stanley. "Eno, before and after," *Melody Maker*, May, 20, 1978.

Scene, Feb. 23, 1978.

Stark, James. *PUNK '77: An Inside Look at the San Francisco Rock n' Roll Scene, 1977* (San Francisco, CA: Stark Grafix, 1992).

Watson, Barbara Jo (Bobbie). Deposition taken on June 15, 1979, in the US District Court Northern District of Ohio Eastern Division case between Robert Lewis, Plaintiff vs. Gerald V. Casale, et al, Defendants.

Chapter 21

INTERVIEWS:

Lewis, Bob. Interview by Rob Warmowski, c. 1996, https://warmowski.wordpress.com/2010/03/01/devo-founder-bob-lewis-my-1997-interview/.

Mothersbaugh, Robert L. Sr. Telephone interview by Jade Dellinger, July 26, 2000.
Smith, Debbie. Telephone interview by Jade Dellinger, April 11, 2001.
Massaro, Susan (Aylward), email interview by Jade Dellinger, Sept. 20, 2000.
Mothersbaugh, Mark. Interview by Michael Pilmer, April 26, 2001.
Watson, Bobbie. Email interview by Jade Dellinger, Sept. 27, 2001.

OTHER SOURCES:
Akron Beacon Journal. "The storm of the century," Dec. 31, 1999.
Canyon Cinema, Inc, marketing materials for "Mongoloid," 1978.
Casale, Jerry, "Drooling for Dollars." *DEVO: The Complete Truth About De-Evolution* (Voyager laserdisc 1993).
Love, Steve and David Giffels. *Wheels of Fortune: The Story of Rubber in Akron* (Akron: The University of Akron Press, 1998).
New York Rocker, July/August 1978.
Photographed copy of Devo's chart comparing record deals.
Scene, Jan. 19, 1978.

Chapter 22

INTERVIEWS:
Barger, Ed. Email interview by Jade Dellinger, Dec. 8, 2001.
Casale, Jerry. Interview by *Toast Magazine*, May 2, 2000.
Czukay, Holger. Email interview by Jade Dellinger, Aug. 28, 2002.
Eno, Brian. Interview by Caroline Coon. "Brian Eno." *RITZ*, October 1977.
Eno, Brian. Interview by Roman Kozak "Math Qualities of Music Interest Eno." *Billboard*, May 13, 1978.Lewis, Bob. Email interview by Jade Dellinger, Sept. 28, 2001.
Licitri, Jennifer. Telephone interview by Jade Dellinger, Oct. 18, 2001.
Mothersbaugh, Mark. Interview by Adam Gnade for *Mean Street*, May 2000.
Mothersbaugh, Mark. Interview by David Giffels, August 1996.
Mothersbaugh, Mark. Interview by Michael Pilmer, April 26, 2001.
Mothersbaugh, Mark. Interview by Music World On-Line, (date unknown).
Mothersbaugh, Mark. Interview by The Onion, July 10, 1997.

OTHER SOURCES:
Casale, Jerry, "Drooling For Dollars," from *DEVO: The Complete Truth About De-Evolution* (Voyager laserdisc 1993).
Devo's original notes for first three albums (Collection of Debbie Smith, Akron, Ohio).
Gill, Andy. "The Oblique Strategist," *Mojo*, June 1995.
Krassner, Paul. *Pot Stories for the Soul*, (NY: High Times, 1999).
Mieses, Stanley. "Eno, before and after," *Melody Maker*, May, 20, 1978.
Mothersbaugh, Mark. Address at the University of South Florida Contemporary Art Museum in conjunction with "Art in the News" (for *The Tampa Tribune*, curated by Jade Dellinger & Margaret Miller).
New York Rocker, July/August 1978.

Chapter 23
INTERVIEWS:
Casale, Jerry. Interview by Melody Maker, Nov. 25, 1978.
Firestone, Rod. Interview by David Giffels, June 2001.
Gold, Harvey. Interview by David Giffels, Sept. 3, 2002.
Mothersbaugh, Mark. Interviews by David Giffels, August 10, 1996 & July 18, 1997.
Mothersbaugh, Mark. Interview by "E. K." for RocknRollreporter.com, 1996.
Mothersbaugh, Mark. Interview by Michael Pilmer, April 26, 2001.
Mothersbaugh, Mark. Interview by *Seconds Magazine*, Issue 5001, 2000.
Mothersbaugh, Mark. Uncredited 1978 interview in Devo Print Collection.
Nicholis, Nick. Interview by David Giffels, June 1999.
Watson, Bobbie. Email interview by Jade Dellinger, Sept. 27, 2001.

OTHER SOURCES:
Casale, Jerry, "Drooling for Dollars," from *DEVO: The Complete Truth About De-Evolution* (Voyager laserdisc 1993).
Christgau, Robert. "A Real New Wave Rolls Out of Ohio," *Village Voice*, April 17, 1978.
Clinton Heylin, *From The Velvets to the Voidoids: A Pre-Punk History for a Post-Punk World* (ibid.)
New York Rocker, July/August 1978.
Terry Southern, Richard Branson, Simon Draper and Ken Berry, *Virgin: A History of Virgin Records*, (London, United Kingdom: Virgin Books, 1996).

Chapter 24
INTERVIEWS:
Barger, Ed. Email interview by Jade Dellinger, April 4, 2002.
Casale, Jerry. Interview by David Giffels, July 18, 1997.
Casale, Jerry. Interview by *Melody Maker*, Nov. 25, 1978.
Casale, Jerry. Telephone interview by Jade Dellinger, June 11, 2002.
Reymann, Dave. Email interview by Jade Dellinger, April 5, 2002.
Reymann, Dave. Email interview by Jade Dellinger, April 6, 2002.

OTHER SOURCES:
Biddle, Daniel R. "Behind the Scenes," *Rolling Stone*, Feb. 8, 1979.

Chapter 25
INTERVIEWS:
Barger, Ed. Email interview by Jade Dellinger, Dec. 9, 2001.
Blocher, Richard. Telephone interview by Jade Dellinger, Oct. 8, 2001.
Casale, Jerry. Address to PROMAX & BDA Conference in Chicago, 1997.
Casale, Jerry. Interview by David Giffels, July 18, 1997.
Casale, Jerry. Interview by *Melody Maker*, Feb. 25, 1978; & Nov. 25, 1978.
Casale, Jerry. Interview by *On Tour* (KCET, Los Angeles), Aug. 1997.
Devo. Interview by *Search & Destroy* No. 8, 1978.
Lewis, Bob. Email interview by Jade Dellinger, Sept. 28, 2001.

Massaro, Susan (Aylward), email interviews by Jade Dellinger, Sept. 17-Oct. 10, 2001.
Smith, Debbie. Email interview by Jade Dellinger, Oct. 7, 2001.

OTHER SOURCES:
Bailey, Dan. "Mark Mothersbaugh Interviwew, June 1988." https://www.youtube.com/watch?v=73kpdVXeiWo
Cincinnati Post, "Chi Chi grips it, whips it: Album cover a weird footnote," Sept. 5, 2002.
DEVO: The Complete Truth About De-Evolution (Voyager laserdisc 1993).
Downing, David. *Neil Young: The Man and his Music* (NY: Da Capo Press, 1994).
Human Highway, Shakey Pictures, 1982.
McDonough, Jimmy. *Shakey: Neil Young's Biography* (ibid.).
Shore, Michael. *The Rolling Stone Book of Rock Video* (N.Y.: Rolling Stone Press, 1984).

Chapter 26
INTERVIEWS:
Barger, Ed. Email interviews by Jade Dellinger, Dec. 4 & 13, 2001.
Devo, uncredited transcript of ca. 1978 interview by "Puddie and Liz," found in the files of Festival East Concerts, Inc. in Buffalo.
Horowitz, Bennett "Bud." Email interviews by Jade Dellinger, May 8 & 10, 2002.
Lewis, Bob. Email interviews by Jade Dellinger, Sept. 30, 2001 & April 3, 2002.
Lewis, Bob. Interview by Rob Warmowski, c. 1996, https://warmowski.wordpress.com/2010/03/01/devo-founder-bob-lewis-my-1997-interview/.
Mothersbaugh, Alan. Interview by David Giffels, Oct. 14, 2002.
Mothersbaugh, Jim. Interview by David Giffels, Sept. 4, 2002
Mothersbaugh, Robert L. Sr. Telephone interview by Jade Dellinger, July 26, 2000.
Myers, Alan. Telephone interview by Jade Dellinger, Jan. 24, 2001.

OTHER SOURCES:
Carson, Tom. Review of *Q: Are We Not Men? A: We Are Devo!" Rolling Stone*, November 30, 1978.
"Reader's Poll," *Creem*, Dec. 1978.
Love, Steve and David Giffels, *Wheels of Fortune: The Story of Rubber in Akron*, (ibid.).
Mothersbaugh, Jim. Address to DEVOtional Fan Convention, Cleveland, 2001 (transcript).
Watson, Barbara Jo (Bobbie). Deposition taken on June 15, 1979, in the US District Court Northern District of Ohio Eastern Division case between Robert Lewis, Plaintiff vs. Gerald V. Casale, et al, Defendants.

Chapter 27
INTERVIEWS:
Barger, Ed. Email interviews by Jade Dellinger, Dec. 1-9, 2001 & May 17, 2002.

Horowitz, Bennett "Bud." Email interview by Jade Dellinger, May 8, 2002.
Lewis, Bob. Email interviews by Jade Dellinger, Sept. 26 & 28, 2001.
Mothersbaugh, Mark. Interview by Michael Hurray, March 12, 1977.
Zoom, Billy. Email interview by Jade Dellinger, May 16, 2002.

OTHER SOURCES:
The Akron Compilation (LP). Stiff Records, 1978.
Bowling Balls from Hell (LP). Clone Records, 1980.
Lewis, Bob. Letter to Ed and Jennifer Dorn, December 1979.
Lewis, Bob. Letter to Ed and Jennifer Dorn. Feb. 8, 1983.
Mothersbaugh, Robert, Sr. Address to DEVOtional Fan Convention, Cleveland, 2001 (transcript).

Postscript
INTERVIEWS:
Casale, Jerry. Interviews by David Giffels, Aug. 10, 1996 & July 18, 1997.
Pop, Iggy. Interview by Jade Dellinger, June 16, 2010.

OTHER SOURCES:
Akron Beacon Journal. "Akron's 'Devo Day' proclamation sounds a little foolish, doesn't it?," March 31, 2021.

Jade Dellinger is director of the Bob Rauschenberg Gallery at Florida Southwestern State College—where he has curated shows, commissioned installations, hosted lectures and held performances with artists including the Guerilla Girls, Yoko Ono, Laurie Anderson, the Go-Go's Jane Wiedlin and DEVO's Gerald Casale. He first invited Mark Mothersbaugh to the Sunshine State in 1999 for a project with the Contemporary Art Museum in Tampa, but most recently world-premiered the DEVO frontman's "Postcards for Democracy" exhibition (with collaborator Beatie Wolfe) at the Rauschenberg Gallery in 2021.

Photo: Tim Fitzwater

David Giffels is the author of six books of nonfiction, most recently *Barnstorming Ohio: To Understand America* (Hachette Books 2020), one of *Library Journal's* Best Books of 2020. His other books include the memoirs *Furnishing Eternity* (Scribner 2018) and *All the Way Home* (William Morrow 2008), both winners of the Ohioana Book Award, and *The Hard Way on Purpose* (Scribner 2014), a *New York Times Book Review* "Editors' Choice." His writing has appeared in the *New York Times Magazine*, *The Atlantic*, *Parade*, *The Iowa Review*, *Esquire*, *Grantland*, and many other publications. He is professor of English at the University of Akron, and serves on the faculty of the NEOMFA creative writing program.